LEGEND

BY
Timothy Young

Dedication

For Skyler and Joe, you show me what matters most
every day.

PROLOGUE

10 Years ago
Colby College, Waterville Maine
High School Championship Football Game

Joe Blackstone stood on the sideline and watched as the clock ticked to zero. The stands emptied onto the field with fans eager to congratulate the Bulldogs on a 56-14 win. The 6'5", 240 pound senior had led the Lawrence High School football team to four consecutive State Championships. Next week he'd join the basketball team, confident the result would be the same. Come spring season, it would be baseball.

Joe's first love was football, and what he yearned for more than anything was a new challenge on a bigger stage. Although he had few close friends, Joe loved his teammates and the tight community of Fairfield Maine. The blue-collar town was a place where people worked hard, knew each other's name and came out in droves to support their high school teams. But Joe longed for the next step. He'd known he was different at an early age, always able to compete and beat older kids at any sport. He excelled at everything he tried, but football was his true love.

Fairfield is home to the premier youth football program in the state of Maine. For years, children up to the age of thirteen had competed in the league. Forging a foundation for the high school's continual success. Although bigger kids had come through the program, never had they been blessed with Joe's speed, strength or skill. So, when Joe was thirteen, the league made it clear to his father, Joe would not be allowed to return to the program, he was simply too physically developed to compete against kids his own age.

Many of the small school districts in Maine could not afford to field junior high school teams so 8th graders were allowed to play freshmen football. Joe was disappointed he couldn't play with his classmates but looked forward to the new challenge. Already 6'1", 190 pounds, he was far from the smallest player on the team, despite being the youngest.

His coach, Earl "Pete" Cooper, had been a second father figure to Joe from the first time they met. After watching Blackstone not only compete, but lead the freshmen to an undefeated season, Cooper had called the young player into his office, it was in this first meeting he told Joe of his expectations for the young man. No, he would not be evaluated against his teammates, no, he would not play freshmen again as a ninth grader, no, he would not be allotted the same time as the other underclassmen to learn the game at the varsity level. Joe was different, and he would be treated differently. Cooper would expect him to work harder on and off the field. The coach was going to challenge Joe in any way he could.

First, Cooper laid out a training regimen that included high target goals he believed would push the young player even if they weren't realistically attainable. Joe attacked his training regimen like no player Cooper had ever coached, hitting new benchmarks on a near weekly basis. By the time his freshman year arrived Joe's strength, speed and stamina had far exceeded what Cooper believed possible. Nonetheless, the coach continued to push and Joe, who was still growing, continued to impress.

Of course, Joe loved the physical nature of the game, but what he loved most was being part of a team. Joe had a special bond with his teammates, in each sport he played, but none more so than football. He believed football required an extraordinary team effort to be successful.

But the balance of effort had become distorted over the past two seasons. Sure, the Lawrence Bulldogs were a talented team with great coaching, but Joe Blackstone had become unstoppable. He was a man amongst boys. Bigger, faster and stronger, all by a wide margin, he was able to make plays at will. If a teammate missed a block, missed a tackle or committed any other error Joe's talent overcame it.

On this particular fall day, Joe sat out the entire 4th quarter of the State Championship game, but still finished with seven touchdowns, three rushing, and four passing. His combined yardage total of six-hundred-four yards broke his own state record.

Joe could take a game over at will, but seldom did, the gaudy stats made him uneasy. For most of his junior and senior seasons, Joe had played cat and mouse with his opponents. Purposely playing a smaller role in the outcome, allowing his teammates to enjoy the spotlight, it was his game within the game. But when his dad called to say he'd be home in time for the championship, Joe decided to go all out.

John Blackstone traveled a great deal for work. It was only the two of them, so Joe had spent a lot of time with friends and neighbors growing up; until he was old enough to stay home by himself. Having inherited his father's mental toughness, along with his impressive stature Joe had much to be thankful for. He'd never been sorry for himself or envied the family life most of his teammates had. In his case, the family dynamics, or lack of, only increased Joe's dedicated work ethic. Sure, he missed his dad, but instead of focusing on it Joe filled his time with sports, school and working out.

His dad had only seen him play two high school football games and both were when he was a freshman. Despite his mature qualities, he was still a kid, so when presented with the rare opportunity to play in front of his dad, he had been determined to make the most of it.

Following the championship game, Joe picked his way through the crowd. He skirted around teammates, coaches, and reporters in search of his dad. "Joe." The familiar voice grabbed his attention, and Joe turned into his father's embrace. His father hefted him off his feet and said, "Great game son."

Basking in his father's pride, Joe said, "Thanks, Dad."

John set his son down, beaming he said, "Joe you were something special today, I've never seen anything like it."

"The guys played great today Dad, everything clicked."

"Nothing against your team Joe but you're what was clicking."

Joe smiled at his father's approval, while at the same averting his eyes and looking at his feet. "It was a good game."

John grinned at the discomfort his praise caused. For all his athletic accomplishments, Joe had never been comfortable with praise. John slapped the top of Joe's shoulder pads and said, "Come on." They started walking toward the locker rooms. "So what's on the agenda tonight?"

There was a big party at Jay Rowe's, but Joe feigned ignorance. "I'm not sure." A part of Joe wanted to grab a burger and hang with his old man, but the part controlled by teenage hormones had another plan. Stacy Higgins had been flirting with him for the past couple of weeks. Joe knew there was a good chance Stacy would be at Jay's and he intended to find out. "I think some of the guys are gonna go out. I'll grab a bite with them and be home later. Okay?"

John gave Joe a knowing smile. "Sure, you guys have fun, be careful and don't ride with anyone who's been drinking."

"Yes, sir."

"I've got some work to catch up on, I'll see you when you get home." Love for his son shined in John's eyes, and he said, "Wow ... you were awesome out there."

"Thanks, Dad." Joe's chest filled with pride as his dad turned and walked away.

Joe disappeared into the locker room, showered and was one of the first players to board the bus back to Fairfield. Eventually, both team buses filled and they pulled out of the parking lot, followed by a caravan of honking horns. A parade of vehicles made the short drive through Waterville to the Fairfield Town Line, where they were met by the small community's fire engine. Instead of heading straight for the school, they traversed the mile stretch that led through the middle of town. Joe watched his teammates hang out from the windows, celebrating with the crowd gathered along the route.

He thought back to this same ride home, after his first State Championship game three years past. The joy of the moment had been so pure, the culmination of hours of hard work and dedication by him and his teammates. Joe was proud to have played in front of his dad, but otherwise, the game had been a mere check on a *to-do* list. He hungered for a challenge and looked forward to putting his mark on the college game and eventually the pros'. Memories of the past and dreams of the future were soon replaced with visions of Stacy and her incredible ass.

The procession ended at the high school, where a crowd was gathered in the gym. The team entered and were met with more applause. Coach Cooper stood with his team and addressed the crowd, congratulating the boys on a tremendous season.

The Bulldogs had no names on the back of their jerseys because Cooper believed strongly that football was a team game and there was no room for individuals. So, Joe was more than a little taken back when he was signaled out. "For four years I've had the pleasure of coaching Joe Blackstone." His words met with loud applause; he waited for the crowd to quiet down. "I've been involved in sports for forty years as a player or coach, never have I come across a more talented or driven athlete. It's an honor to coach every young man who comes through this program. I hope you all realize what a privilege we've had as coaches, fans, and teammates to watch this young man don the blue and gray these past four years." Coach Cooper looked directly at Joe and said, "You've made us all proud son." Again the gym erupted.

Since Joe was always deflecting praise and crediting teammates for his accomplishments, not a single player held any resentment or jealousy toward him. The entire team chanted "Joe, Joe, JOE ..."

Coach Cooper's words and his teammate's mantra hit him with more force than any on-field collision ever could. It dawned on him, he would never play another game for Earl "Pete" Cooper; a man he admired, respected and loved. For the first time, today's game held real meaning outside his father's attendance. Sure, he would join several of his teammates on this very court for basketball next week, and in the spring, they'd have baseball. But never again would he play a game with *this* football family.

Joe fought to keep his composure in check, walked to coach Cooper and embraced him in a hug. "Thank you for everything you've done for me, coach."

Amidst a chorus of noise Cooper said, "Son, you're going to be the best damn player this game has ever seen."

Joe was swarmed by reporters and several college recruiters before finally getting out of the school. He caught a ride with his buddy Chris Buck, who had been waiting for him. When they finally got to the party, he learned Stacy had left with Andy Adams. Andy was a good player, but his real talent was with the ladies, rivaling that of Joe's on the field. Realizing the fun ship *Stacy* had sailed, Joe hung with his teammates reminiscing about the season before again catching a ride home with Chris.

Buck dropped Joe off around eleven. He bound up the steps to the darkened house and reached for the doorknob. At that moment a strange light raked across the two small windows atop the door. The hair bristled on the back of Joe's neck, and he froze in his tracks. He listened to the night, hearing nothing but a distant vehicle and the occasional gust of fall. He hadn't even had a beer at the party so surely, he couldn't be seeing things.

Joe gripped the doorknob and slowly attempted to twist it, but it didn't budge. Confused, he backed down the steps. It wasn't like his father to lock the door. Joe went to the garage, leaned down and peered through a small window. His dad's car sat right where it belonged. He hadn't gone out.

After a moment, Joe chastised himself for being paranoid. Light from the neighborhood must have shone through a window, and reflected through the door; which his dad had decided to lock. So what? Big deal. It wasn't like he didn't have a key. Returning to the door, Joe unlocked it and stepped inside.

He tossed his keys on the counter and headed to the stairs. A voice in his head screamed something was off. Upstairs, he turned toward his father's room, which ran along the front of the small house. A slight crack in the bedroom door allowed light from a street lamp to spill into the hallway. Anxious why his dad had gone to bed so early, Joe knocked and whispered, "Dad?" The house was silent, but the door crept inward.

Joe's attention was drawn to peculiar shadow on the rug. But the *shadow* sat directly in a stream of light, and it was red. His heart raced, and he pushed the door wide open; terror gripped his soul.

John Blackstone was lying on the floor, battered and bruised. The digits from his right hand were scattered across the rug. Joe staggered toward the still form and collapsed to his knees. One inert eye was open, the other was swollen shut. Joe reached out and touched his father's disfigured face. The warmth of his blood branded itself to Joe's memory. "Dad." Tears filled his eyes.

Again, Joe pleaded with fate. "Dad please."

A shadow fluttered across his father's lifeless eye, and Joe sensed a slight vibration on the floor. Deep within himself, a rare instinct kicked in. Casting aside a flood of sorrow, Joe reacted. He sprung off his knees while turning to his right. A blade arced in his direction, glistened as it cut through the night. With his feet coiled under him, but not yet upright, Joe sprung to the side. The blade missed his back but found flesh of his right forearm. Joe spun around, ignoring the gash, he squared off against his attacker, his father's killer.

He was big, nearly as tall as Joe with broad shoulders and thick arms. Clad in black, he glided across the room with the grace of a much smaller man. Mockingly, he tossed his knife from hand to hand, steel and blood shined in light cast through the window. He backed Joe into a corner and said, "Is the big football star gonna cry? Maybe I'll cut that golden arm off—"

Joe's eyes darted to his father's hand.

"—like I did your daddy's fingers."

Rage ignited the adrenalin coursing through Joe's veins. He exploded forward; momentarily catching the intruder off guard, and drove his shoulder into the killer's sternum. The blow knocked the big man backward, they landed, and Joe was rewarded by the sound of ribs breaking.

The killer howled but still held the knife. Before Joe could gather himself from the hardest tackle of his life, white-hot pain pierced his shoulder. The blade sliced through flesh, nerves, and tendons before grinding against bone. His right arm useless, Joe drove his left thumb into his attacker's eye socket. The man howled and lost his grip on the knife. Joe reared back and unloaded a left hook that connected square on the man's temple. Again and again, Joe pummeled him. Long after the assailant's body went slack, Joe stopped and pulled the blade from his shoulder. Pain, anguish, and rage torched his soul. Joe leaned forward until his face was inches from the unconscious man. He placed the tip of the knife beneath the killer's chin, roared with the voice of a stranger, and thrust the steel through the man's mouth and into his skull.

With his chest heaving and right arm hanging limp, Joe pushed himself off the floor and struggled to his feet. The room spun, and he staggered against the wall. Joe spotted the phone on a table beside the front window. With blood leaking from the sleeve of his jacket he stumbled toward it, picked it up and dialed.

"911 what's your emergency?"

Before he could respond, Joe heard a noise and turned. A bright flash blinded him, and the wind was knocked from his chest. He never noticed the second flash, only the pain cutting through his side. The two 9mm slugs hurled Joe's 240 pounds toward the window. He crashed through the cold glass and fell into darkness.

CHAPTER 1

Present Day
Fairfield, Maine

The further you drive on I-95 in Maine, the greater the distance between towns. In the early hours of this cold winter night, the black road cut a lonely void between the pines. Each town a small island in a sea of darkness, drifting forever more remote.

A lone truck pulled off exit 35. At the top of the ramp, it turned left toward a single oasis of light. *Truckers International* lit a hilltop beside the endless stretch of asphalt. The small-town truck stop was known to locals and long haulers alike. Open 24/7/365, it offered fuel, food and alcohol. Whether, having grown up in central Maine or passing through, you quickly learned it took all three to survive the long cold winters.

The black truck pulled past the pumps and into a spot to the right of the main door. The lot held more vehicles than the new arrival had seen in the last hour. A frigid wind nipped at his exposed skin when he stepped from the truck. Stiff from the long drive, he blew a warm breath into his hands and stretched his tall frame. He strode to the entrance, pulled the second set of double doors open, and warm air wash over him from above. His stomach growled as an assortment of aromas filled his nose.

The diner was decorated with furniture and pictures that were intended to be nostalgic but had instead landed on generic. Over thirty tables and booths filled the space, a dozen of which were occupied. A sign directed the patrons to seat themselves, so he made his way to the back and choose a spot with a good view of the room. He shed his jacket and settled onto the worn leather.

Based on their appearance, and the number of rigs in the parking lot, most of the customers at *Truckers* were truckers. Undoubtedly on the back end of a long night or front end of a long day. The new-comer pegged the remaining few as mill workers, also on one end of a long shift.

A young waitress approached with a smile, menu and a pot of coffee. All three were welcomed. Her name tag read *Becky*. Kind blue eyes, smooth skin, and high cheekbones highlighted her beautiful face. Her nose, a touch too large, added to Becky's appeal. She wore her black hair in a girlish ponytail, but a skin-tight T-shirt and stretch pants revealed a seductive figure. Her 5'3", 110 pounds of curves would've been tough to conceal in any attire, but clearly, concealment was not the objective.

She placed a menu in front of him and said, "Good mornin'." Her voice resonated a youthful innocence, it was a sharp contrast to her body.

"Morning," he replied.

"My name's Becky," she said and poured him a cup of coffee.

"Thanks."

"Our specials are on the back of the menu. I'll be back to check on you in a minute okay." Becky said and hurried off.

He pegged her as nineteen maybe twenty. And chastised himself for enjoying the view of her retreat a little too much. Feeling like a dirty old man he thought, *her poor father.*

He scanned the menu and decided on the *Truckers Special* a three-egg omelet, home fries, bacon, and toast. Soon Becky returned to take his order, refilled his mug and headed to the kitchen.

As she vanished, two more people walked into Truckers. His first thought was, *they don't belong here.* The taller guy was about 6'3", 280 pounds and wore his black hair slicked back into a ponytail. The other was about 6'0", 250 pounds with a shaved head. Both appeared to be in their late twenties or early thirties, but it was hard to tell because each had a bloated face associated with steroid abuse. The most obvious thing about them was, neither wore a jacket despite the frigid temperature outside. Both wore black slacks and what had to have been custom tailored dress shirts.

Having spent lots of time watching others and being sober for the first time in three weeks, the observer noted two things. First, no reaction to the temperature inside or out, not a shiver coming in from the cold or a glance above at the rush of hot air gusting from above the entrance. Second, they didn't take note of their surroundings. Sure, they watched where they were walking to avoid walking into things, but they never scanned the room. When people walk into an unfamiliar place, they tend to check out their surroundings. It's a part of the human psyche that has been ingrained over tens of thousands of years. No way were these regulars, yet they acted like they owned the joint. It went against basic human nature these guys were trouble.

Any hope he was over reacting dissipated when the bald guy hollered, "Look at this fucking place."

His buddy cackled and said, "Hopefully this dump has something edible I'm starved."

The two men laughed and strutted through the maze of tables. An air of discomfort enveloped the room. All but one set of eyes avoided contact with the pair. Nonetheless, the tall guy, Slick, pointed to a portly man of about fifty and said, "Holy shit! Look at this fat bastard. I hope he didn't eat everything they have."

Trembling, the fat man kept his head down, staring at a half-eaten mound of pancakes, willing the pair to leave. But Kojac slammed his fist on the table, leaned over and said, "Is that true fat man did you eat everything?"

The stranger was silent, sharing the fat man's desire to forego a confrontation. This was not his problem, not his concern. Yet, his breathing slowed, and body became still. Like a predator tracking its prey.

The kitchen doors snapped open, and Becky backed through carrying two plates of food. Slick tapped Kojac to get his attention and pointed toward Becky. The pair shared a knowing smirk and picked a table near the back.

Becky distributed the food, grabbed a couple menus and approached the newcomers. She laid them on the table and asked, "Good mornin', would you guys like coffee?"

"We were thinking about something a lot better than coffee," Kojac said.

"Okay," Becky said. "What'll it be?"

"I'd like a taste of this," said Slick as he cupped Becky's back side.

Once again, the stranger fought to control his anger. He was impressed when Becky deftly brushed Slick's hand aside, forced a smile and said, "I'll be back to take your order in a sec."

Kojac grabbed her wrist, "Wait, my friend can be a little rude sometimes."

"That's okay, I know he was kidding."

He pulled her closer. "You dumb bitch, he wasn't kidding. He was rude because he was being selfish and forgot to share. We both want a taste of your white trash pussy. And we take what we want."

Becky snapped her arm back with surprising strength for such a small girl. As she hurried away, the pair broke into a chorus of, "*She's a brick … house.*" They nearly rolled out of their chairs laughing at their own joke. Becky turned toward the restrooms and the man sitting alone in the back was able to see her face. The smile was gone, and her kind eyes glistened with tears.

The patrons throughout the diner continued to keep their heads down, content to mind their own business. The man in back decided he was not. Ashamed he'd not intervened sooner, he slid out of the booth. No stranger to guilt or anger he channeled a fresh dose of both and approached the pair. At their table he stood silently, imposing his will, forcing them to speak first.

"What the fuck do you want Hillbilly?" Asked Slick.

Every patron in the diner stared intently, safe now, able to gawk in anonymity behind the stranger.

"I asked you a question." Annoyed, Slick repeated himself, "What … the fuck … do … you … want?"

The tension in the room was palpable, yet the stranger said nothing. He didn't blink or look away, he kept staring at Slick with cold blue eyes.

Kojac didn't bother to look up when he spoke. Instead, he made a show of polishing his manicured nails with a napkin. "I'm gonna give you three seconds to get lost before we throw your ass out."

Without a trace of levity, the stranger said, "That's funny."

Still focused on his nails, Kojac's asked, "Really, how so?"

The stranger's eyes remained locked with Slicks. "I've been standing here trying to decide if I'm going to *LET* you leave."

Kojac lost all interest in his nails and snapped his head up. "What? You dumb motherfucker!"

Adam Owad pulled into Truckers, deciding if he had to be up at this ungodly hour, he was at least going to grab a quick bite. When he opened the door and entered the warm dining area, he heard a loud "... *motherfucker.*"

Adam quickly surveyed the scene and headed toward the back. A tall guy, easily 6'5", was standing over a table, his thick beard made it tough to pinpoint his age. Loose clothing partially obstructing his appearance but broad shoulders and a thick neck put him over 250 pounds. Two guys were sitting at the table. Both pumped up with the kind of bulk that comes from years in the gym and plenty of steroids. The trio held the room in rapt attention. It didn't take a genius to know he'd walked in on trouble.

At their table he noted the intensity splayed across everyone's face but took a greater interest in their hands. "Good morning gentlemen." A moment passed in silence. Adam raised his voice. "I said good morning ... gentlemen."

The pair who were seated turned toward the new arrival but offered nothing but a scowl. Without looking at Adam, the third man said, "Good mornin' officer."

Adam wasn't even sure the big man had seen him approach. "Is everything okay here?"

"As soon as these two clowns learn a little respect everything will be fine."

The bald guy looked at Adam and pointed at the man standing beside him. "I don't know what kind of bum fuck town you're running here, but you better get this Hillbilly outta our face."

"Everybody needs to calm down, Sir why don't you take a step back for a second."

The bearded man had yet to move when Becky returned from the restrooms. Spotting the young waitress, Kojak couldn't resist, licking his lips he goaded the bearded man. "Mmm-mmm the things I'm gonna do to her."

His buddy roared with laughter and said, "Nothing finer than tight young pussy."

Adam was furious, but he needed to get Becky away from them, so he escorted her back to the kitchen.

The stranger stood perfectly still. In a hellish tone, he whispered, "You're not walking out of here."

The two laughed. "Last chance Hillbilly," Slick said. "Get the fuck outta here before we kick your ass."

"Please, try." A smile pulled at his beard.

Slick stood and lunged forward to shove the bearded man. Before his hands even made contact his left wrist was snatched by a vice like grip. In his drug altered state, Slick was slow to process what was happening. His wrist was twisted behind, and up his back, a gruesome popping noise echoed through the diner. He howled in pain but fell silent when the bearded man slammed his head through the table.

Adam heard a crack, like a bat and ball, as pushed through the kitchen doors. Turning toward the noise, he saw both man and table crash to the floor, battered and broken. He'd taken two steps toward the wreckage when he saw the flash of steel. Knowing it was already too late, Adam reached for his gun.

The stranger had spotted the bulging ankle holsters when the pair had first entered the truck stop, it was a habit, like breathing. In the event of an altercation, they'd be dispatched with haste and finality.

Kojak was getting up as he raised the weapon, but before he was able to level his aim, the big man kicked a chair in his direction. It struck Kojak's forearm, knocking it and the gun into a wide arc. With startling quickness, the stranger took one step and delivered a thunderous blow to Kojak's jaw. The bald man's body went rigid and his eyes rolled back in his head, both he and the pistol fell harmlessly to the floor.

Weapon at his side, Adam approached. He glanced at the two still figures sprawled across the worn linoleum and studied the man who'd put them there. Before he could say a word, Becky plowed through the kitchen doors. She took one look, threw her hands in the air, and screamed, "Dad, what did you do?"

Violent eyes dissolved into amusement and the bearded man couldn't help but laugh. Under the scrutiny of every eye in the room, he walked back to his table, sat and waited for his breakfast.

CHAPTER 2

Uncertain how to react, Becky quickly got back to work, she brought his food as the first ambulance arrived. She offered an awkward thank you, which contained as much curiosity as gratitude. He ate and observed as the diner transformed into a hive of activity.

Two State Troopers, two local Officers, and a County Sheriff had all arrived to join their colleague, Chief Owad, Fairfield's Chief of Police, Becky's dad. Outside, emergency lights danced a rainbow across the diner's frosty windows.

Once attended to, the two goons were cuffed and strapped to a stretcher. Both were conscious but as promised neither would be *walking* out.

Numerous times, one of the officers had glanced his way, but none had approached. They spoke to each other, Becky and several other patrons but not him. He doubted he was in any real trouble and more importantly, he didn't care. He'd been in much bigger trouble, and truthfully, he hadn't cared then either.

The stranger watched two ambulances, and a pair of cruisers pull tear of the parking lot and form a small convoy on their way to the hospital. Becky cleared his empty plates and poured another cup of coffee.

The last two officers at the scene, Chief Owad, and the Sheriff were in a heated debate as they stepped outside. If the Sheriff's animated gestures were any indication, he was not happy with the outcome. After a less than friendly farewell, he left, and Owad came back inside.

The Chief strode to the big man's table and said, "We need to talk."

He used his chin to point to the bench opposite his but didn't speak.

Chief Owad removed his coat and took a seat. "I'm Sheriff Owad."

"I know."

"You do? Well, then I guess you have me at a bit of a disadvantage." Owad waited, but no answer was offered to the implied question. Clearly irritated, the Chief said, "Listen, I've spent the last forty minutes spreading a pile of horse shit all over this cluster fuck. I've broken more procedural rules than I care to list and I'm just getting started. I did it because you laid those two assholes out which kept me from doing something stupid." He lowered his voice. "How about you cut the shit and just tell me your name."

"Joseph Blackstone"

The recognition was instant but still took a moment to process, when it did the Chief's face softened. A decade later memories of that night still gripped his soul, as it did everyone in town. For the people in Fairfield, the sun did rise the next day, and life did go on. But don't try and tell them time heals all wounds. Pride and promise, once the foundation of everything in the community, had yet to heal. To Adam, no place symbolized that more than the high school gym. A stream of blue and gray banners hung on the walls, symbols of success and achievement. But the flow of victory had come to an abrupt halt ten years ago, leaving an ugly void. Over time, the void had grown into an ugly reminder of lost dreams, and become a prophecy of heartache.

"The same Joe Blackstone who," Adam grasped for something other than what he was thinking, "attended Lawrence High School ten years past?"

"And whose dad was murdered," said Joe, answering the real question.

"Listen, Joe, I'm not sure if you remember me but I ..."

"You were on the force back then. You were the first one on the scene. That was a long time ago, let's worry about today."

"Yeah, I guess we should." Relieved to be focused on current events, Owad said, "Both these guys were carrying concealed weapons, and neither had a permit, we also found twenty pounds of meth in the trunk of their car. You did everyone a favor so I'd like to do one in return."

"I'm all ears."

"Because of the weapons and drugs, the State and County guys wanted in on this, but I squashed it. Those guys would have interviewed you all day and night. Come by the station, and we can put your official statement together. I'll get you in and out in an hour or so."

"I've been on the road all night," Joe said. "I'd like to get some sleep. How 'bout I come by this afternoon."

The Chief hesitated but relented. "O.K. come by the station later today and will knock this out."

Joe nodded and said, "I'll be there."

They stood, and Adam pulled the bill off the table. "Breakfast is on me." He extended his hand and said, "Off the record and as Becky's dad, thanks, I loved what you did to those guys."

Joe shook Adam's hand, "No problem, so did I."

CHAPTER 3

Philadelphia, PA

Plush carpeting muted their footsteps when they exited the elevator. Having concluded a tour of the Philadelphia Freedom football team's facility, John Pollard led Mike Mealey to the owner's office. When they entered, Sky Marie Taylor rose and stepped around her desk to greet them. "Good morning gentlemen." She extended a hand to Mealey. "Coach, thank you for coming in on such short notice."

Mealey couldn't decide which was more surprising, the firm handshake from such a feminine hand or her natural beauty. He'd seen Taylor on TV many times, but in person her long brown hair and hazel eyes were breathtaking. At Fifty-two years young, she retained the beauty and grace of women half her age.

"It's a pleasure to be here Mrs. Taylor, I appreciate the opportunity"

"Please just Miss, Mrs. Taylor died with Mr. Taylor."

The late Jonathan Taylor had purchased the franchise in the early eighties. Despite only moderate success on the field, the franchise, like most others in the World Football League, continued to climb in value. When Mr. Taylor died of a sudden Heart attack in 1995, most people assumed his young wife, Sky Marie Taylor would cash in and sell the team. What she did instead turned Philadelphia into one of the league's premier franchises on and off the field. Not since the fifties, before the mergers had Philadelphia won a professional football championship. Under Taylor's leadership, they had won four titles, built a new state of the art stadium and were a fixture on the list of the top ten most valuable franchises in all sports.

At the conclusion of an injury filled 10-6 season, longtime coach, Mike Mikalonis, announced his retirement. The following day, Ms. Taylor held a press conference and vowed to find the coach who would bring a fifth world championship to Philadelphia. The bulk of that task fell squarely on the broad shoulders of Philadelphia GM John Pollard. Pushing fifty, John hadn't retained much of the light brown hair of his youth but his blue eyes still burned with excitement for the job. He stood a shade over 6'0", and was a lean 205 pounds. When Ms. Taylor inherited the franchise, John had been a young assistant in the personnel department. He stayed there for the first two years of Ms. Taylor's ownership. During that time, few changes were made to the coaching staff or front office, and the on-field success was underwhelming. At the conclusion of year two, Ms. Taylor announced she was terminating both her GM and head coach. Her first order of business was to find a GM, and she interviewed all the top candidates, but it was twenty-eight-year-old John Pollard who impressed her. He had designed the most advanced statistical analysis software in the league and possessed a willingness to buck the establishment. But it was only through sheer persistence he was even able to secure an interview. John requested the opportunity so many times Ms. Taylor realized she had two choices, fire him or interview him. Luckily for Philadelphia, she decided on the latter. Under heavy criticism, Pollard was hired as the Philly GM, and after three straight years of remarkable improvement, Philadelphia sat atop the WFL as World Champions.

John would be the first to say, his team's success had and would continue to be a team effort. But no individual had contributed more than he. Possessing a keen eye for talent, John often found it in places the competition wouldn't dare look. Mikalonis had been Division II college coach with no pro experience when John had hired him, it was his first hire as GM, and it made him a national punch line. But the jokes stopped when the winning started. Since then, he'd hired scouts from smaller schools to comb the countryside for prospects. With Ms. Taylor's direction, they'd hired some of the best event coordinators on the planet to handle team travel and logistics. He even hired the hostess from Capital Grille to be the team's new community relations manager.

The team owner and GM sat on a large sofa, opposite Mealey, who sat on an identical one. Coffee and tray of pastries had been laid out on the table between them. The office was large and tastefully decorated. Since she'd never had children, there were no pictures of such to fill the space. In fact, there were only five photographs in the entire office, four of championship winning teams and one of her late husband. Each of the five photos held a special place in the owner's heart, and each displayed her level of expectations.

Ms. Taylor was quiet while Pollard questioned the coach at length about his potential staff, schemes, and expectations for Philadelphia should they hire him. They already knew his resume, National Championships at Division III Maine Maritime Academy, Division I (FCS) University of Maine and Division I (FBS) Miami. At each stop, Mealey had taken a program from worst to first in their conference within three years, winning a national title within five, most recently Miami had won two. Sky Marie studied the man, at five foot ten Mealey was of average height, with average brown hair and an average build neither heavy nor lean. But there was nothing average about the intensity burning in his brown eyes or the passion with which he spoke. Having heard enough, she asked, "Why would you be successful making the jump from college to the pros when so many of your peers have failed?"

Mike knew Philadelphia had interviewed several candidates with extensive WFL experience. But having seen a glimpse of the culture Taylor and Pollard had created he wanted in. Turning his complete attention to Sky Marie, Mike's eyes bristled with excitement when he spoke "I don't fail. We can talk scheme and strategies all day long, but the bottom line is ... I don't fail. It's simply not an option for me. Lots of people say they're competitive, talk about their desire to win or how they hate to lose. For me failure is simply not an option, in that regard, I believe we're the same."

Ms. Taylor pursed her lips and traced the side of her jaw with a manicured nail. "You've peaked my interest, Mike. Please, explain."

Waving a hand toward the walls, Mealey said, "The reason you only have pictures of your championship teams is, in your mind, they were your only four successful seasons. You don't see your other teams as failures. You just ran out of time before you could get them where they needed to be." Mike leaned forward, and his enthusiasm grew. "Philadelphia hasn't won the whole thing in four years, and a lot of the players from that championship are gone. But we all know you're closer than most people think. The QB is young and talented with plenty of weapons around him. The offensive line is big and athletic. The defensive line is so-so, but the secondary is excellent. The only weakness I see right now is at linebacker, and that can be addressed through free agency and the draft. I won't fail you, give me this job, and I'll give you a few more pictures worthy of these walls."

CHAPTER 4

Joe woke midafternoon to the familiar tug of alcohol but resisted the temptation. For reason's unknown, even to himself, he needed to accomplish today's task with clear eyes. There'd be plenty of time for drinking later, it wasn't like he had anything else to do.

The clock said 3:12, he was over three hours late for an appointment he never intended to keep. Ten years ago, the quick reaction of then Patrolmen Owad had undoubtedly saved Joe's life. Despite that, Joe believed he owed the man nothing. Owad's daughter had been harassed by two goons, and Joe had hammered them, he didn't owe Owad, or anyone else, a damn thing. He had no intention of making any statements and planned to be gone before he was missed.

After a quick shower and a fresh change of clothes, Joe left the room he had checked into that morning. He knew the address but had never been to the storage facility he was now headed to. While Joe lay broken in a hospital, a coworker of his fathers, whom he'd never met, had packed up their simple home. Everything deemed saving had been put in storage, everything else was sold with the house. Later a rental contract and key were mailed to the rehab facility Joe was recovering in. The first year had been paid in advance, Joe had made it a priority and paid the last nine. When he called to take care of the most recent bill, Joe was told the facility had been sold, everything had to be relocated, or it would be disposed of. He'd never had the urge to visit these relics from a different life, but he couldn't let them go either.

A portly man of about forty greeted him in a sparse office. After showing his ID, Joe was led into a large warehouse. Rows of different size storage lockers ran the length of the building. They passed garage-sized units and smaller ones about half as big before reaching Joe's, which was no larger than a small walk-in closet.

The clerk pointed to some dolly's and said, "You can use the carts to wheel stuff out, just make sure you return them. If you need anything else, I'll be out front."

Alone with his reservations, Joe opened the door. A dozen boxes were inside. Slowly, he picked through the memories. In one box Joe found pictures of his Mother, each a relief to the fragile and faltering memory of a six-year-old boy. He pulled a glass frame from the box, warm blue eyes he struggled to remember held his gaze. In another there was a picture of his dad, his smiling face a brief reprieve from horrific images Joe would never forget.

Joe took his time inspecting each box before packing them into his truck. They filled the rear of the seat and a good portion of the passenger side. Clear eyes had replenished his memory with images of his parents, but now they were neither needed nor wanted.

CHAPTER 5

Chief Owad kept a sharp eye on the clock hanging in his office. As it spun past noon, his disappointment filled the cramped space. The indifference in the Blackstone's eyes had been a clear warning he had no intention of showing up to sign a statement, but Owad had let personal feelings cloud his judgment.

Had Blackstone not been at the diner, Adam wasn't sure how he'd have handled the two goons. What he did know was every scenario he played in his mind would have landed him in a lot of trouble. Still, if it had been anyone else he would have hauled them to the station, but this wasn't anyone else, this was Joe Blackstone. This was the kid who'd been a hero to an entire community. This was the kid who walked in on his father's murder, the likes of which Central Maine had never seen. This was the kid who won a savage battle for his life. This was the kid who was stabbed and shot twice before falling from a second-story window. This was the kid lying motionless on his front lawn when Adam rolled up that night.

Finding Blackstone in a fragile state between life and death, Adam's training had kicked in, and he administered CPR. Even now he could recall the horror of having to revive the young man he'd cheered for just hours before. Adam had been a thirty-eight-year-old patrolman, and he still struggled with the memories. How could an eighteen-year-old, with no family, possibly recover from that kind of tragedy?

Chief Owad hadn't treated Joe Blackstone like anybody else because he wasn't like anybody else.

Curiosity got the better of him, and Owad decided to run a search on Joe. The events of that November night were prominent on every resource available to the Chief, a black mark for his departs failure to close the case. But nothing else. After that night not a single record existed of the Joe Blackstone he knew. Scratching his head, he thought, *What the hell, how could that be?*

His patience faded with the late day sun. Frustrated, the Chief turned out his office lights and headed home. *I'll find Blackstone tomorrow, get a statement and maybe even a few answers.*

CHAPTER 6

Joe drank the first six pack in the lot below the field. There were three other cars scattered about, but he hadn't seen anyone exit or enter the sleeping school since he'd arrived. Joe grabbed the second six pack and got out of the truck. He yanked a can free, popped the top and took a long pull.

The fragrance of burning pine filled the crisp air. Soft clouds sagged beneath the stars and teased of snow. To Joe's left, a single light hung off the back of the gym, illuminating a paved walkway that ascended to his right. Climbing the path Joe fell further into the past with each step. He crested the hill, again a single light illuminated one end of the field, Keyes Field. To Joe, the frozen grass was aglow with memories, his private field of lost dreams.

Finishing a beer, he put the empty can in his coat pocket, unwilling to defile sacred ground. He opened another and walked across the field.

Before every game, he listened to the same music in his room before leaving home. He'd arrive at the school, put his bag in the locker room and take this same walk. Each time starting with the same song, AC / DC's, *If you want blood you got it*. It was a song that had motivated him, Joe never imagined it would come to define him.

As had been his pre-game ritual, Joe sat alone on the bench. Drinking greedily, he watched a catalog of memories play out before him. Entire games flashed by. Most, lopsided triumphs. These were supposed to have been a small part of his story, where it all began, not an irrelevant cliff note.

Joe shook his head, unable to ignore the one game he treasured most. He still carried pride, disappointment, and shame with the memory of it. It was the only time he was tested.

Thirteen Years Earlier

Only two minutes remained in the 3rd quarter when the Cony Rams scored to go up 19-0. Their fans erupted in a sea of red, while the Lawrence crowd fell eerily quiet. All hope of victory seemed lost. Standing helplessly on the sideline, Joe watched as Cony players taunted his teammates in the end-zone. One strutted toward the Lawrence bench. "You guys ain't shit," he said. "This is our field now."

It was the first time rage burned in Joe's veins.

Coach Cooper gathered his team, but before he could say a word, Joe cut him off. At first, the coach was pissed, but when he looked into his young stars eyes, he saw pure determination.

All attention now on Joe, he stepped to the center of the group and looked intently at his teammates. In a steely tone, Joe asked, "Did you see what they did?" His stare settled on one teammate after another. "Do you see what they think of us? They have no respect for us." He paused a long moment, his glare burning into the will of each player. "And they sure as hell don't fear us." Joe pointed across the field and hollered, "Let's teach them some respect and put the fear of God in 'em!"

Under Cooper, the Bulldogs traditionally ran a Power I offense, featuring a speedy tailback, punishing fullback and disciplined line. Joe's sophomore year, Cooper installed a shotgun spread package. It was a wrinkle Lawrence ran a few times a game. The *GUN* package, as it was referred to, consisted of only three run and three pass plays but it made the defense account for Joe as a runner. While commonplace in today's game, few teams were running it then.

After Cony had kicked the ball into the end-zone, Cooper pulled Joe aside. "From here on out we're in the gun. The game is yours now son, you lead the way, and they'll follow."

Already sitting atop a mountain of adrenaline, Cooper's words took him to new heights. With gritted teeth, Joe said, "Yessir."

Coach Cooper gave him the play. "Let's run blue gun 12 power."

Without another word, Joe trotted to the huddle and said, "First play is blue gun 12 power." Joe looked at Roland Lavoie who would line up beside him. On this play, Roland was supposed to block the defensive end. "Lavoie let the D-end go and block the outside linebacker instead. That fucking D-end has been a pain in the ass all day, and I'm sick of his shit." Joe was the only sophomore starter on the team, but from the way, his teammates hung on his every word it was clear who their leader was.

At the line of scrimmage, Joe looked over the defense and settled into the moment. Both sidelines melted away. He heard Cony's safety call out, "Blue special gun … blue special gun."

Troy Hill was split wide right, he settled into a crouch with his fist oddly high like he normally did. Cony's middle linebacker slid to his left and pointed at Lavoie. "Key 22 … Key 22."

"Ready — Set — Hut." Joe caught the snap and immediately stepped to his right.

Cony's defensive end on that side was their most physical player, if not their best. Richard Toothaker, was a 6' 5", 260 pound senior. Lawrence had been unable to block him all game, and he'd made them pay for it time and time again.

On the sideline, Cooper grimaced when he saw Roland blow right past Toothaker without blocking him. By the time Joe took his third step the big defensive end was barreling down on him. Right before contact, Toothaker dropped his eyes and hurled himself into the impending collision.

Lavoie sealed the outside linebacker, offensive tackle Shawn Fennell buried the defensive tackle and guard Jay Rowe out smothered the inside linebacker. As soon as Toothaker dropped his eyes, Joe launched himself. Unfortunately for Cony, he launched himself with a jump step that seemed to teleport Joe five yards to his right. Toothaker came up with nothing but air and hit the ground with a thud. Joe landed and shot upfield inside Roland's block. Troy made a vicious crack-back block on the safety, and Joe cut it to the outside. Only the cornerback stood between Joe and the end-zone. But battering ram disguised as Joe's right arm knocked him off his feet.

When he reached, the end-zone Joe turned and casually flipped the ball to an official. Ecstatic, his teammates charged toward him. Unlike Joe, they had yet to see the yellow flag. When they did, Joe saw their excitement bleed away.

"God dang it," Copper hollered. Reeling from the rollercoaster of emotions he watched his team walk back to the huddle dejected. He was thinking about his next play call when he heard Joe yell out "On the ball, run it again."

"What the hell is he doing?" Cooper asked anyone brave enough to answer. "Joe, JOE … HUDDLE UP!"

"On the ball, run it again!" Joe repeated. The determination on Joe's face smothered his team's disappointment. The offense hustled back to the ball and lined up. Cony was taken off guard but quickly recovered and lined up across the ball.

On Joe's command, Timmy Martin snapped the ball. Again, Lavoie trucked past D-end and let him come free. This time, Toothaker's advance was less aggressive. Mirroring the previous play, Joe lowered his pads to gather himself. This time, Toothaker stopped his advance, anticipating Joe's cut to the outside. It never came. Instead, Joe exploded through Toothaker who was flat-footed and absorbed the full force of the blow. Joe's cleat ground against Toothaker's facemask as he ran over him. The rest of Conys' defense had over-pursued, anticipating of the same play, and were out of position. Joe's teammates did an excellent job of staying on their blocks. A rule Cooper always preached was, *"If a defender cheats too much in one direction and you can't block him the way you want, use his momentum against him and block him the way he wants to go."* And that's what his team did. The outside linebacker fought inside so hard, Rolland buried him there; taking out two more defenders with one block. Joe read it perfectly and bounced outside.

Troy anticipated Cony's error and knew Joe would look to cut outside. So when he saw the safety back up, he attacked the corner, who was closer to the play, with a textbook stock-block.

For a moment, Cooper wasn't the head coach of the Lawrence Bulldogs; he was just another screaming fan and hollered, "Nice block Troy!" Blackstone slipped outside the final Cony defender and hit the sideline with a full head of steam. Cooper saw Cony's safety, Robin Weed, had been playing deep and had a good angle on Joe. Weed, a 6' 1", 210 pound senior had already scored two touchdowns for the Rams and happened to be the defending state champ in the one-hundred-meter dash. The coach knew Joe couldn't out run him with the angle Weed had but hopeful his quarterback could put a move on him.

Joe raced up the Lawrence sideline like a breakaway train. But his foot speed paled in comparison to his mind. Joe saw Weed bearing down on him, he knew Weed was a track star and the defending state sprint champ. Joe didn't care because he played baseball in the spring and knew if he ran track, Weed would be the runner up. Minutes ago, Weed had taunted Joe and his teammates. The smart move for Joe was to cut back behind Weed, but that would be too easy, he wanted to embarrass him. *"The prick might have an angle,"* thought Joe, *"but I got a whole new gear."* He flew past the sideline, only a few feet from his coach

He's going to score, Cooper thought. The Coach had never seen such determination on a player's face; the safety's angle didn't look so good anymore. Joe pulled away and Weed dove at the back of his legs. But it was too late, Joe was gone. In awe, Cooper raised his hands to signal the score.

When Joe crossed the goal line, the score was 19-6 in favor of Cony, but Lawrence had seized the momentum. Flush with resolve, Joe's teammates rushed to the end-zone. The home crowd was electric and for the first time in the game, doubt settled upon the Cony sideline.

The PAT team came on the field, and Joe jogged over to Cooper. Before the coach could say a word, Joe said, "Put me in on D." it wasn't a question or demand. Joe didn't say it because he *wanted* to go in he *needed* to.

Cooper pointed to his defensive coordinator. "Roderick put Blackstone in for Leclair at strong side backer."

"Got it, Coach." Justin Roderick was the defensive coordinator and assistant head coach. He wore a headset to communicate with two coaches in the booth above the field. Hearing the exchange over Justin's mic, one of the coaches said, "Justin if Blackstone gets hurt on defense we're screwed."

"Really coach? The kid just ran for eighty and ninety yards on back to back plays. On the second one, he ran by the state hundred-meter champ like the kid was standing still, and he's not even winded. He's going in."

The extra point sailed wide left, and after a short kick, Cony took over own their own 37-yard line. On first down, the Rams ran a sweep in Joe's direction, but he slipped a block and dropped the running back for a four yard loss. On 2nd down, Cony's quarterback dropped back to pass. Rabid, the Bulldogs chased him from the pocket, he scrambled to his right, and stepped out for no gain, bringing the 3rd quarter to a close.

Expecting a pass on 3rd and 14, Roderick called a blitz. The ball was snapped, and Joe rushed hard off the edge, easily beating the two blockers assigned to pick him up. But Cony caught the Bulldogs off guard and ran a quick pitch to the weak side of their formation, away from Joe. Lawrence cornerback Chris Buck reacted perfectly, Buck was in great position to make the tackle, until he slipped, leaving no one between Robin Weed and the end-zone.

Joe was on the opposite side of the field and four yards deep in the backfield when Weed cleared the line of scrimmage. He took off like a rocket, sliced through everyone between them, and caught Cony's fastest player as he was crossing the 20-yard line. Weed had messed up by carrying the football in his inside arm, and Joe was intent on making him pay for it. He stretched his right hand in the air, swung at the ball, and chopped it free. Weed stumbled, and Joe charged over him. They both tumbled out of bounds while the ball skidded across the grass. Buck, who hadn't given up on the play recovered the ball on the 17-yard line

The Cony fans sat in shock while the Lawrence following erupted. Chris' mom was so happy, her shrill voice cut through the crowd when she hollered, "Way to go Chris Buck!"

Joe ran to the sideline. "What do you think?" he asked Cooper.

Cooper adjusted his hat and said, "If it ain't broke..."

"Don't fix it," said Joe, sharing the same thought.

Joe took the field and gathered his team. "Nothing fancy guys, we're gonna keep pounding the rock down their throat. Same play blue gun 12 power. Then we're gonna line up and run it again."

This time when Lawrence lined up, Cony crowded the line of scrimmage. Determined to stop the run, the Rams were begging the Bulldogs to pass the ball. Joe and his teammates didn't care. Play after play, a big and physical Lawrence line fired off the ball rocking the more athletic, but smaller, Cony front. When the safeties and linebackers filled the holes, Joe ran through them, dragging two, three and four players at a time. The Cony defenders wilted under the Lawrence assault, constantly looking to the game clock, they moved slower after each play. Eighty-three yards and twelve plays later, Lawrence punched it in and again missed the extra point. Unable to stop Joe and his teammates, Cony clung to a 19-12 lead and willed the clock to expire.

There was 6:23 left on the game clock when the Cony offense took the field on their own 29. The Lawrence defense held tight on first and second down, but after no gain on third down the Rams picked up a first, thanks to a defensive holding penalty. Again, the offense ran a couple of conservative plays draining time off the clock. Faced with 3rd and 4 Cony surprised the Bulldogs with a play action pass to their tight end for a twelve yard gain.

The gutsy call helped Cony regain some momentum, more importantly, each additional play would drain valuable time off the clock. If they could convert one or two more first downs, the game would be over. On the next two plays, Cony ran up the middle, gaining a total of four yards. On 3rd and 6 they ran off tackle, away from Joe. The back made a nice cut at the line of scrimmage and surged close to the first down. The official spotted the ball, looked to the sideline and signaled for a measurement. The markers were carried onto the field and a hush settled over the crowd. One official pinned the chain to a yard line while the other pulled the first down marker toward the nose of the football. With the chain pulled tight, the official set the first down marker an inch past the nose of the ball. A mix of groans and cheers filled the air.

With 1:44 left in the game Cooper, used his last timeout and jogged onto the field. In the huddle, his players looking tired but focused. "I don't think they'll punt. They only need about six inches for a first, they're going to try and win it right here. Let's go goal line. They like the quarterback sneak in these situations, so I want the D-line to pinch. Joe, you switch with Heath; move to inside to linebacker, and key the QB." Eleven faces stared back at Cooper, each a mask of determination. "If they do come out in a punt formation, drop back into our regular return."

The official hollered, "Timeout's over, coaches off the field."

Cooper looked over his shoulder, gave the official his best *hold on a second* stare and turned back to his team. A huge grin spread across his face, and he said, "Guys this is what it's all about. Stuff 'em, and we'll win this thing."

"YESSIR!" His players bellowed

On 4th and inches, the Cony offense broke the huddle. They were going for it. A first down would seal the win, with no timeouts left, Lawrence would be unable to stop the clock.

The Fennel brothers Shawn and Derrick were lined up in the gaps to either side of the center. Joe was confident the Cony quarterback would not have any luck there. More likely he would let the center power forward and follow him. Joe knew he couldn't let that happen. As soon as the center's hand twitched Joe sprung forward.

The quarterback was already leaning forward when the snap hit his hands. The Rams signal caller was pulling the ball from beneath the center when Joe struck. Before the quarterback could gather the ball, Joe battered him with his own teammate. Joe drove both players to the ground five yards behind the line of scrimmage. The ball would have been fumbled had it not been pinned between the two Cony teammates.

Once again Joe had ignited his sideline, and fervent teammates surrounded him.

Joe was all business in the huddle. "Grey gun quick on the first play and gray gun smoke on the second. When we complete the first pass I'm going to yell *run it again*, everyone gets it?" A few grins broke out in the huddle, and everyone nodded. "Alright let's do it. Ready … Break."

The offense hustled over the ball. The Rams secondary was playing deep expecting a long pass. On the snap. Troy took a jab step at the cornerback. The defender, already twelve yards away, was backpedaling. Troy gathered himself, turned inside and caught a bullet from Joe. He sprinted up the field. Ron Mayo, the slot receiver, made a great downfield block on the cornerback. The two safeties finally converged to bring Troy down but not until he reached the Rams 36-yard line.

With less than 50 seconds left Joe directed his team. "On the ball, run it again. Hurry up on the ball."

On the next play, Troy made the same jab step. Joe pivoted and started his motion, and Troy readied himself for the ball. This time the cornerback attacked and slipped inside Mayo's block. Joe pumped the ball in Troy's direction, but instead of releasing it, he pulled back and lofted a tight spiral down the sideline. The entire stadium held its breath while the ball hung in the air. It dropped into Mayo's hands, and he dashed in for the score. The divide between the two sidelines couldn't have been greater.

Despite all the excitement Cony still led 19-18.

"No way are we kicking this coach," Joe said when he got to the sideline.

Cooper shook his head. "Not a chance, what do you think about QB power again."

"I think you read my mind."

Back on the field, the offense gathered around, and Joe said, "One more time blue gun 12 power. Does anyone have *ANY* doubt?" His teammate's faces were a mask of grit and determination.

Cony had nothing left, not even Toothaker managed any kind of push. The line opened a huge hole, and Joe trotted in for the two-point conversion untouched. Lawrence led 20-19 with 0:29 seconds left.

Cony was unable to handle the squib kick, and Lawrence recovered, sealing the victory. Joe took a knee, and the game was over.

Lawrence fans emptied onto the field, creating a jubilant sea of blue and gray. Joe was mobbed with praise and found himself encompassed by reporters. He listened to their questions and gave all the right answers.

What he recalled most was teammates celebrating with loved ones; and envy. Out of beer and nauseated by memories he headed back to his hotel.

CHAPTER 7

The bar was already buzzing with the happy hour crowd, which Joe knew would be dominated by locals. The small community was not a vacation destination and other than the paper mills there was little business to call on. Pete & Larry's, as the bar was known, catered to those who lived in the area and those who were back visiting a place they once called home. Joe wanted to avoid running into anyone from his past, but he wanted to continue drinking more. Figuring his long hair and beard would make him difficult to recognize he found an empty stool at the bar.

A short while later he sipped at his sixth glass of Patron Silver on the rocks. True to the task, the cold liquid had dulled his senses. A swelling crowd stood two deep all the way around the central bar. He'd recognized a few faces, but no one had recognized him. Joe was staring at two enormous breasts when someone walked in from the lobby and impeded his view. Drawn to them, he squinted and studied the new arrival with blurry eyes. After a moment, a familiar face came into focus. He polished off his drink and ordered another.

Joe watched the man walk around the bar toward a small gap in the crowd. Wedging into the void he signaled for a beer. His face was fuller, and hair thinner, than the last time they'd seen one another.

Troy Hill had been like an older brother. They had met the summer before Joe's freshman year and became inseparable; playing football, baseball, and basketball together. When they weren't playing, they were training. Although he didn't possess Joe's natural gifts, Troy was a good athlete with a tremendous work ethic. When Joe's dad was away for work, Troy and his family had always welcomed him at their house. He'd been a great friend to Joe, but distance and circumstance had caused them to lose touch when Troy went away to college.

Joe watched his old friend take a pull from his beer and scan the crowd. Troy's eyes drifted past Joe, stopped and snapped back with recognition.

Joe had planned to leave before anyone knew he was in town. He didn't have any place to go, but he didn't want to be there. Had he been close to sober, he would've left the bar as soon as Troy walked in, but he wasn't. Joe held his glass up to acknowledge his old friend and took a long pull from his drink. Troy's face filled with disbelief and he circled the bar.

Joe stood, and the crowd parted as he stepped away from the bar.

Troy stopped in front of him. "Joe?" he asked, stunned.

"How you been Troy?" Joe extended his hand.

Troy grabbed the offered hand and pulled Joe in for a hug. Joe staggered. The two men embraced and slapped each other on the back. "My God," Troy said. "I haven't seen you since ..."

Joe slurred his words and said, "Yeah I know it's been a long time."

"I tried looking you up about a thousand times but when you left it was like you vanished."

Joe expression was blank

It was obvious, his friend had been drinking for a while so Troy asked, "You wanna get outta here?" Let's go someplace quiet so we can catch up."

"I gotta better idea," Joe said. "Let's stay here and keep drinking."

Troy looked toward the back of the bar and pointed to an empty table. "OK, let's grab a seat." They walked over and sat down. "So where've you been?" Troy asked. "What've you been doing?"

Joe had prepared an answer for this question if he was recognized while in town. "Pretty much all over, Dad left me a little bit of money. So I've sorta been, hanging out." It was a boring answer describing a pathetic existence most people would choose not to follow up on. Joe wasn't looking for pity, but he did prefer anonymity. The problem was he hadn't expected to run into Troy.

Troy's face twisted into a quizzical frown and remembered the day he met Joe. School had let out, it was his first summer in Maine. Looking for a game of hoops he took a drive to North Street playground in Waterville. It was about six o'clock, and there was a full game going with six or eight guys waiting for the next one. Troy recognized several of the players. Most were upperclassmen or recent grads from one of the nearby schools. One player stood out, Danny Carr was last year's Mr. Basketball in the state of Maine. He had graduated from Waterville and was going to the University of Maine on a basketball scholarship. Carr was 6'6", and a solid 225 pounds. When Troy finally got on the court, his team was matched up against Carr, and four guys he knew had already graduated. Troy knew three of the guys on his team, one was going to be a senior and two were juniors like him. He didn't know the other guy but assumed he was older when he pointed to Carr and said, "I'll take him." The stranger was giving up an inch or two but looked thicker and stronger than Mr. Basketball. They were easily the two biggest guys on the court.

Not liking his team's chances, Troy was counting the growing crowd trying to determine how long he would have to sit waiting for another game.

Carr hit a three on his first trip down the court. At the other end, Troy dribbled the ball off his foot, setting up a fast break the other way. Carr went in for an easy layup, but the new guy came from nowhere and pinned the ball against the backboard. Everyone on Troy's team and those waiting for the next game went nuts.

"Goaltending," Carr said and motioned that the basket was good.

Everyone on Troy's team argued it except the guy who'd made the play, he was laughing as he jogged back up court. Eventually, the rest of his team followed suit.

"Dude that was bullshit," said Troy.

"No big deal," — the stranger rubbed his hands together — "it's not gonna matter."

"I'm Troy, what's your name?"

"Joe."

The rest of the game was physical, chippy and downright nasty. Joe smothered Carr, despite all the picks and screens his teammates set for him, Mr. Basketball couldn't get a shot off. On the other end, Troy and his team kept feeding the ball to their big man. The more Carr's team fought to slow Joe down, the better he played. He beat double teams, triple teams and powered through hard fouls.

They ran away with the game and stayed on and won seven more before calling it a night. While they were walking off the court, Troy asked, "Where you from Joe?"

"Fairfield."

"No shit me too, did you play ball at Lawrence?"

"Yeah still do."

Confused Troy asked, "What do you mean still do? I was on the team last year, and I'm pretty sure I'd have remembered you."

"I played for the middle school, I'm going to try out for the high school team this year."

Troy a smile creased his face. "Oh, I get it, you're Blackstone, the monster 8th grader who dominated freshman football last year. I've heard about you. Making varsity isn't gonna be a problem."

The two had become fast friends. What had always impressed Troy, was how hard Joe pushed himself. Not only was he the most gifted athlete Troy had ever seen, but the hardest working as well. Troy had assumed Joe's future was as a pro football player. After what had happened to him, it was easy to envision Joe's life going in a different direction, but it would have gone in *SOME* direction.

His voice dripping with skepticism, Troy asked, "So you've been … *'hanging out'*?"

"Yep."

Troy didn't believe the answer, but he faked a smile. "Cool," he said and waved his hand to get the attention of a nearby waitress.

She strutted to their table and asked, "What can I getcha?"

"I'll have a bottle of Shipyard," Troy said, "and my brother here would like?"

"I'll take a double Patron Silver on the rocks," added Joe.

"Be right back," the waitress said and strutted off.

"Are you home for good?"

Not wanting to mention his trip to the storage shed Joe replied, "Nope, passing through."

"Oh, that's too bad," said Troy slouching in his chair. "How long will you be here? Where're you staying?"

"I have a room here. I'm rolling out tomorrow."

Troy shook his head. "No way, you're staying with me."

"I already —"

"Not up for discussion," Troy said, cutting him off. "Don't make me drag your big ass outta here."

Joe smiled because he had no doubt Troy would try. "Okay, you win, I'll crash with you. Besides, I might as well see the Hill Mansion while I'm in town."

Troy laughed. "Shut the hell up, or maybe I will let you sleep here."

"Troy I know you're not living with your parents and I know you ain't renting an apartment because ... 'that's a bad investment'," said Joe, mocking Troy with his own favorite phrase. "I'm sure you're living some place nice, and I'm sure you own it."

Troy raised his hands in mock surrender. "Alright enough. You are right, I bought a place. And no, it doesn't suck."

They both laughed.

To Joe, the conversation was both foreign and familiar. He hadn't joked and laughed like this in years, yet he was able to do so with Troy like they'd seen each other every day since they were kids. Joe wasn't sure how much the tequila had to do with it, and he didn't care, it felt good.

Troy had intended on stopping for one drink before heading to The Point Afta, for a late dinner with friends. He considered inviting Joe along, but none of them had known Joe, only of him, so Troy blew them off. The two old friends drank and talked. Troy told Joe his parents had retired to Florida and his sister was doing good and living in the area. They talked about old football games, relieved basketball tournaments at the Bangor Auditorium and badgered each other about who hit the longest home runs in baseball.

Their table filled with empty drinks and the night raced by. By the time the lights were raised, neither was in any condition to drive, but both were far too drunk to know it. After settling their tab Joe and Troy staggered outside. Troy, who normally only had two or three drinks, fell twice as they were walking to his Tahoe. Joe was much bigger and had been drinking almost every day for ten months. Despite having not eaten since his early breakfast; and having drunk much more than Troy, Joe seemed to be holding the alcohol better, or so he thought.

"Troy I'll drive, you can't even stand up."

"Nah, I'm fine, I can drive."

"You can't even walk," said Joe, "give me the keys or I ain't going."

"You sure? You drank a shit load of tequila."

"I'm used to it." True. "I'm fine, I can drive." Not so true.

Troy handed Joe the keys, and they piled into the SUV. Joe managed to get out of the parking lot without hitting a car. He drove slow and focused intently on the salt-stained pavement. Despite his best efforts, he was all over the road. Troy was late telling Joe where to turn a couple times which almost landed them in the ditch. Through sheer luck, they made it to Troy's driveway without causing an accident or getting arrested. Joe pulled down the long drive and stopped in front of a large home. A porch wrapped around the otherwise modern design.

"Nice place," Joe said as he turned the ignition off.

"Thanks." Troy's head was resting against the passenger window. "I'm starving."

"Me too, you have anything to eat?"

Troy sat up and looked at Joe. "Nope, not a thing."

"Fuck it, let's go to Truckers."

"Let's do it," Troy said.

Joe backed out of the driveway, nearly hitting Troy's mailbox in the process. Less than a mile later their luck ran out when Joe veered away from the bright lights of an oncoming car. Right before the two vehicles passed, the Tahoe's front passenger side tire slipped off the pavement. Joe's reaction was late and too severe. He jarred the wheel away from the rough terrain. When the tire regained contact with the asphalt, the Tahoe lurched to the left and shot across the oncoming lane, missing the rear end of the other vehicle by less than a foot. Had they been traveling any faster the SUV would have rolled over. As it was, they were propelled off the road. They plowed through the remnants of the last snow storm, and a dozen small trees before slamming into a large pine. Airbags punched both passengers back into their seats.

Startled by the near miss, the young girl driving the car looked over her shoulder as the Tahoe dove into the woods. She stopped, settled her nerves and dialed 911. Next, she called her dad while executing a three-point turn, and headed back to where the Tahoe had gone off the road.

His voice was thick with sleep when he answered, "Hello."

"Dad."

"Becky, are you okay?"

"I'm fine, but I just saw a car go off the road."

"What? Where?"

"About two miles from the house, toward town."

"I'll be there in five minutes."

He was. The Chief parked behind the flashing lights on his daughter's car and shined his searchlight along the side of the road. *Fucking idiots,* he thought, spotting the SUV with a trail of mangled trees in its wake. He left the searchlight on, climbed out of his car, and trudged into the woods. Half way there, Owad recognized the two men leaning against the SUV, talking with his daughter.

Becky broke off from them, hurried to her father and said, "They seem, fine Dad, barely a scratch."

Reading his daughter's face, Adam knew there was more. "But?"

Becky hesitated and said, "They're pretty drunk."

Adam heard a car approaching and knew the scene was going to be a zoo within the next few minutes. "Tell me exactly what happened."

Becky took him through what she had seen, how the Tahoe veered off the road, climbed back onto the pavement, and shot behind her, ending up in the woods.

One of his officers was approaching when Adam asked, "How close did they come to hitting you?"

Becky could see her dad's anger rising and said, "Dad I'm fine."

"How close."

She grimaced and said, "Pretty close."

Adam looked past Becky; toward Joe and Troy. "Go home," he said and turned toward the young officer who'd arrived. "Get these two morons checked out, and bring 'em to the station."

"Yes, sir."

The officer left to do his job, but Becky stayed. "Dad," she said, pleading. "I know you're mad, but this mornin' —"

"Becky," Adam said, his voice rising. "I don't care about this morning, you need to leave, right now."

Becky climbed out of the woods and went home. A paramedic checked on Joe and Troy. Afterward, they were taken to jail.

CHAPTER 8

The next day, Joe woke up in a small cell. His body was stiff from the hard cot and his head splitting. He rose slowly walked to the toilet, relieved himself and splashed water on his face before returning to the thin mattress. From his cell, he couldn't see anything but an empty hallway, so he sat and tried to piece together the events of the previous night. He remembered drinking with Troy and driving to his house. The details were fuzzy, and Joe wondered, *didn't we make it back to Troy's? How the fuck did I end up in jail? And where the hell is Troy?*

His eyes were closed and head in his hands when he heard a door open. He turned toward the sound of approaching footsteps. Chief Owad stepped in front of Joe's cell, unlocked the door and said, "Let's go, follow me."

Joe followed the Chief back the way he'd come from. They passed through the door at the end of the hall and into an open room with a half dozen cubicles, all but one were occupied. Joe was well aware all eyes were on him, the fact that he recognized a couple people in the room added to his self-loathing. He followed Owad into a private office off the main room. The Chief took a seat behind the desk and pointed Joe toward a small chair in front of it. Joe eased his large frame onto the chair and waited.

A vein popped out in Adam's neck while he stared daggers at Joe. I was a full minute before he said a word. When he spoke, his voice was saturated with contempt. "What the hell is your problem?"

"Excuse me?" asked Joe.

"I said, what the hell is your problem?"

"I don't have one."

"Oh, let me tell you something. You are one hundred percent wrong about that. You've got a couple problems. You jerked me around yesterday, you were drinking and driving last night, and you almost hit my little girl. From where I'm sitting you have all kinds of problems."

The pounding in Joe's head grew stronger.

The Chief continued, "*YOU* of all goddamn people." Joe's eye's flashed with anger, and Adam's rage pushed him further. "Do you know how many DUI accidents I've had to respond to? The first time was about two weeks after I'd joined the department." Adam leaned forward. "Do you know when that was?"

"I don't need to listen to this shit."

"Well, you're gonna. You almost hit my little girl last night, so I don't give a shit what you want. If I'd lost *my* mother to a drunk driver, I'd be a little—"

Joe sprung out of his chair, crashed through the desk and was on the Chief in a flash. Gripping Owad's throat, he had the smaller man, still seated in his chair, pinned between the back wall of the office and his desk.

Officers rushed in when they heard the commotion. But they couldn't pull Joe off until he recognized his own rage in the Chief's eyes and surrendered.

CHAPTER 9

Philadelphia

Before a near capacity crowd in the team's auditorium, Ms. Taylor introduced Mike Mealey as the team's new head football coach. Following the introduction, Mealey stepped to the podium and addressed the media for the first time in his new role. Although welcoming, each member of the press was searching for their own nugget. From the start, Mealey was brash and pulled no punches. When asked what he thought of their franchise quarterback, Mealey answered, "Jeff Pergine is young, talented and cocky. What's not to like?" When asked how many games he expected to win this upcoming season his replied, "All of them." Neither answer was entirely truthful.

Mealey told the assembly he expected to introduce his offensive and defensive coordinators within the next couple weeks and thanked them all for coming.

After the conference, Mealey went directly to his new office. All he had was a desk, chairs, phone, computer and secretary but that's all he needed. Knowing his ultimate goal was to be a head coach in the WFL, Mike had been building a database of potential staff members for years.

His two top choices were available, and the first thing he needed to do was meet with the Freedom's current defensive coordinator. Kevin Pickell had been hired as a linebacker coach on Mikalonis' first staff, three years later he had been promoted to Defensive Coordinator. During Philadelphia's Championship years, it had been Pickell's defense that had garnered much of the credit, constantly among the best in the league at rushing the passer and creating turnovers. Often fined, and once suspended for an entire season, Pickell had been one of the most controversial figures in pro football, if not all of pro sports. The same mayhem that made him such a great coach was largely to blame for his never getting the nod for the top job. Over the past few seasons, the one-time lightning rod had faded from the spotlight and so too had his side of the ball. No longer among the leaders, Philly's defense had been mired in mediocrity. Most assumed the game had passed him by and at 62 he would soon retire.

Twenty minutes after Mealey settled into his office, Pickell knocked on his open door. "You asked to see me, Coach?"

"Yes, I did." Mealey gestured to a chair and said, "Please have a seat."

"Congratulations on the new gig," Kevin said as he parked himself in front of Mealey's desk.

"Thank you." Getting right to business Mike said, "You've had a hell of a run here."

"Yeah, we've won a few games over the years."

"What do you think of the current roster?" Mike asked.

"The offense has some players and the defense is loaded with dead weight."

"You sure it's not a scheme issue?"

Pickell did nothing to hide the animosity in his voice. "Scheme issue? Have you even watched this team play?"

Mealey stayed calm but continued to goad the DC. "Yes, I have watched this team play, and the defense you've been running doesn't look much like the one you ran five years ago."

Kevin stood and pointed across the desk. "Coach how about you go fuck yourself, I've gotten more outta the slop I've had to work with over the past few years than any hot shot you're going to bring in here to replace me. Instead of wasting my time why don't you be a fucking man and say what's on your mind."

"I guess you're anxious to retire and go golfing with coach Mikalonis?"

"I know what this is, somewhere you have a list with a bunch of hot shit coach's, that you're going to sell to Pollard as God's gift to defense so you can replace me. You're the boss, and you can do whatever the fuck you want but know this, I'm not going to go crawl under a rock. I'll sign on with someone, and when I do, I'm going to take your team apart every time we play each other." A wide grin spread across Mealey's face, raising Pickell's anger to a boil. "What the fuck is so funny? I swear to God I'll mop this fucking floor with you."

"It doesn't look like you've changed as much as everyone says." Pickell remained standing with a dark expression on his face but held his tongue. Mealey continued, "Coach Pickell, please sit back down."

After a moment's pause, Pickell eased himself back into the chair. He retained a fiery glare but his brow curled with curiosity.

Mealey held the older man's glare. "I've watched the film, and like you said the scheme is not the same. I also know it's not the same because you haven't been given the tools you need to be successful. Even John admits the defense was overlooked due to the needs of the offense and available talent. He and I both agree, the defensive line, and more so the linebackers need to be upgraded. The secondary has a few players, but no *hot shit* coach is going to have success unless we can pressure the quarterback." Mealey leaned back in his chair. "What I *didn't* know was if you even cared anymore. It seems you do, so, it looks like we've got two options."

Pickell took the bait. "And those would be?"

"We can get you the tools you need and keep you on as the defensive coordinator, or we can fucking fight because if you ever talk to me like that again, we're going to. What's it going to be?"

"Why choose?" said Pickell. "Let's do both."

***

Fifteen hours after Pickell agreed to stay on as the Freedom defensive coordinator, Mark Lafond arrived at the Philadelphia facility. In addition to the greatest head of hair since Jimmy Johnson patrolled the sidelines, Lafond was known throughout the WFL as an offensive genius. But after two unsuccessful stints as a head coach, his star had lost its luster, and he'd been out of coaching for two seasons. His first stint as the head man had come early in his career but lasted only eighteen months. The popular opinion was that he failed due to lack of experience. His second stint, while longer at three years, had been equally forgettable. This time the press labeled him as lazy and unorganized. Mealey had always been fascinated by Lafond's offensive principals, game plans and play calling. After speaking to several former players and colleagues, Mike was convinced Mark Lafond was the perfect guy for his team. During both his tenures as a head coach, ownership had forced personnel and staff members on Lafond; that more than anything had led to his teams' failures. Supporters had not come forward to back the Head coach for fear of losing their jobs, while others made him their scapegoat. He was a talented coach with original ideas and a tireless work ethic. Mark Lafond was no longer the popular pick for jobs around the WFL, but he was Mike's pick.

Pollard's secretary met Lafond in the lobby and escorted him to the head coach's office, where Mealey and Pollard awaited. Introductions were made, and once everyone was seated around Mealey's desk, the Head coach asked, "So Mark why haven't you gotten back into coaching."

Lafond spoke in an easy rhythm, like an old friend. "I've had several offers, but none of them interested me. So I decided to enjoy the time off and spend it with my family I got to watch my boys play more ball over the last two years than the previous ten."

Pollard asked, "But you're interested in getting back on the sideline now?"

"Yes, my youngest son is graduating in a few months, and the other graduated last year. Either on the sideline or in the studio, it's time I get back to work."

"Why didn't the other jobs interest you?" Mealey asked.

"Throughout my career, I've tried to be the best coach I could. On the field and within front office my goal has always been to win. I was lucky enough to get offered a couple head coaching jobs, and despite some reservations I took them." A mix of frustration and regret twisted the side of Lafond's mouth into a frown. "I ended up spending more energy working around the internal politics than coaching, and ultimately failed. Moving forward I won't take a job where there's a power struggle or conflicting ideologies within the building."

John and Mike glanced at one another and shared a silent thought. "Let's take a tour of the facility," said John.

The trio continued their conversation while John led them throughout the facility. Genuinely impressed Lafond said, "This is one heck of a compound."

"Thank you," John said, "but I saved the best for last. Our Sports Science Center, or as we call like to call it, the SSC, is the crown Jewel of the entire complex. Follow me."

Pollard led them around a corner where a two-story glass wall revealed a cavernous gym. In addition to the conventional equipment you could find in most gyms, Philadelphia had over two dozen pieces of proprietary equipment. Philadelphia had partnered with Newton Performance, a manufacturer of the most advanced training equipment on the planet. NP provided the franchise with the latest in training technology, in return Philadelphia allowed them to collect and study the data generated by their players.

Inside the SSC, Lafond was wide eyed as he examined the machines. Mounted on the right-hand wall, an odd looking array of cameras and electronic equipment caught his eye. "What's that?" He asked.

Pollard answered, "It's our virtual reality chamber. Players can use it to refine their reflexes and instincts. It monitors body mechanics and gives the athletes feedback on how to improve."

Holding the chamber door open as Lafond stepped inside, Mealey said, "I don't know about you, but this thing impressed the hell out of me when I first saw it."

Three-dimensional images surrounded Lafond, giving him the impression he was in the middle of a live game. Lafond shook his head and gasped. "Holly shit, this is incredible."

When Lafond exited the simulator, Mealey said, "The only ideology I see when I walk in this building is to be the best. If you agree, I'd like to offer you the offensive coordinator position. What do you say?"

Mark extended his hand. "I'm in."

CHAPTER 10

That same night, twenty miles away in Lower Gwynedd, Philadelphia Freedom star quarterback Jeff Pergine arrived at his new neighbor's house. He was an hour and twenty minutes late, mainly because he knew he could be. Civilians like his host for the evening would never complain, and Jeff enjoyed taking advantage of that fact. They were eager for the privilege of his company, it gave them something to brag about.

Two weeks earlier, the fat husband had driven up Jeff's driveway while his furniture was being delivered. Jeff had almost howled in laughter while his portly neighbor struggled to remove himself from a shiny red Porsche, but Jeff's face had remained a mask of friendship. He met the man at the bottom of his front steps with an extended hand and said, "Hello."

They shook, and Jeff's neighbor said, "Hi, I'm Lewis Leary, Welcome to Oak Meadow, I live across the way with my wife, Cindy."

What Jeff wanted to say was go back where you came from fat man and don't bother me again. But he was as cunning off the field as on. Long before he was a football star, Jeff Pergine had learned how to read people and give them what they wanted, all the while hiding his true desires.

"Jeff Pergine pleased to meet you," he lied.

"It's a pleasure to meet you, I'm a huge fan. I've been watching you play since before you won the Heisman."

"Thank you," Pergine said with a rehearsed smile.

"I won't keep you, I'm sure your busy. My wife Cindy and I wanted to invite you to dinner at our house tonight if you don't already have plans."

"I have to get some things settled here, and tomorrow I'm headed out of town to do a commercial, maybe I can take a raincheck?"

"Sure thing, anytime. We can touch base when you get back." The two said bye and Lewis crammed himself back into his car and drove off.

Jeff had never intended to have dinner with his pathetic neighbor, but two weeks later he'd seen Lewis' wife, Cindy, checking the mailbox at the bottom of their driveway. Her ass looked incredible in black yoga pants, so he stopped, rolled down the window and introduced himself. It was a mild winter day, but still, the cool air caused Cindy's erect nipples to poke through her fitted sweatshirt. It took all Pergine's considerable skill to keep eye contact with Lewis' young bride. "Hi, I'm Jeff, your new neighbor."

Cindy pranced over and rested her elbows on Jeff's open window. Arching her breast forward she said, "Well hi there neighbor, it's about time we meet." A coy grin spread across her face, and her blue eye's sparkled with mischief.

This chic is looking for more than her husband has to offer. She wants excitement, she wants danger, and I'm going to give it to her, thought Jeff as he flashed his million dollar smile. "I hope I was worth the wait," he said. Leaning back, he gazed at Cindy's figure, taking his time to soak in her supple breast. His eyes drifted back to hers, and he pursed his lips. "Because *you* sure were *Mrs. Leary.*"

Cindy's face glowed with excitement. "Mmm, you're so bad."

"Mrs. Leary maybe we should have the dinner Mr. Leary mentioned, I promise I can be good."

Despite his flirtatious words, Cindy couldn't read Jeff's eyes. She'd always controlled men and bent them to her will. But her lack of it now warmed her with anticipation.

"Why don't you come by tonight at six?"

"Sure, that could be fun, see you tonight *Mrs. Leary.*" Jeff put his SUV in drive and Cindy jumped back as he pulled away without another word. He looked in his rearview mirror and Cindy was still standing where he'd left her, watching, as he sped up his driveway. She was a predator, and now she knew she wasn't alone, Jeff looked forward to showing Cindy her place on the food chain.

Theirs were the only two properties accessible via a private drive. The houses sat opposite one another, each with its own driveway bracketed by large oak trees. Despite their old-world design the homes were ultra-modern and contained every possible convenience. Two brothers, owners of a large construction company, had purchased the land years earlier. Their business had skyrocketed with the housing market in the late 90's. After six years of record profits, they rewarded themselves by building the twin mansions. But their business had softened while the homes were under construction. They had barely moved in before the construction bubble had burst. Shortly after, their company collapsed. They had to file for bankruptcy, and the bank assumed ownership of both homes. Initially listed at over twelve million dollars apiece, both of the twenty-six thousand square foot homes were empty for several years. Unwilling to maintain the properties until the housing market recovered the bank continued to reduce their asking price.

A middle-aged bachelor, Lewis Leary had been working as a used car salesman, when he'd purchased the sole winning ticket for a two hundred and fifty-million-dollar jackpot. An opportunistic real-estate agent had shown Lewis the properties. He offered the bank four million dollars, they'd accepted, and Lewis had substantially upgraded from his one bedroom apartment.

A few weeks later, Lewis met Cindy, on a trip to Atlantic City. The buxom blonde was working as a cocktail waitress at the Borgata. She'd waited on his blackjack table, and the balding millionaire was immediately taken back by Cindy's beautiful face and seductive body. He tipped her handsomely and asked if she'd join him for dinner, which she declined. On her fourth trip to his table, Cindy overheard Lewis, while he was recounting his lottery story to a trashy divorcee seated beside him. Cindy gave him a new drink, and when he'd tipped her, she leaned in close and said, "Thank you. If you're sticking around, I get off at eleven. I'll be at the Gypsy bar downstairs."

Lewis had been waiting for her when she arrived. Impossibly tight jeans and a skin-tight halter top had left little for his imagination. Lewis never stood a chance. From that moment on, the round Romeo and the hottie half his age had been an item.

Lewis answered the door wearing khaki shorts and a blue Nike golf shirt, "Good evening neighbor."

Jeff hid his disappointment, smiled and said, "Hello." Wishing it had been Cindy who greeted him.

"Come in, come in. What's your poison?" Lewis laughed as he led Jeff through the three-story entryway. "I've always loved saying that."

Lewis was several drinks into the evening. *What an idiot, this guy's clueless,* thought Jeff. Playing the friendly neighbor, he said, "I'll take a vodka and cranberry if you have it."

"Coming up," Lewis said and led Jeff to a large granite bar adjacent to a vaulted family room; both nearly identical to those in his house. His host hit a button behind the bar, and Jeff cringed inwardly, as country music filled the air.

Fixing the drink, Lewis said, "I'm so glad you could make it. Cindy is still getting ready, but she should be down any second, you know how women are. I had my chef pick up some dry aged strip steaks and lobsters. I hope you like surf and turf?" Without waiting for a response, Lewis rambled on.

Jeff feigned interest with an occasional nod or smile, all the while thinking, *I can't wait to bang your wife*. The clatter of heels against a marble floor captured his attention. Cindy entered through an archway on the opposite side of the grand room. She wore a light knit mini skirt, and Jeff doubted anything else. The blue material collared her neck, stretched tightly over her toned body, and stopped pleasantly high on her thigh. An inviting section of material was cut from the center of her chest to her navel, only carefully placed laces held the garment to some level of concealment.

"There she is, it's about time," Lewis said, rushing his words. "I thought we were going to have to eat without you."

Jeff greedily drank Cindy in as she approached. He stood to greet her, her body brushed purposely against his when he kissed her on the cheek.

"Sorry I'm so late," she said.

"Oh, that's fine, I just got here myself."

Cindy asked for a glass of wine, so Lewis suggested they go to the wine cellar where he had already decanted several bottles. Their chef, an Argentinian, whom Lewis introduced as Chef Martin greeted them on their way through the kitchen. "Good evening sir, it's an honor to cook for you. How would you like your steak?"

"Rare," answered Pergine, not wasting words talking to the help.

"Very well," the Chef said and returned to his work.

The wine cellar was located in the basement along with another large bar, game room, and home theater. The lower level had been designed with dark wooden beams, old stone, and exposed brick. It gave the entire area an antique vibe. Again, the layout was similar to Jeff's, but the styling contrasted the ultra-modern look of his basement and made this space much more appealing. The realization flooded him with jealousy, only his desire for Cindy's lithe body kept him from storming out. Focusing on that hunger, Jeff's façade never faltered.

Inside the wine cellar, a tray of antipasti sat on a round table in the center of the room. Several thousand bottles of wine were displayed on mahogany racks, which covered the walls. Lewis gestured toward the table and said, "Please, have a seat." Cindy and Jeff made themselves comfortable. And Lewis retrieved one of the decanters he'd prepared, from a counter built into the wine rack.

While pouring a glass for Jeff, Lewis said, "This is a 2007 Joseph Phelps Insignia Cabernet, Cindy's favorite."

Jeff took a sip. Although he usually didn't drink wine, he found the full-bodied taste pleasant enough, "Very nice," he said with earnest appreciation.

Had Lewis not been pre-occupied, making ridiculous slurping noises, he may have noticed the way Cindy's eyes consumed their guest when she echoed Jeff's words. "Very nice indeed." And then, took her first sip of wine.

Throughout dinner, Lewis and Cindy peppered their guest with questions. Jeff, himself, his own favorite topic, charmed his hosts with stories of his many accolades, often drawing a friendly pat on the lap or grasping of his forearm from Cindy.

The delicious food and wine coupled with the abundant conversation about himself had Jeff flying high. He had planned on slipping Lewis enough Rohypnol to knock him out, but now he had a better idea. Jeff excused himself to use the bathroom. Once alone, he removed a small bottle from his pocket and extracted half of his usual dose with the dropper. Before going back into the wine cellar, Jeff stopped at the adjacent bar and poured three shots of tequila, adding the Rohypnol to one of the glasses.

He sauntered in with the shots and said, "I hope you don't mind, I helped myself to these. Some of the guys on the team and I like to drink a shot of tequila after a nice dinner, it's kind of our thing." He lied, "I thought we could do the same."

"Let's do it," Lewis said, yelping.

Cindy nibbled at her lower lip and raised a provocative brow.

Jeff handed out two of the glasses. They raised the shots, and Jeff said, "To a fun night and getting to know each other better, cheers." They touched glasses and each tossed back the fiery liquid.

When Lewis suggested moving to the game room for after dinner drinks, Jeff wondered, *did I even need the roofie?*

While her husband stumbled to the bar, Cindy added a little extra sway to her hips as she made her way to the sitting area. Glancing back, she was pleased to see Jeff following her, his eyes riveted to her ass. "Well hello there," Cindy whispered when he joined her in a love seat. She sat up and looked over the leather backing and saw Lewis was still fixing drinks. A warm hand slid between her thighs, her body tensed and she snapped her head around. Exposed by the forbidden touch, her pulse raced to a fevered pitch.

As Jeff had suspected, Cindy was not wearing any panties. His gaze searched her eyes; unveiling her fear, his pulse to quickened. The tension rose between them, until a last, her eyes fell shut and she eased back against the cushions. A shallow gasp escaped her, and his mouth twisted into a mischievous grin.

"Alright, let's keep this party rolling." Lewis' words were slurred as he staggered over with their drinks.

At her husband's approach, Cindy pulled at Jeff's hand. Resisting, he enjoyed the panic on her face. He waited until Lewis was rounding the couch before he allowed Cindy to remove his hand. Pleased with himself, Jeff twisted toward his pudgy neighbor and asked, "What did you make us?"

"Nothing but the best, Macallan 25." Lewis boasted. He managed to hand Jeff and Cindy their glasses before tripping over a coffee table and careening into the seat opposite theirs.

While Lewis pawed at the golden liquid soaking his shirt, Jeff offered Cindy a private toast. "To a night you won't forget." His hungry eyes set her ablaze with desire. Jeff turned to Lewis and said, "Hey buddy, can we get some dance music in here?"

Lewis shimmied forward, leaned toward the coffee table and said, "I can get you any song you want with this." He grabbed a remote off the table and aimed it at a rack of stereo equipment behind the bar. Lewis fumbled with the buttons but eventually found a satellite station with good club music, he turned it up and sat back with a triumphant grin.

The music was loud enough that Jeff had to raise his voice for Lewis to hear him. "Great music man, I bet a guy like you can really dance."

Overcome by drugs and alcohol, Lewis' head rolled from side to side. When he shook it no in response to Jeff's question, he looked like a bobble head in slow motion. He closed his eyes for a moment and said, "Not me ... I'm too fat, Cindy can dance, though, she's great."

Jeff glanced at Cindy with a devious grin. She knew where he was heading. "You're awful," she said, but an eager expression betrayed her words.

He looked back at Lewis. "She should dance for us when we have team parties the wives do it all the time. Cindy's as pretty as any of them, but damn! Some of those girls get wild. You wouldn't believe how sexy they can dance." The truth was, Jeff rarely socialized with his teammates, yet alone their wives. He preferred his own *activities* but knew Lewis wouldn't be able to resist the challenge.

Right on cue, Lewis said, "Come on honey sh … show Mr. All-Pro what an all-st … star really looks like." He roared at his own joke.

Cindy shook her head and looked at Jeff. "I'm not gonna dance."

Jeff jumped up so abruptly it startled her. He slid the coffee table out of the way, offered his hand, and said, "Yes you are." They locked eyes, ignoring Lewis until Cindy relented. Jeff helped her up, gave her a pat on the ass, and sat back down.

Cindy picked up the remote and browsed the stations until she found a song with a steady but slower beat. Moving toward her husband, her hips pulsed with rhythm, and manicured nails traced a sinful path over her body. Before long, she was grinding on Lewis' lap while his meaty hands groped awkwardly over her breast. All the while, her eyes never left Jeff's. Another song played, and she rose from her husband's lap. Fixing herself between the two men, she continued dancing for her neighbor.

Jeff leaned to the side so he could gauge the inebriation on Lewis' face, satisfied, he crooked a finger and summoned Mrs. Leary.

Flaunting herself between Jeff's legs, Cindy placed her hands against the back of the couch, leaned forward, and grazed his face with her breast. She spun and settled onto his lap. Her arousal grew with his as her hips rocked against him. Arching back, she twisted her head until her cheek rested against his lips. In a tremulous voice, she asked, "Is that what you wanted?"

"No, not even close." Jeff wrapped one hand around her waist and the other sunk between her legs.

Surrendering to desire, Cindy lost all concern for her husband. She moaned as her body shuddered with his touch.

"Slide your dress off," said Jeff. It wasn't a suggestion. Cindy stood and pulled it over her head while Jeff freed himself from his jeans. Savoring the view, he licked his lips, *my God what an ass.*

Wearing nothing but heels, her chest heaved with excitement as she turned to face him. Their eyes met in an erotic embrace. She straddled his lap, and they moved as one. Unbridled lust resonated between them, transforming a steady wave of pleasure into a frenzied storm. Succumbing to the moment, Cindy bit her lower lip, stifling a blissful cry as her body trembled. Spent, she collapsed against Jeff's shoulder, holding him tight as he thrust against a rising tide.

Jeff met the look of horror splayed across Lewis' face with a demonic grin. A tear rolled down the fat man's face, and Jeff roared with delight.

CHAPTER 11

Fairfield, Maine

Adam reached into the darkness, searching for his phone, as it screeched atop his nightstand. He heard a curse, wasn't sure if it had come from himself or his wife, and finally grabbed the phone. With his eyes still shut, he held it to his ear and mumbled, "Yeah." He listened for a moment, despite his confusion, he shot up straight in bed. He was rubbing the sleep from his eyes when a familiar voice came on the line, "Yes I …" Adam listened and nodded agreement, sitting in the early morning darkness of his bedroom. "Yessir, I understand … Absolutely sir."

"Excellent," replied the voice in his ear before abruptly ending the call.

His wife stirred beside him. "Who was that?" she asked.

Adam lowered the phone to his lap and said, "No one honey go back to sleep." He stared at the screen until it went dark, thinking, *she wouldn't believe me if I told her.* The only thing he was certain about, was that he had no clue what was going on, but would do exactly as he'd been told. His mind shifted from the caller to Joe Blackstone, where had he been the last ten years and what the hell was next? Wide awake, Adam swung his feet out of bed, once again beginning his day much earlier than he'd prefer.

CHAPTER 12

Earl "Pete" Cooper sat in his kitchen while his wife, Mary, made breakfast. In their mid-fifties, the Coopers were an active couple, and it was reflected in their appearance. Mary's eyes still sparkled with youthful enthusiasm, and Pete retained much of the physique that had made him a three-sport star. Their home, while modest, reflected the treasures of a life well lived. Adolescent pictures of their two grown children, blended with memorabilia from Pete's coaching career, filling their home with happy memories. Cooper had retired nine years ago, sighting his age and claiming he lacked the energy to continue coaching. In his mid-forties at the time, and in better shape than most men half his age, nobody had accepted his reasons at face value. But, who was going to tell the best coach in school history twenty-five years wasn't enough?

Cooper wasn't immune to the sorrow that had befallen the tight-knit town. The Blackstone tragedy was always with him. Never more so than when he was at Keyes Field, everywhere he turned he saw reminders of the past. Pete had pushed through the sorrow for one season. He believed he owed it to the kids. And hopped the ghost would fade beneath the Friday night lights, but they hadn't. He retained his teaching job and followed the program from afar. He'd been presented with numerous opportunities to return in a variety of roles, gently declining them all. Despite driving by it every day he hadn't stepped on Keys Field since retiring. In his absence, the program had gone through four head coaches, was currently looking for number five, and held a combined record of 18-63 with no playoff appearances.

Mary set a plate of eggs whites, turkey bacon and whole-wheat toast in front of her husband. He remained quiet, staring out the front window. Mary frowned and raised her voice a tad. "You're welcome."

"Huh? Oh sorry, Mary. This looks great, thanks."

Mary joined her husband, favoring a lighter fare she ate grapefruit instead. They sat quietly, when she was finished Pete's plate was mostly untouched. "So are you going to tell me what's on your mind?"

Pete greatest strength as a coach had been motivating his players. His ability to tap into their emotions, raise them to new heights, and unleash them on an opponent, was nothing short of mystical. Despite his mastery of human emotions, he wasn't always forthcoming with his own. Pete turned to his wife and said, "Joe Blackstone is back in town."

Mary took a minute to process the effect that had on her husband. "How long has he been back?"

"A few days I think, I got a text from Chief Owad. He said Joe got himself in some trouble and asked if I could talk to him."

"So, when are you going to see him?"

"I don't know that I am, I haven't even gotten back to the Chief yet."

"Earl Cooper, you and I both *know* you're gonna go talk to that young man, so it's time to stop thinking and time to start doing."

Pete leaned over and kissed his wife. "What would I do without you?"

"God only knows," Mary said with a smile and shake of her head.

He arrived at the station and waved through the protective glass at the lone dispatch officer who doubled as a receptionist. The door buzzed and Cooper walked through. Other than Adam's office, the lights were low, and desks empty on this Sunday morning.

Adam saw him and pushed himself out of his chair. "Thanks for coming in coach."

"Good morning Chief," Cooper said and extended his hand.

Adam had been an overachieving safety on one of Cooper's first teams. Other than his father, he had more respect for his former coach than any man alive. "Coach, please, just Adam."

"Sure," said Cooper. "What's going on?"

Adam relayed the events from the diner, Joe blowing off their meeting, the accident and the previous day's altercation. He didn't mention the call he'd received or how he'd been instructed to charge Joe, which, despite everything, he had not intended to do. Instead, Adam said, "There is no way around it I have to charge him with reckless driving. If he doesn't agree to my offer, I'm going to charge him with driving under the influence and assaulting a police officer." He explained what he had in mind.

When he finished, Cooper shrugged and said, "It looks you have everything under control here, I'm not sure what I can do to help?"

"Coach, it's not like I even knew Joe. But, he seems," — Adam paused and searched for the right word— "lost, he seems lost. Don't get me wrong he's angry enough too." Adam pulled at the collar of his shirt. Cooper's eyes narrowed when he saw the black and blue marks, but he stayed silent and let Adam continue. "I figured you're about the closest thing to family he's got. And if I was ever in a bad way and needed a good talking too, I reckon you'd be the best man for the job."

A bond Cooper hadn't known in years swelled inside him.

Aware of which players needed a kick in the ass or a timely placed pat on the back, Cooper had pushed his teams to the verge of perfection. Motivation had been their fuel, but hard work was the furnace which forged the steel within each player. Those lucky enough to have played for Cooper had become a family, and like all families, they shared a bond. It's what had caused Adam to reach out to his coach, and now it motivated Cooper to help Joe.

Joe was laying on the cot when he heard the outer door open. He kept his eyes closed and listened to two sets of shoes approach. He assumed Owad had enlisted someone to join him after their last encounter. His cell door opened, someone entered, and the other retreated. Curious Joe opened his eyes to steal a glance. Surprise filled his face, but embarrassment brought him to his feet when he saw Cooper standing above. "Coach," he said and scrambled to his feet.

"I always hoped you'd come home, but I never expected it to be like this." A subtle shake of his head added sting to the blow. Blackstone cast his eyes to the floor, unwilling to meet Cooper's. "Have a seat let's talk," Cooper said. Joe sat on the bunk, and the coach grabbed a chair Owad had placed inside the door. He positioned it across from Joe, sat and waited for Joe to look him in the eye. When his former player finally did, Cooper asked, "Where have you been son?"

It was a question Joe was neither willing nor able to answer. "All over coach, I've been around."

"But now you're back?"

"No." Joe explained how he came back to clean out his storage shed and planned to head right back out of town.

"You better change your plans."

Joe crossed his arms. "Why do you say that?"

"Chief Owad is going to make you a proposal, and it isn't going to go well for you if you don't accept. I've known the man for a long time, and I assure you he's not playing around. I have no idea where you've been, what you've been doing or where you're running to, but you need to stop."

"What do you mean, *stop*."

"You suffered more than any young man should. I wasn't the only one around here who looked for you after you disappeared, lots of people did. It's clear you don't want to talk about where you've been or what you've been doing, and that's fine, but people here haven't forgotten about you. You're in a bit of trouble, and you need to pay the price, in the scheme of things it's not a big deal. But the people here still care for you, they love you, and they hurt for you. Whether you like it or not you ain't going anywhere, so you can either stay the course you're on and become an embarrassment to yourself, or you can get your shit together. The people here will help, they'll stand beside you like they wanted to ten years ago."

The embarrassed high school kid was gone. "I don't owe this town anything," Joe said, bristling with anger.

A sadness clouded Cooper's face and said, "Son, you're not listening, we owe *you*."

CHAPTER 13

Someone had driven Troy home from the station, he wasn't certain who. That afternoon, he woke up with a pounding head but no vehicle. After he'd collected himself and taken a shower, he called the station to check on Joe. Chief Owad had been unavailable but left word that Joe wouldn't be going anywhere for another day or two. Realizing there was nothing immediate he could do for Joe, he focused on his transportation issue. It took three calls to learn the frame was bent on his Tahoe, it would likely be totaled, and he'd need to borrow or rent a car for at least a week until the details were worked out. Depressed about the possible expense, Troy left a message for his sister, Carrie, and went back to bed.

Carrie Hill had been flying home when her brother called. She got his message when her plane landed in Portland. Too late to call, she texted, "SURE THING BIG BROTHER, I'LL BRING THE JEEP BY IN THE MORNING :)"
***

"Are you gonna sleep all day or what?"

Troy's eyes squinted against the light. Carrie was sitting on the side of his bed, shaking his shoulder "What the hell are you doing?" He asked, in a tight voice.

"What am I doing? You're the one who wanted to borrow my car, now get up, you have to drive me back home."

Troy sat up and said, "I expected you'd have one of *your people* drop it off." Through pure chance, Carrie had landed a role in a major movie. Beauty and natural talent had made her a star. Although exceedingly proud of his little sister, Troy relished every opportunity to tease her about being a big shot, the fact she was the most grounded person he knew, did little to dissuade him.

Carrie punched him on the arm. "You better move your ass before me, my people, and my Jeep leave," she said and hopped off the bed and strolled out of the room.

"Fine," said Troy, groaning. "I'm coming, let me grab a quick shower."

After a shower, Troy met his sister, and the welcoming aroma of coffee, in his kitchen. She handed him a cup, and he eased onto a stool at the center Island. "Thanks, I needed this."

Carrie took a sip of her bottled water and raised an eyebrow. The silent gesture a clear signal it was time to fess up.

"Okay, okay … I had a little accident with my Tahoe." Carrie's expression turned to concern. "I'm all right, and nobody got hurt," Troy said.

"Thank God," Carrie said.

Troy told her about running into Joe on Friday and how the evening ended with his SUV buried in the woods.

When Troy finished, Carrie's nose crinkled and she asked, "Why would you two drive like that? And what the hell were you thinking going back out to get something to eat?"

Troy held his hands up in surrender. "I know, it was stupid. We were both so messed up neither of us was thinking straight."

Carrie's expression softened, and she asked, "How's Joe?"

"I'm not sure. I called the station yesterday, but they wouldn't let me speak to him. They said he was going to be there until at least today, possibly tomorrow."

"No, I mean ... *how* is he?"

Troy's mouth twisted with concern as he thought how best to answer his sister's question. Finally, one word came to mind, and he said, "Sad."

They sat quietly, each with their own thoughts. After a moment, Carrie broke the silence. "I never told you about this. After the summer, before my freshman year, it must have been before Joe's Senior year, I went to the pits with Becky Kincade and her sister Rachelle." *The pits* were an old gravel pit where high school kids went to drink and fool around. Troy frowned but hearing the gravity in Carrie's voice he held his tongue. "We met three guys there Rachelle knew from the KV Tech College football team. It wasn't even dark out, but they were already drunk when we showed up. They gave us each beer, Becky and I were scared stiff, but Rachelle started making out with one of the guys right away. The other two were all over Becky and me, she kind of went along with it but I was scared to death. I'll never forget it, the guy was grabbing me and trying to kiss me ... I can still see his face." Troy fought his rising anger but kept quiet. "He pinned me up against the car and was trying to slide his hand down my pants ..."

"Motherfucker," Troy said, his temperature rising.

Carrie held her hands up to silence her brother. "Anyway, I screamed, and I scratched him. He hollered, stepped back and grabbed at his face. His friends thought it was all a big joke, they were laughing their asses off. But when he pulled his hand away from his face and saw blood, he freaked out. I stood there frozen even though I knew he was gonna hit me. He grabbed my hair and cocked his hand back, but someone yelled '*STOP.*' Everyone turned, it was Joe, and he was running right at us. The guy let go of my hair and started to say something but Joe never stopped, he ran right through him, decked him, they landed about ten feet away, and Joe started wailing on him."

"Good."

"Troy, it was scary, his friends couldn't pull Joe off, they were big, bigger than Joe even but he kept tossing them aside like they were little kids, I thought he was going to kill the guy."

"Fuck him," Troy said, "that prick got what he deserved." The Hills were a tight-knit family, and Troy knew what it had meant to Joe to be part of their circle. It dawned on him that the rage he felt at Carrie's retelling of the story must pale to what Joe had felt at the time. "Shit, I'm surprised he didn't kill him."

"Like I said, I thought he was going to, but when I yelled for Joe to stop he did. It was weird, in the chaos of a fight he heard me and stopped cold."

"What was he doing there?"

"He'd been running the hill you guys always used to work out on and was jogging home. If he hadn't been, I don't know what would have happened. He saved me that night."

"Let's go," Troy said and jumped up.

Standing, Carrie asked, "Where are we going?

"We're gonna get Joe outta that place, one way or another."

CHAPTER 14

Joe was quiet when Owad returned and led them back to his office. Once they were seated at his desk, the Chief said, "Here's the situation Joe. Too many people know about the events of the last few days, so this is what's going to happen. You're going to plead guilty to reckless driving and receive a 6-month suspension of your license. You're also going to plead guilty to a charge of simple assault and serve a three-month probation for the shit you pulled in here yesterday. I've talked with the DA, and he's onboard. You're welcome to counsel by your own attorney, but if you don't agree to this deal, the DA is gonna charge you with driving under the influence and felony assault, which carries up to a ten-year sentence."

Owad and Cooper waited for a response.

Joe wasn't convinced there wasn't an option C, but he let the thought slide. Deep down he loathed his behavior, unable to stand the sight of himself in the mirror. Even from within his own darkness Joe could see the kindness in these men. Before he responded, they were interrupted by a commotion coming from the front of the station. Angry voices were heard yelling at one another, frustrated the Chief stood and marched out of the office to ascertain the cause.

When Owad entered the lobby, Troy and Carrie Hill were in a heated debate with his dispatched officer, "Can I help you two?" He asked in a commanding tone.

The Hill's didn't flinch. Troy answered, "We wanna see Joe right now."

Adam sighed. "Listen —"

"No Chief you listen," said Troy, shaking his head. "He's been here over 24 hours, and I'm not leaving until I talk to Joe and know he's okay."

Carrie placed her hands on her hips and waited while the two men glared at one another.

Owad wasn't in the mood to screw around, and he wasn't about to take orders from civilians, but they could help offer a solution. Tight-lipped he considered his options. Deciding on a course of action, he pointed at the Hills and said, "You two follow me."

Joe and Cooper turned toward the approaching footsteps. When they reached the office, Owad returned to his seat, the Hills exchanged an awkward hello with Cooper, and Joe a managed a silent nod before centering his attention back on Owad. With no place to sit, Troy and Carrie stood behind the two occupied chairs.

Carrie was stunned by Joe's appearance. His long hair and thick beard were a sharp contrast to the All-American boy she had known growing up. But it was the sorrow seeping from his blue eyes that hit her the hardest. Even after he had looked away, they stayed with her.

Owad scratched the stubble on his chin and waved a hand toward the new arrivals. "Your friends here demanded to see you. Apparently ... they have serious concerns about your well-being while you're my guest here."

Reading the room, Cooper decided to interject. "Joe, you have anything you'd like to tell them?" he asked. "It might alleviate some of their concerns?"

Joe squeezed his eyes shut and took a deep breath when he exhaled and re-opened them, Owad noted the change. The tension on his face and anger in his eyes were gone. *Not gone, hidden*, Owad corrected himself.

Speaking over his shoulder, Joe said, "Everything's fine." He looked back at Owad. "We were talking about how I may be staying in town for a while."

Confused, Troy and Carrie said nothing; hoping someone would explain what was going on.

CHAPTER 15

Four Months Later

As had become his routine since moving in with Troy, Joe woke early. He fixed a full breakfast of eggs, bacon, sausage, toast, and ate heartily. He was finishing his coffee when Troy walked in. "Everything is still hot," Joe said. "Grab a plate."

"Jesus, I've gained fifteen pounds since you moved in," said Troy. "How the hell can you eat this shit every day."

Joe gave Troy's gut the once over and chuckled. "Maybe if you worked out once in awhile you wouldn't be so fat."

Troy grunted and fixed himself a plate. "I've got an early meeting, you want me to drop you off at work?" Referring to the job Joe had taken at a local Gym.

"Nah I'm good, I like the run."

"Suit yourself," Troy said before shoving a strip of bacon in his mouth.

Joe grabbed his backpack and left. He started his run at an easy jog, gradually increasing his pace. Six miles later he sprinted into Elm Plaza, past JC Penny, and arrived at Champions Fitness Center; where he'd been working as a manager and trainer for three months. The massive gym housed tennis courts, racquetball courts, an aerobic room, full gym and a nightclub on the upper level. To Joe, it was a playground.

Shortly after He unlocked the doors, the first members of the day trickled in. He enjoyed these early hours most of all. The few members who were present at that time mostly kept to themselves. Joe took advantage of the relative peace by throwing himself into his training.

The laidback environment, which Joe had submerged himself in since returning to Fairfield, had been a blessing, rejuvenating Joe's mind and body.

***

Friday was the last day of School at Lawrence High before summer vacation. Pete Cooper strode purposefully through the front doors. But instead of following his normal track to the left, toward his classroom, he turned right and headed to Jim Maracio's office. When he arrived, Cooper knocked once and opened the door without waiting for a response.

Maracio was hired as school's Athletic Director shortly after Cooper retired. Having worked in the same building for years, the two knew each other but had never been close. At the intrusion, Jim looked up from his laptop. "Pete, what can I do for you?" he asked and signaled toward a chair opposite his desk.

Cooper remained standing, in typical form he got straight to the point. "Who's coaching the team this year?"

"Football?" Embarrassed as soon as the word left his mouth Marciano continued, "We've got some applications, and we're looking at multiple candidates."

"So nobody."

It wasn't a question, but the intensity in Cooper's eyes compelled the AD to respond, "No, not really."

"Good I want my job back."

"Pete I …" Maracio hesitated.

Poker-faced, Cooper waited.

The suddenness of the request had caught Maracio off guard, but when he paused to consider it, he couldn't think of a downside. "Coach we'd be thrilled to have you back." Maracio stood and shook Cooper's hand.

"Great, I guess I better get to work."

"I got to ask … why the sudden change of heart?"

"It's time we start winning again."

***

Finished with his last client of the day, Joe was straightening up loose weights when he spotted Carrie Hill, easily every guy's favorite gym member. He caught a glimpse of her in a mirror and thought, *if that girl's ass isn't the reason God invented yoga pants I don't know what is.* Averting his attention, Joe continued racking scattered weights.

A moment later he felt someone approach. "Hey, Joe. Do you mind giving me a spot?"

Joe turned into the gaze of Carrie's emerald green eyes and stammered. "Ah ... Hi ... Yeah sure." Joe didn't want to subject anyone to his demons, especially not Carrie, so he'd purposely kept their conversations limited and light. Nonetheless, he enjoyed the view, and he followed Carrie to the squat rack.

"I'm gonna do 12 reps," Carrie said. "I should get 'em, but keep an eye on me in case I get in trouble."

Keeping an eye on her was all Joe wanted to do and had been fighting unsuccessfully to avoid. "Sure," he said.

Carrie ducked under the weight, lifted and stepped back.

Nervous, Joe's eyes swam laps from Carrie's backside to the mirror in front of her. One moment they bore into the thin black material stretching across the outline of her thong, the next they slipped within the cleavage spilling from her top. Realizing he was holding his breath, Joe gasped; inhaled her scent and knew he was in trouble.

"Nice ... nice form," Joe said, as he warmed with embracement.

On the last two reps Carrie's pace slowed, Joe moved closer, ready to grab the bar. The heat radiating from her body caused his temperature rise. Her taunt muscles strained beneath the weight but did not falter. Finished, she re-racked the weight and spun out from beneath the bar. Her face and chest were flush and glistened beneath a sheen of exertion. Joe stood frozen and stared.

Suddenly aware he was in her personal space, Joe stepped back. Carrie grinned and said, "Thanks for the spot."

"Sure ... I mean no problem, yell if you need another one." Joe turned to walk away.

Carrie smacked him on the butt.

Surprise was splayed across his face when he wheeled around.

"Don't worry," Carrie said, "I will."

Unblinking, Joe stood frozen as Carrie strode away.

***

It was late afternoon when Joe left for the day, he jogged at an easy pace all the way to coach Cooper's house. He had seen his former coach every day since their conversation in his jail cell. Warmer weather had moved their daily conversations from Cooper's kitchen to the porch wrapped around his house. They had talked about many things, but what they hadn't talked about was football, sports yes, but not football. Today would be different.

Cooper was sitting on the porch when Joe arrived. "Hi, Coach."

"Afternoon Joe, help yourself to some iced tea," Cooper said. An icy pitcher perspired on a small table between Cooper's chair and an empty on. An extra glass had already been set out.

Joe sat and helped himself, draining half the cold drink with his first sip. As was often the case, they sat quietly and watched over the street while an occasional car or bike rolled by. All the ice in the pitcher had melted by the time Joe spoke. "Last day of school today right coach? Whatta you gonna do with all your free time?"

"Same as you I guess."

"You joining the gym?"

"Nope, you're joining my staff."

Joe twisted in his seat to face Cooper, who was focused on a squirrel climbing the side of his neighbor's house across the street. "What do you mean … *your staff?*" asked Joe.

Cooper turned to meet Joe's eyes. "I took the team back today, and I want you to help me." Joe was silent, so he pressed him and asked, "What do you think, will you help me?"

Joe's voice echoed with doubt when he said, "I … don't know if I can."

"After everything you've been through, I'd understand if you don't love the game anymore, but you might enjoy coaching."

"That's just it coach, I do love it, I always have, it's just …" Joe's expression filled with pain.

"What is it, Joe?" Cooper knew losing his mother at such a young age and losing his father in such a violent manner had left Joe deeply scared. Still, he sensed there was more, he'd seen it in his eyes while sitting in Joe's cell and he saw it now. "You can tell me, son."

As if a curtain had been drawn, the pain vanished, and Joe stood. "I've got to go, thanks for the iced tea."

Cooper watched as Joe disappeared around the corner at Western Avenue. It was clear Joe still had a lot to work through, but after hearing his former star admit he still loved the game, the old coach grinned as a plan formed in his head.

CHAPTER 16

Philadelphia

Mealey sat alone in his office, reviewing film from the Freedom's last Mini Camp. Already the rookie coach had spent five times as many hours studying film from the five-day camp than the team had spent on the field.

When Mealey paused the video to review his notes he couldn't help but be excited about his offense. At 6'7", 325 pounds Foamagulla "Foam" Anderson had developed into one of the best left tackles in the game. The two guards, Kevin Carter and Bill Luger, were strong, nasty and athletic. Shawn Lutz possessed the smarts, and talent Mealey wanted at center. Only aging veteran Jim Schank, at right tackle, was on the downside of his career, even so, Mealey believed the former all-pro had couple productive season left in the tank. Billy Bates provided a big and versatile target at tight end and returning all-pro wideout Dwayne Wilmot was a burner on the outside. Another wide receiver, rookie free agent Ryan Barrett, had been a pleasant surprise at camp and Mealey hoped he would continue to impress. Second-year running back Kirk Mathieu looked poised to improve on last season's rookie of the year performance. With all-pro Jeff Pergine under center, Mealey expected Philadelphia to be atop the league offensively. He'd been impressed with how quickly the entire unit was learning Lafond's offense, especially Pergine. There was something about the young QB Mealey found odd, but he had to admit the kid was near flawless all camp. With size, speed, a strong arm and pinpoint accuracy, he was already considered among the league's best.

Mealey wasn't nearly as pleased with the defense. For the tenth time this afternoon he picked through his notes hoping to find something that wasn't there, frustrated he dialed coach Pickell's extension.

"Yeah." came the brisk reply on the third ring.

"Coach, can you join me in my office?"

"Be there in five," Pickell said and hung up.

While Mealey waited, he marveled at how little his defensive coordinator had to work with over the past couple years. Despite Pollard and Mealey's effort to address these shortcomings, Pickell continued to voice concerns. Concerns Mealey quietly shared.

Pickell shuffled into Mealey's office and dropped himself in a chair facing Mealey's desk. "What's up?" he asked.

Mealey rubbed the back of his neck. "Whatta we gonna do with this defense?"

"Fucking pray," said Pickell.

"Come on, I know we have problems, but it's not like John, and I haven't tried, we've traded for, signed or drafted six guys who should be able to help at linebacker and D-line."

Pickell's face took on a serious expression. "We upgraded depth at those positions and a few of the young guys may even turn into something down the road, but that's down the road."

"You don't think any of the new guys are better than last year's starters?"

"Chris Harris can probably start at nose tackle, he's the best of the lot, but George George is the second most talented and he ain't nothing special. I mean Jesus Christ even his own parents knew he was too stupid for two names," — Pickell shook his head — "George fucking George, Jesus Christ."

Mealey couldn't help but laugh. When he stopped, he said, "So we're pretty much screwed."

Pickell knew the GM and head coach had done everything in their power to plug the holes on defense. Unfortunately, what they needed above all was a pass rush, and that coveted talent wasn't available. Every club in the league knew a strong pass rush was the foundation of a good defense. Most teams constructed their rush using talented players at multiple positions; a lucky few relied on a single superstar. One player who could rush the quarterback and create havoc all by themselves, despite opponents concerted efforts to contain them. Lacking overall talent, Philadelphia needed this kind of rare player, but there hadn't been any in the draft, and no team lucky enough to have such a talent would part with him. "With our improved depth, I can rotate more players in and outta the game. By keeping guys fresh, we'll be a little better, but unless one of the rookies turns into a monster, we still won't have shit for a rush."

Deflated Mealey said, "Well I guess we better keep looking, thanks, coach." Signaling an end to the meeting. After Pickell had left, he sat back in his chair and rubbed at his temples. He sat up when his cell phone buzzed atop the desk, without checking the caller ID he silenced it and resumed watching the video.

***

In West Philadelphia, Harvey Litt stood behind Jeff Pergine. Seated at a small table, Litt's client had been autographing posters for a group of youth football players for the past hour. The short, rodent-faced manager made a show of checking his watch. "Sorry kids that's all for today," he said. "Jeff is late for another appointment."

Pergine smiled, quickly scrawled his signature on one last poster and handed it to a wide-eyed boy standing in front of him. A local news crew captured the moment and would share it during their evening broadcast.

When Jeff stood, he was pleased to receive the applause his mere presence warranted. Still, he had to fight back the bile as it rose in his throat. Jeff considered the people from this impoverished section of the city beneath him, and it sickened him to be amongst them. Even Harvey, who was well aware of his client's true feelings, couldn't see the malice Jeff concealed as he waved goodbye and said, "You all make sure you root for the team this season!"

Jeff continued to wave as he climbed into a limousine sitting idle in the narrow street. Only when Harvey closed the door, shielding them behind the dark glass, did Jeff's disguise melt away. He glared at Litt with hostile eyes and said, "Enough of this bullshit, I'm not doing any more appearances in the hood."

"JP, listen I know how you feel. But this is the kind of publicity that will pay off. You just need to be patient, a little while longer."

Litt was the only person whom Pergine made no attempt to conceal his true self. "Fuck patience, I must have checked my wallet twenty times while we were there. I shouldn't have to be around these people."

Litt still marveled at the contrast between the *real* Jeff Pergine and the public image they'd crafted. He didn't begrudge him for it, after all, it was people like Pergine who accounted for the whole of Litt's small but lucrative client list. Litt worked quietly, and off the radar, for the top sports management firms. When an agency grows concerned over their clients' image, they call Harvey Litt. He or a member of his team will then manage that client. His firm specialized in preventing the behavior, and occasionally erasing evidence of such, that would cast their clients in a negative light. Pergine was unique, he was the only client to have initiated contact himself. Under the guise that he was asking for a teammate, Pergine had asked his agent whom he could contact for the kind of services Litt offered. Without question, Litt believed Pergine was a psychopath, but he took great pride in the job he had done to hide that from the rest of the world.

"I know Jeff, and I'll see to it we limit these appearances for a while," said Harvey in a tone reserved for a child. "The season is right around the corner, and I know you have a lot of work to do." He paused to let Jeff calm. "Remember you have a lot riding on these next few months. We're close to locking up one of the big apparel companies in a long-term deal. Add to that, the new contract we're going after next year, and you're looking at over one hundred and forty million. All you need to do is keep your eye on the prize."
***

Fairfield, Maine

When Joe arrived back at Troy's, he grabbed a bottle of water, devoured it in one swig and headed to his room. He turned on the shower and for the second time today stripped off his gym clothes. He stood beneath the cool stream, wishing it to wash away his conversation with Cooper. Instead, his urge to forget cast light upon old dreams. He longed for the competition, to be part of the game, part of a team, a family. He turned his face upwards, inches from the spray. Engulfed in water, Joe imagined he was drowning in his own guilt. Yet, in his imagination, no matter how far he sank he could still breathe. "Fuck!" he hollered into the spray and turned the faucet off. After he had dried off, Joe threw on a pair of shorts and headed to the kitchen for another bottle of water and something to eat.

Joe was rummaging through the refrigerator when Troy walked in. He surveyed the scars which marked Joe's sorrow, it wasn't the first time he had seen them, yet it still pained him to do so. They reminded of a tragedy Troy knew well and implied of others which he knew nothing about. Saddened he thought, *what the hell have you been through Joe?* Troy shook it off and said, "Hey grab me a beer."

Unable to find anything he was hungry for, Joe pulled a bottle of water and a beer from the fridge and closed the door. He handed the beer to Troy, who took a sip and collapsed exhausted on a stool at the center island. "Long day?" Joe asked.

"Yeah, we had a ..." The phone rang, cutting him off, he picked it off the counter and answered, "Hello." He listened for a second, then held it out for Joe without saying a word.

Joe had only received three phone calls since moving in, and those had all come from work. He assumed this would be the same. "This is Joe," he said.

"Hi Joe," said Carrie.

His surprise transparent, Joe met Troy's stare and said, "Oh hi, what's up?"

"I'm getting ready."

"Ah … ready for what?"

"To come pick you up."

Riveted to Joe's call, Troy sipped at his beer.

Joe cleared his throat and said, "I don't know …"

"Listen, I'm coming," Carrie said. "I love my brother and all but come on, you need to get out. Besides, I don't have a date, and I wanna go to dinner. I'll see you in an hour." The line went dead.

"Ok," Joe said to himself and hung up the phone.

Troy raised an eyebrow and asked, "What was that about?"

"That was your sister," Joe said, stalling.

"No shit, I know it was my sister. I answered the phone remember? What the hell did she want?"

Battling the tides of angst and excitement, Joe attempted to sound casual. "She wants me to do her with something." He missed his mark by a wide margin.

"What the fuck did you say?" Troy asked, getting to his feet.

"No … no," Joe said. "I meant she wants me to go somewhere with her."

Troy sat back down, hiding a smile.

Knowing how tight Joe and Troy had become again, Carrie had called her brother at work. She liked Joe and if the way he acted around her was any indication she was confident he felt the same way. Not wanting to put Joe in and awkward position; Carrie had given her brother a heads up and informed him, in no uncertain words, he'd better not have a problem with her asking Joe out.

To Carrie's surprise, Troy had been thrilled to hear the news; Joe was a welcome change from all the uppity assholes she'd dated of late. His sister was grounded despite her movie fame, and most of the people she had grown up with treated her the same way they always had. Still, Carrie was always anxious about going places that served alcohol, all too often an inebriated stranger wanted to be her best friend, or worse. With Joe around Troy knew she'd be safe. Regardless, Troy relished Joe's discomfort and planned to bust his balls for as long as possible. Rallying his self-control, Troy suppressed his laughter, cast a hard glare at Joe and said. "What do you mean … *go somewhere?*"

Joe held up his hands in surrender. "Hey man … listen it's not what you think."

"No? Then what the fuck is it?" asked Troy. He fought to hold a furious appearance, but the awkward silence and apprehension on Joe's face overtook him. He dropped his face into his hands and burst into laughter.

"You motherfucker," Joe said as he shoved Troy off his stool.

Still laughing as he regained his balance, Troy fought to compose himself and mocked, "*She wants me to go somewhere with her.*" Again, he howled.

Joe laughed with him.

When they settled down, Joe turned serious, and he asked, "You sure you're cool with us hanging out?"

"I couldn't pick a better person for my sister to spend time with."

Joe's eyes filled with appreciation. "Thanks," he said. "That means a lot."

As Joe was heading back to his room to get dressed, Troy said, "Hey, word of advice."

Joe turned. "What's that?"

"Lose the beard."

"Will do."

CHAPTER 17

Sixty minutes later, on the dot, Joe heard Carrie walk in and say hi to her brother. Leaving his room Joe caught his reflection in a hall mirror, the clean shave hinted of someone he had once been. When he walked into the kitchen, the siblings fell silent.

Troy's jaw dropped. Joe's hair was still long, but his freshly-shaven face brought Troy back to the day they'd met on the basketball court.

Carrie had no such flashback, she was busy enjoying the moment. The corner of her mouth quirked up as she drank in the handsome, square-jawed man with piercing blue eyes.

Joe looked back and forth between the two, noted the difference between his t-shirt and jeans and the little black dress clinging to Carrie's sculpted figure and asked, "What's the matter am I underdressed?"

"You kiddin' me," said Troy. "I'm shocked you showered for a change."

Joe bit his tongue and gave Troy a sarcastic smile.

"You look great Joe, come on you've been subjected to enough of my brother's immaturity, let's go."

The host greeted Carrie by name when they arrived at Amici's Cucina. He made a big deal of the *special table* they would have for *her* in a few minutes.

The bar was full, but they snatched a pair of seats when a handsome middle-aged couple stood to leave. A heavy-set bartender mixing a drink to Joe's right looked past him and gawked at Carrie. Focused on a loud group at the opposite end of the bar, Carrie was unaware of the lingering gaze. Joe leaned into the bartender's sight line and drew his attention. His mouth twisted into an appreciative grin and he asked, "What'll it be?"

Joe patted Carrie on the lower back, his hand lingered, and her eyes smiled at his. "What would you like to drink?" He asked.

The warmth of Joe's touch surged through her dress and ignited her skin. With feigned composure, Carrie turned to the man waiting behind the bar and said, "I'll take a Cabernet please."

"And a bottle of Shipyard," Joe added.

"Coming up." The bartender busied himself with the task.

Joe's hand feathered across Carrie's back. And his eyes devoured the fullness of her lips before falling into her emerald eyes.

Carrie's pulse quickened, she longed for the passion branded upon her by his touch. Only when the bartender presented their drinks did they break their lustful gaze.

At the interruption, Joe's expression reverted to a mask of concealment and he pulled his hand away. Lost in their thoughts, they each took a sip from their drink before Joe broke the silence. "So ... I was kind of surprised you called."

"Why?"

"I don't know," said Joe. "I'm sure you know a lot of people, who're much more interesting than me to have dinner with; plus ... you know."

"When it comes to *interesting* you're tough to beat, and what exactly is it *I know*?"

"Troy, you're his little sister, and he's my friend ..."

"Oh … yeah … I get it." Mocking him with a deep, playful voice, Carrie said, "You're talking about guy code."

Joe chuckled. "Yeah, something like that."

"That's cute and all, but I could care less."

Anxious to change the subject, Joe was relieved when the host appeared and said, "Ms. Hill if you'll follow me your table is ready."

Joe stood and threw a twenty on the bar for the drinks. With a broad smile, he offered an arm and teased. "Ms. Hill … if you'd allow me to escort you to *your* table, it would be a great honor."

Carrie punched Joe on the arm but took his has hand instead. With a crooked grin, she said, "Let's go smart ass."

Joe was amazed at the attention Carrie garnered on the way to their table. For years, he had worked diligently to blend in and go unnoticed, a daunting task considering his physical stature. Walking with Carrie, Joe took comfort in the shadow she cast.

The host led them to a high-backed booth that offered ample privacy. Carrie ordered a bottle of wine, and they were left alone. "So let's have it," Joe said. "How the hell did you end up in the movies?"

"It's pretty silly and kind of a long story."

"I've got no place to go let's hear it."

"Alright, you asked for it," said Carrie. "The summer after my senior year of high school a couple of friends and I took a ride to Acadia National Park. None of us had ever hiked to the top of Mt. Cadillac, only driven up, so we parked at the bottom and started up. When we came outta the trail at the top, you know the one by the parking area?"

"Yeah, it's right before the observation deck," Joe said.

"That's it," Carrie said. "We saw a guy right there, trying to change a flat on his Mercedes. His wife was disgusted, and his kids were whining. When we walking past, I asked if he needed help. My friends all laughed because they remembered a story I'd told them a million times. About how my dad made me change a tire myself before he'd let me drive alone."

Joe laughed. "That sounds like your dad."

Carrie nodded her agreement. "Anyway, the guy ignored me because he thought I was a smart ass, so I walked right up to him and told him he was doing it wrong. You should have seen the look he gave me. But his wife let him have it and told him to let me try. Apparently, he'd called AAA three hours before. They hadn't shown, so he had been trying to change it himself for over an hour. It was easy because my mom had a little Mercedes SUV I used to drive, so I knew about the individual slots along the bottom of the frame for the jack. I had his car up, and the tire changed in fifteen minutes."

Joe sat up straight and said, "You continue to impress."

Carrie tilted her head in a playful manner before continuing, "This guy was shocked. So as a thank you, he asked my friends and me to join his family for dinner that night. He wouldn't take no for an answer, so we agreed to meet them at the Acadia Inn in Bar Harbor. When we got to dinner it was a real fancy place; we were underdressed, so they put us in a private dining room. He'd given us his name earlier, but none of us knew who he was. It turned out, he's a big-time Hollywood director, Michael Zimmerman maybe you've heard of him?" Joe shook his head no. "Neither had we, but while we're at dinner he kept asking me questions like, what were my plans for school? Do I like movies? Had I ever done any acting? What do I wanna do for a career?" Carrie waved her hand dismissively. "I figured he was making small talk, no big deal. Well, he finally explained who he was and asked for my cell number because he had a project coming up and said I'd be perfect for one of the characters. We all figured he was full of shit, showing off and acting like a big shot, but I gave him my number anyway. After dinner, we said our goodbyes, and I didn't think much about it until he called me a couple of weeks later."

The waiter arrived and asked if they were ready to order. Neither Joe nor Carrie had looked at their menu yet, so they asked for a few more minutes. They each browsed through it and as soon as they set the menus back down their waiter returned.

Joe ordered the veal chop, and Carrie selected the branzino.

When the waiter left, Carrie asked, "Am I boring you yet?"

"Not at all, it's a crazy story."

"Yeah it was a whirlwind, they flew me to LA, and I thought I was auditioning for a small role but it turned out to be the female lead. I had done a few school plays, but nothing can prepare you for all that."

"Troy never told me any of this, but we did watch *Lost Innocence* and the sequel. What was it called?"

"Redemption."

"Yeah, I liked them both. I haven't seen many movies lately, but they were good." Joe's throat tightened, and he said, "And you looked incredible."

"Joe Blackstone … are you flirting with me?" Carrie asked, a devilish grin tugged at the corners of her mouth.

Joe smiled. "I'm trying, but I'm a little outta practice."

Dinner came, and they continued talking about her acting career while they ate. Carrie told him about the projects she had turned down because she had needed a break from that lifestyle, how the time off had rejuvenated her, and she was ready to return.

Their plates had been cleared away, and the bottle of wine was empty. They were sipping what was left in their glass when Carrie said, "All night we've talked about me, I wanna know where you've been and what you've been up to."

"Nothing to tell," Joe lied.

The wine was having its effect, but Carrie could still sense Joe's discomfort at the mention of his past. "You know I had the *biggest* crush on you when you were in High School," she said, changing the subject.

"Sure you did," Joe said, drawing out the words.

"Oh come on, that can't be a surprise. All the girls had a crush on you, even a lot of the moms."

"Yeah okay, I think maybe you've had too much to drink." Joe smiled and shook his head. "I better get us a cab."

Carrie wanted to pay the tab, but Joe insisted dinner was on him and took care of the bill.

Twenty minutes later they were riding in the back of a beat-up Crown Vic. The seats were tattered, shocks nonexistent and the car reeked of cigarette smoke. Nestled beneath Joe's arm, Carrie had settled herself against his chest. Much sooner than Joe would have preferred, they cab slowed and bounced off the pavement and onto Carrie's camp road. Its lone headlights pushed back the night as they wove between tall pines. Rocks and gravel crunched beneath the tires until they emerged from the trees and stopped in front of a large, well-lit log cabin. Carrie peeled herself from Joe, and they slid out of the car. Joe asked the driver to wait.

Joe held her hand as they strolled along her walkway, neither of them in a hurry. "Nice place," Joe said when they made it to the front door.

"Thanks." Carrie turned to him and asked, "Would you like to come in?"

There's nothing I'd like more, he thought but said, "I should go."

Carrie squeezed his hands, stretched up and kissed him on the cheek. "Call me."

"I will," Joe promised. He waited until she was inside before returning to the cab. Leaving Carrie felt like the most unnatural thing he had ever done, on the ride back to Troy's, Joe decided he wasn't going to repeat it.

CHAPTER 18

The next day, Joe was pacing in the kitchen when Troy trudged in. It wasn't even noon yet, and he'd already been to the Gym and detailed his truck. He wanted to call Carrie but wasn't sure about the etiquette. Joe hadn't dated since high school, and even then, he hadn't had any serious girlfriends. It wasn't as if he'd been celibate, far from it. Over the years, Joe had plenty of desires and no problem fulfilling them. His time home was the longest he had gone without quenching his thirst in years.

"Mornin," Troy said as he climbed on a stool and opened the paper.

"Huh," Joe said, "did you say something?"

Troy peered over the paper. "*I said* good mornin'."

"Oh, hey good mornin'," Joe said and centered his thoughts back on his friend's sister, she had been there throughout his sleepless night and his early trip to the gym. Their evening had cast light on the part of Joe he had closed off long ago. For the first time since he could remember he was looking forward to something good, something pure. The unfamiliar sensation invigorated him, but uncertain why such good fortune had befallen him and untrusting of his intentions, Joe filled with angst. *Was it lust he felt? Lust for her perfectly toned body, catlike eyes, and pouty lips.* He glanced at Troy. *No, it was more than lust.* Joe continued to busy himself by cleaning the kitchen. He was certain he had done nothing to deserve Carrie but could not suppress the dormant emotions she had stirred.

After Joe had wiped the same section of countertop for the third time, Troy set his paper down and said, "Call her."

"What?" Joe replied as he stepped to the refrigerator, surveying its contents for the fourth time without removing anything."

"You're driving me crazy pacing around like a schoolboy with a crush. Carrie obviously likes you, or she wouldn't have called yesterday, and you like her; I'm cool with it. Stop being a pussy and call her for fuck sake." Troy picked up his paper and resumed reading it. He smiled when he heard his friend snatch the phone off the counter and retreat down the hall.

A moment later Joe yelled, "Hey Troy, what the hell's Carrie's number?"

At the end of her dock, Carrie closed her eyes and raised a smile to a cloudless sky. Anxious to enjoy the first warm day of summer, she hopped in her boat, hefted a cooler off the dock and set it beside her. As she reached for the ignition that would bring the boat to life and officially start the summer, her cell phone chirped. She saw her brother's name on the tiny screen and answered, hoping not to hear Troy's voice. "Hello."

"Hi Carrie this is Joe, I hope I didn't catch you at a bad time."

Carrie smiled. "Not at all."

"Oh good." Joe paused, gathered his nerve and said, "I had a great time last night."

"So did I," Carrie said. "I was gonna take my boat out, you wanna join me?"

"Sure, that would be fun, I'll see if Troy can give me a ride. Otherwise, I'll see you in about forty minutes."

"Relax Forrest, I'll come pick you up, see you in a bit." Carry hung up, grabbed a mesh cover-up she had laying on the seat beside her and climbed out of the boat.

Back in the kitchen with Troy, Joe said, "Hey, Carrie's picking me up, she's taking me out on her boat. I don't have swim trunks, is there any place on the way where I can grab some?"

"Check my room, on top of the dresser," said Troy. "I got a couple of pairs at Marden's last week. They were two for one, but the fuckers are too big, should fit you, though."

"Thanks," Joe said. He found the shorts and tried them on, they looked ridiculous, but he was pleased with the fit. Since he didn't have any sandals, he put sneakers on. He was stuffing an extra t-shirt and shorts into a backpack when he heard Carrie's Jeep. Joe put his hands in his pockets and took stock of his wardrobe, *what the hell Joe, you think it's time for some new clothes?*

Carrie's eyes danced behind dark glasses when Joe emerged from her brother's house. He was chiseled, and she had admired his broad shoulders, long muscular frame and thick thighs at the gym. Anticipating an afternoon on the water with him brought a smile to her face.

Joe opened the door and slid into the seat. "Hi, thanks for picking me up."

Carrie lowered her sunglasses, and her emerald eyes sparkled as they traced a seductive path along his physique. "My pleasure."

Despite his crimson face, Joe returned the gesture and removed his sunglasses. He devoured her tan body, prominently displayed beneath a mesh cover up and tiny white Bikini, and replied, "No, I'm pretty sure it's my pleasure." In what was becoming a habit, Carrie smiled and punched him on the arm.

On the ride to Carrie's, Joe asked, "What kind of boat do you have?"

"It's a 23-foot ski boat, a Moomba, Mojo. It has the same engine as the Ford Raptor F-150's."

"Wow, sounds nice."

"I like it. I get together with friends and ski or wakeboard whenever I can, but most of the time I cruise around by myself and enjoy the sun."

Joe looked at Carrie as she drove, as much to himself as to her, he said, "That sounds peaceful."

When they arrived, Carrie parked in the driveway and led Joe to the left around her garage and down a flight of stone steps. At the bottom, the yard leveled out and stretched sixty feet to the water. A neon green boat with black markings was tied to the end of a teak dock. Joe followed her to the shiny watercraft.

When they were settled on board, Carrie fired up the engine. "Can you free the lines for me?" She asked.

"You got it, Captain."

Once untied, Carrie nudged the throttle, and they eased away from the dock. After they had gained a little distance from the shore, she sat up in her swivel chair, slipped out of her flip flops, and pulled the cover-up over her head. Joe sat sideways, facing Carrie, on the bench seat that lined the rest of the deck. He kicked his sneakers off and struggled to keep his tongue in his mouth. Her little biking was an erotic contrast to the tanning oil glistening on her defined, yet feminine body. And her every movement provoked a carnal urge which Joe fought to suppress.

Carrie navigated around two other boats, setting a starboard course and giving Joe something else to admire about her. "You handle this thing like a pro," he said loud enough to be heard over the engine.

"Thanks, have you spent much time on boats?" Asked Carrie.

Joe turned away and looked out over the water. *Not with daylight*, he thought but said, "Some." He twisted in his seat and stretched his legs along the soft cushion. Facing aft, Joe settled beneath the warm mid-day sun. His left hand found Carrie's thigh, and he traced an easy path back and forth from her knee to her hip. The simple touch generated more energy than the sun above. Carrie swiveled her seat ever so slightly, offering Joe a more intimate path. With each stroke, his hand crept closer to her inner thigh, and their shared hunger grew.

With less than ideal concentration, Carrie adjusted their heading to a small island in the middle of the lake. She pushed the boat as fast as she dared, and then a little bit beyond.

When they got to the shallow water near the island, Carrie throttled back. Joe swung his legs off the bench and staggered his feet around Carrie's, who was now facing toward the center of the boat at a forty-five-degree angle. His hands continued to explore, while Carrie slid the boat into a shallow cove created by the crescent shaped island. A crop of rock and trees afforded them three hundred degrees of privacy. They were in effect invisible, hidden from every property on the lake except those too far away to see them. They were visible to passing boaters, which heightened their excitement.

Finding the sweet spot, Carrie reversed the throttle and brought the boat to a near perfect stop. She sprung out of her seat and over Joe's leg. At the bow, she tossed an anchor into the water and was tying it off when he grabbed her.

Joe stood when Carrie got up. The sight of her bending over the bow became too much. He was on her in an instant, grabbing both her arms he pulled her upright, jarring her into his chest.

Startled by Joe's sudden aggression, Carrie shrieked. Undeterred, Joe coiled an arm around her shoulders, pinning her to his chest. His other dove beneath the white fabric of her bikini, eliciting a gasp. Not until she surrendered to their hunger did he release his hold on her. She turned to him, and they tore at each other's clothes. Naked, he spun her back around and pushed her forward, over the bow of the boat. Water slapped against the hull as the boat quaked beneath them. Overwhelmed by the moment, it didn't take long before their release echoed as one across the water.

Their clothes were scattered. Joe collapsed on the bow of the boat, spent. Carrie draped herself on his lap, and he held her tight.

Carrie's heart was still racing when she broke the silence. "Wow." Joe was quiet, so she straddled his lap. His big hands clasped her waist; she searched his eyes. For the first time, she caught a glimpse of the whole man. Despite — maybe because of — the aggression with which he'd taken her, she was more drawn to Joe than before. She saw tremendous violence in him but was comforted by his presence and the security it promised.

Easing herself back, Carrie's eyes surveyed, and her hand explored. Her finger grazed a jagged scar on Joe's shoulder; her thumb brushed over a thin line on his forearm. She cupped a hand over three separate circles sprouting from his chest and torso. She placed a soothing hand on another half dozen wounds. Raising her eyes, she whispered, "What have you been through?"

"Enough."

The one-word reply conveyed an abundance of pain. "It's okay," Carrie assured him, "you can tell me."

Carrie's eyes meet Joe's with a kindness he'd never known. He found the tone of her voice comforting, her intentions pure, and Joe believed he could trust her. But he couldn't burden her with the weight of his past despite a desire to be truthful. "I've seen people do a lot of bad things, and I've done just as many ... more even. I can't change my past, and I'm not going to burden you with it. Until you came back into my life, I hadn't thought about my future because I didn't care if I had one. I know I don't deserve you, but if you can believe me when I say all that's in my past, I'd like to see where this leads."

Carrie's hands swam along Joe's torso as he cradled her face with a delicate touch. His fingers slid behind her head, kneading her thick mane as he pulled her close. She inhaled the lemongrass scent of his hair while he savored her neckline. He nuzzled along her jawline until their lips came together. The embrace stirred Joe and Carrie raised up and reached for him. She lowered herself upon him, and they made love, slowly, savoring one another with all their senses.

They spent the afternoon talking, laughing and loving. The day spilled into night, and before Joe realized it, the weekend was over. When Monday came, Joe found himself thinking of their perfect weekend and longing for more. Every hour was a new dawn, an awakening, a resurrection. Because every minute Joe spent with Carrie or guiltlessly thinking about her, he healed. At first, he dreamt of Carrie and what their future together could hold. Her light revived him, promise replaced guilt, and broken dreams emerged from the darkness.

CHAPTER 19

Lower Gwynedd PA

Jeff was in his upstairs bathroom, with his neck and body twisted to ensure the needle he held found the proper mark on his backside. Satisfied he jabbed the two-inch tip into his flesh and pushed down on the plunger. He wasn't concerned with the league's policy against performance-enhancing drugs. He paid Harvey Litt handsomely to alert him well in advance of any *random* testing. When all the liquid drained from the syringe, he removed the needle. A small dot of blood appeared where the needle had punctured his skin. When Jeff turned and stretched for a towel, he spied something from his bathroom window and froze in his tracks. His eyes narrowed, and a dark expression filled his face as he watched a small dog squat on his patio.

Jeff hiked up his shorts and tore out of the bathroom. Within seconds he was on his back porch standing above the small pile of feces. Jeff's right hand held the bronze statue he had received for winning rookie of the year. He centered his attention on the dog, tracking it as it sniffed its way around the perimeter. With long scraggly hair and beady eyes he guessed it was some kind of Chihuahua, but to him, it was a rat. Jeff crept forward, only after he'd stepped off the stone steps did the dog take notice. He knelt and rested his hand on the grass. "Come here, boy." Jeff tapped on the ground, and he continued calling the dog in a high pitch voice, masking his ire. Tongue hanging and tail wagging it approached, covering the last several feet in an excited hop before it rolled beneath his hand. A smile spread across Jeff's face, and he rubbed the tiny stomach. Hiding his malice beneath a jovial tone, he said, "Good boy ... Gooood boooy!"

Elated with the attention, the dog wiggled with excitement. Despite the tiny heart thumping against Jeff's palm, its body reminded him of the miniature footballs he played with as a boy. He met the dog's joyous expression with an icy stare, his lips pulled back into a snarl, and his hand thrust downward. The dog squealed in agony, and something burst within its fragile torso. Pinned to the ground and mortally wounded, it eyes pleaded with Jeff. His free hand lifted the heralded award high in the air and delivered an answer to the small creature's plea.

Jeff stood, his focus was glued to the carnage at his feet. The dog's head was crushed and nearly decapitated from its distorted body. Golden-brown fur blended with bones and blood, creating a gruesome collage. With a deep breath, he inhaled the image; savoring the moment

Jeff took his time removing the mess from his patio, lawn, and award. He busied his mind trying to decide what he had enjoyed more, the sensation he felt when one of the animal's organs had burst or the site of its smashed head? Ultimately, he decided both were equally spectacular.

That afternoon his new Ferrari F12 Berlinetta was delivered. Sliding into the cockpit, Jeff was uncertain which was better, the plush leather passenger compartment or its' sleek red body lines. *They're equally spectacular*, he reflected; a wicked grin filled his face.

As he neared the bottom of his driveway, he saw Cindy jogging away from hers. Since their dinner party, Lewis had kept his distance, but Cindy had gone out of her way to let her intentions be known. Seldom pursuing the same conquest twice, Jeff had blown her off, in a less than polite manner. But her chosen attire on the warm summer day offered cause for an exception. Jeff tapped the gas and spun the wheel. The Italian sports car bound forward, tore from his driveway and surged toward his neighbor. He covered the distance in a flash.

Cindy screeched and jumped to the side before the carbon-ceramic brakes brought the car to a halt inches from her quivering legs.

Smiling in the driver's seat, Jeff powered down his passenger window and said, "Looking good Cindy."

"Are you fucking crazy?" Cindy hollered, "You almost hit me!"

He leaned over the center console and similar to the booty shorts and a tube top she wore, his eyes clung to her figure. Quenching his thirst, Jeff licked his lips and said, "Mmm-mmm, I'd never hurt such an incredible piece of ass." His smile widened. "Unless you asked."

Cindy shook her head, and her jaw hung slack as she ducked into the open window. "Oh ... you ... are so fucking bad." Her mouth twisted into a mischievous grin.

"You have no idea."

Appraising the car's interior she whistled and said, "Nice wheels, you just get it?"

"Yeah, I treated myself … for being so good."

With a raised brow, Cindy tilted her chin and pursed her lips.

"So how's Lewis been?"

She looked away, and Jeff found pleasure in her discomfort.

"He … um, he …, he was kind of upset about what happened."

"Were you?" He asked, already knowing the answer.

After a guilty pause, Cindy replied, "No."

"Good, then we'll do it again sometime."

Jeff revved the engine, but before he could pop the clutch, Cindy hollered over the chorus of seven-hundred horses. "Hey wait … have you seen my dog?"

He let the engine settle; his expression revealed nothing. "What?"

"I adopted a Chihuahua from my friend Colleen," she said, smiling. "It's so cute, but I haven't seen it since I let it out this morning."

"Sounds adorable, what's its name?"

"Carlos."

"I can't wait to meet him."

CHAPTER 20

Having spent most of the week with Carrie, little of it sleeping, Joe stayed in bed late on Saturday. He had the day off, and she had flown to Los Angeles for a meeting with her agent the night before, so he took advantage of the opportunity to get some extra rest. As he was getting dressed, he heard the garage door slam, and a moment later his truck driving off. In the kitchen, Joe fixed himself a light breakfast and thought about his last conversation with Cooper. It was the only thing, other than Carrie, he had thought about all week. Having avoided his former coach long enough, Joe figured it was time to see the man. He placed his empty plate in the dishwasher and took off for a run.

Without a backpack to weigh him down his pace was faster than usual. His mind replayed the week with Carrie, while his legs raced across the asphalt. Joe couldn't recall a more enjoyable time. It had been a great escape, but it was time to face Cooper. When last they spoke guilt had prevented him from admitting he thought about the game every day. How he could remember the tiniest details from high school games but couldn't remember his parent's voice. He didn't want Cooper to know how he had felt when the doctor told him about the damage to his shoulder. How he had cried, how the tears rained down his face while he lay in bed for days following his father's murder.

Those were the early days of a journey filled with pain and guilt. Along the way, he'd found outlets to deal with both, many in fact. But they only pushed him further into darkness. Being back in Fairfield had given Joe a glimpse of light and Carrie guided him to it.

Before setting a destination for his run, Joe arrived at one. Cresting a slight rise, he pulled up and slowed. With hands on hips, Joe walked a small circle until his broad chest settled to a normal rhythm. From the back road to the high school, Joe looked down at the practice field. It was vacant except for one kid at the far end of the field, who was filling a target with footballs from twenty yards away. He was a tall, lean lefty with decent feet and a tight spiral. After a few minutes of observation, Joe noticed how the ball occasionally sailed high of his intended target. Without thought, he walked down the hill, into the shallow valley, and across the grass, he'd spent so many hours on.

As Joe drew near, he turned and said, "Hey what's up."

He stood about 6'3", and Joe guessed his weight at a little under 200 pounds. His eyes looked familiar, and his face carried an easy smile. "Not much," Joe answered. "You look good, you play for Lawrence?"

The kid grinned with youthful innocence. "Yep … I heard Coach Cooper's coming back, so I gotta get ready."

"What's your name?" asked Joe.

"AJ."

Joe extended his hand. "Hi AJ, I'm Joe nice to meet you."

"Hi." AJ shook Joe's hand. "Did you play here?"

"About fifty years ago kid."

"Cool."

Confident the teenager hadn't grasped the sarcasm, Joe smiled and asked, "You mind if I show you something?"

"Not at all," AJ answered and handed him a ball.

Joe gripped the leather, looked at it and for a moment he was eighteen again. He inhaled the leathery scent as he knit his fingers between the laces

"Are you okay?" AJ asked.

"Yeah ... I'm good." Back in the present Joe said, "Every now and then, you drop your elbow and cut your hand under the ball." Joe demonstrated with his empty hand and his thumb pointing up. "That's why the ball is sailing high sometimes. Keep your elbow up and finish with your thumb down, you'll have more control." Joe threw the ball, the spiral was loose, and the ball lacked velocity, but it hit the intended target.

"Hey thanks," AJ said, oblivious to the frustration on Joe's face.

He threw a dozen balls and they all hit their mark. "I see what you mean," AJ said. "Thanks again for the tip."

"No problem, enjoy your workout," Joe said and walked away.

AJ called after him. "Did you ever play for Coach Cooper?"

Joe stopped and turned. "I did."

"Cool ... what else should I work on?"

With a light-hearted snicker, Joe said, "You better put the footballs away and start running."

AJ's face sank. "Yeah?"

"Come on kid," Joe said. "I was gonna finish my run, but we can do some conditioning and agility work instead."

"Great man, thanks."

They marked off a distance of about forty yards. After jogging it a couple times, so AJ could get loose, they stood beside each other and Joe counted down. "Ready ... set ... go."

Joe finished well ahead, coasted to a stop, and turned back toward their starting point.

AJ hustled to catch up. "Holy shit," he said, "what the hell?" His mouth hung open.

"Let's go, kid, no time to dog it."

They repeated the process nine more times, and each time Joe finished a little further ahead. Next, he laid the footballs out, and they did a series of agility drills, shuffling in, out, and around the balls. Invigorated by the familiar setting Joe pushed himself and AJ harder with each drill. When they finished, his lungs burned, and his shirt was drenched. AJ took a greedy gulp of water from an oversized jug. Finished, he offered it to Joe, who took it and sipped the cold liquid. Handing it back, Joe studied AJ. The kid's long brown hair was soaked and matted to his head, his easy gait had vanished, and his face burned red with exhaustion. But he hadn't wavered.

Every muscle in AJ's legs burned, each step a sizeable task requiring great effort. The water did little to quench the fire in his lungs, and he fought to keep his hand from trembling when he handed the jug to Joe. He clasped his hands together atop his wet head and took deep breaths. Embarrassed, he looked toward the road, avoiding the older man's eyes. The guy had been smiling the entire time they were doing drills, he never slowed and was he barely winded. Refusing to give in AJ had pushed through the pain, but this guy had run circles around him. Pissed off and determined to work harder he thought, *No friggin way should some old dude be able to outrun me.*

Joe heard a car approach and looked up at the road. When it came into view, he recognized it was Chief Owad, "*Now what?*" He thought.

"My dad's here I got to go."

Joe stifled a laugh. "I guess AJ stands for Adam Junior?"

"Yep, you know my dad?"

They gathered AJ's footballs and packed them in a large duffle bag.

"Sort of." Joe glanced in the older Owad's direction. The Chief was sitting in the car with the window rolled down. They exchanged a wave and Joe looked back toward AJ and said, "Kid you keep working like you did today, and you'll have one heck of a season, I promise you." Joe raised a fist in front of his shoulder.

AJ thumped Joe's fist with his and said, "Thanks, man, I appreciate that. You kind of kicked my ass today."

"Let's do it again," said Joe when they were walking across the field. "I'll be here Monday night after work, say 5:00."

"Okay, yeah sure. I'll see you Monday."

They crested the hill beside the Chief's car, and Joe said, "Your boy's an athlete Chief."

"Thanks, Joe, you need a lift anywhere?"

"Nah … I'm good, thanks. Have a good one Chief, and I'll see you next week AJ." Joe turned and jogged off. Energized by the prospect of a new challenge, for the first time in many years, Joe's mind focused on the game he loved instead of the guilt it caused.

AJ watched Joe run off and again marveled at his endurance. He shook his head, tossed the duffel bag in the back of his dad's car and dropped into the front seat.

Adam spotted the disappointment on his son's face and asked, "What's the matter?" AJ stared straight ahead and said nothing. "What's the matter?" Repeated Adam in a more demanding tone.

"I need to get faster," AJ said, rubbing his face, "and in a lot better shape."

The corners of Adam's mouth turned up into a grin.

AJ frowned. "Dad it's not funny … I'm serious."

Feigning concern, Adam asked, "You couldn't keep up with Joe?"

"No … I know he's in good shape in all, I mean look at him … the guys a house, but how am I gonna get a scholarship if I can't even outrun an old dude."

Adam shook his head and laughed at his son.

AJ smacked his hand on the dashboard. "Why is that funny?"

"Son I love you, but sometimes you sound like a stupid Pollack." AJ stared blankly, and Adam said, "That *old dude* is only twenty-eight. You didn't ask him what his last name was, did you?"

AJ shook his head no.

Realizing his son still hadn't put it together Adam rolled his eyes and said, "Blackstone … you were working out with Joe Blackstone."

Comprehension widened AJ's eyes, realizing he'd just worked out with a local legend he brightened. "Oh! … no wonder."

"Yeah, *'no wonder'*." Adam dropped the car in gear and pulled away.

"Dad he can friggin fly, he's like a machine or something; doesn't even get tired. I don't remember watching him play, but everyone still talks about him. He still holds most of the state records, he's a legend … man, he must have been something."

"He still is AJ … he still is." Adam had no idea how true his statement would prove to be.

***

Joe arrived at Cooper's house and found him in the driveway under the hood of his old Cadillac. "Hi, Coach."

Cooper replaced the dipstick and looked up. "Morning Joe." He waved a hand at Joe's sweaty clothing and said, "Looks like you've been working out."

"Coach, I've been thinking about what you said, and I'm sorry, but I can't coach with you." Joe paused, Cooper was silent sensing he had more to say. "I can't coach because I wanna play … I'm gonna play in the league." A wide grin spread across Cooper's face. A frown tugged at Joe's mouth, and he said, "I know it sounds crazy, but I thought you'd support me on this?"

"Son … I've spent all week trying to figure out how I was going to talk your stubborn ass into this." Cooper slammed the hood shut on the old car. "You go get cleaned up, and I'll be by to get you within the hour."

"Where are we going?" asked Joe.

"To do an old friend a big favor."

CHAPTER 21

Philadelphia

400 cc's rumbled beneath the hood as Mealey eased his 1967 GTO from the garage. He gripped the wooden wheel and the car pulsed in his hands. The old Pontiac roared with approval when he goosed it onto Gulph Road. Traveling beneath a canopy of trees, the red muscle car jumped in and out of the early light spilling through the foliage. Mike choose a path between Philadelphia's Main Line mansions, in awe of the extravagant old money estates. Before long he crossed over City Line Avenue and into West Philadelphia. The dilapidated row homes a stark contrast to the opulence of the Main Line. He bounced along the broken streets and merged onto Cobb's Creek Parkway. Engulfed by its namesake park, the timeworn road snaked through an oasis of green, reminding of more prosperous times before spilling into a sea of concrete. Stadiums, hotels, parking lots and warehouses sprawled across a massive grid which represented ground zero for Philadelphia sports. There wasn't a car in sight as Mike rolled down Broad Street. The baseball and football stadiums rose to his left, the hockey and basketball stadium was dead ahead, and shrubs hid the Freedom practice field on the right.

He turned right at the intersection of Broad and Pattison. In the distance, he saw a blue Caddy sitting across the street from the Freedom's gated entrance and assumed the old car had broken down. When Mike got closer and saw two people sitting in the front seat, he became suspicious. As he slowed to turn the pair emerge from the car. At first, Mike thought the passenger was a Freedom player, tall and broad shouldered he'd easily fit in amongst the team. Something about the driver looked familiar, but the man's face was partially hidden behind what Mealey guessed was a phone. He waved, but Mike ignored him, spinning the wheel sharply to his right, the heavy car swung around the turn and bounced to a stop in front of a bright yellow gate. A security guard approached from the adjacent office. He was about to ask the guard how long the Caddy had been sitting out front when his phone vibrated. He chuckled when he saw the 207-area code. Looking in the chrome mirror, he answered the call and returned his old friend's wave.

Cooper first met Mealey back when he had been a young Division III head coach at Maine Maritime. The two coaches had attended some of the same clinics and had many conversations about Lawrence prospects, even Joe. They lost touch when Cooper retired, but he had retained the younger coach's cell number. Cooper had called several times but was unable to connect with anything other than a generic voice, confirming the mailbox he had reached was full. He considered texting, but couldn't confirm he had the correct number, so he decided a face to face visit would be best.

WFL owners meetings were scheduled the following week in Florida. Since head coaches typically accompanied their owners, Sunday would be the last chance for Mealey to get any work done before the trip. Familiar with Mealey's work ethic he had guessed correctly that the coach would be in at the crack of dawn on Sunday. After a few hours in a hotel, Cooper and Blackstone had woken, well before sunrise, and positioned themselves at the front entrance. He had recognized the 67 Goat as soon as it rounded the corner, he would have heard it even sooner, had it not been for the noise coming from nearby Interstate 95. His plan had been to wave Mealey down, confident he'd be recognized and granted a few minutes of the man's time. But he worried when the Philly coach ignored the wave. When he looked through the rear window and saw Mealey answer his phone, Cooper relaxed; they had cleared the first hurdle.

Two minutes later they were pulling into the player's lot. Both the old coach and his former player gawked at the home of a professional football franchise. A large box structure, they assumed was an enclosed practice field, stood to their left, a two-story office building to their right and straight ahead stood a large modern building. They climbed from Cooper's car and walked toward Mealey, who was parked in a reserved spot directly in front of them.

Mike met them with an extended hand and said, "Coach, it's been a long time."

"Too long." Cooper shook Mealey's hand and introduced Joe. "Mike Mealey, this is Joe Blackstone."

They shook hands. "It's a pleasure to meet you, coach."

"Pleasures mine Joe." Mealey turned back to Cooper and pointed to the big blue Caddy. "I can't believe you still have that thing."

Cooper tilted his head toward the GTO and said, "Look who's talking?"

Mealey laughed. "Yeah, I guess you're right, creatures of habit." He turned on his heel and said, "Come on, I'll show you around the place, and then you can tell me what the hell you two are doing here."

Mealey led Blackstone and Cooper throughout the facility, pointing out the modern amenities. He explained the basic structure of the organization, and how resources were employed to assemble a team and manage it from week to week. He was pretty sure he recognized the young man's name, even if he was mistaken, Blackstone's size was a pretty big indicator as to why they had driven here to see him. Mealey had always liked Cooper and had been familiar with Blackstone's legendary high school career. But he wanted the pair to see how far away the WFL was from high school football in Maine. That way, when he politely declined the request he was expecting, it would be easier for them to return to Maine and leave dreams of the WFL behind.

The tour ended in the team cafeteria. Like the rest of the building, it was asleep at the early hour. Mealey pointed to a counter with fountain drinks, a coffee machine and a cooler of bottled water. "Can I get you guys anything to drink?" he asked.

"I'll take a bottle of water please," said Joe.

"I'm fine, thanks," Cooper said.

Mealey plucked two bottles from the cooler, tossed one to Joe and pointed to a round table. When everyone was seated, he looked at Cooper and asked, "So?"

Cooper looked Mealey in the eye and said, "Coach you know why we're here and I'm sure you remember Joe. You were at U Maine when he played for me. We spoke about him more than once. I also know you're being polite, because I'm sure you think we're out of our mind."

Mealey smiled. "Pete you never were much for bull shit, I always liked that about you. I remember Joe. He was a hell of a high school player ... *in Maine.*" He focused on Joe and said, "I was real sorry to hear about what happened to you, and your dad. No one should have to go through something like that." Mealey sighed, and his expression turned serious. "This is professional football, and every guy we invite to camp was a stud in high school *and* college. Have you even put the pads on since high school?"

"No sir."

"Have you been throwing the ball?"

Joe shook his head. "I can't, my shoulder's fine, but I've got some nerve damage and scar tissue, there's no zip on the ball."

Mealey held his hands up. "Whatta we even talking about then?"

"I can play tight end."

"Joe I can see you're in shape, I respect your enthusiasm, but the guys around here are elite athletes, they're bigger, faster and stronger than anything you could imagine, you ..."

Joe stood and started walking out of the cafeteria.

Confused, Mealey turned to Cooper and asked, "Where the hell's going?"

Pete couldn't contain himself. A toothy grin broke out on his face, and he said, "We kinda figured you were gonna say something like that. He's going to get a change of clothes, and I'm going to make you a proposition." Mealey listened with a wary stare. "You pick three drills, and I bet you, Joe will meet or beat whatever your team-best is."

Out of patience Mealey stood and said, "Pete, it was good to see you, but I don't have time for this. Let me know if you can get back for a game, and I'll get you tickets." He stood and started for the exit. "I'll walk you out."

Cooper held his ground and hollered, "Mike … MIKE." Mealey wheeled around. A vein was bulging on his temple. Cooper was holding his hands up in surrender. "I know you think this is nuts, but did I ever steer you wrong on a player?"

Mike's expression softened. "Nope … no, you didn't," he admitted.

"I know what you think about the level of play in Maine." Cooper pointed in the direction Joe had gone. "But you never saw that kid play. I'm not talking about a highlight reel or clip on the news. I mean live and in person. If you had, you'd know I'm here to help you as much as him." Mealey raised a brow. Cooper continued, "I give you my word, you won't be disappointed. Pick 3 drills, and he'll set new team best."

Pollard strolled in with Joe, who had a gym bag slung over his shoulder. "I found this young man out front, he says he has a tryout."

Mealey fixed his gaze on Joe and held it. After a moment he rolled his eyes and said, "Yeah, I guess he does." He pointed to the locker room they had toured earlier. "Get changed, I don't have all day."

Mealey, Pollard, and Cooper stood together while Joe loosened up in the team's cavernous Sports Science Center. The head coach had decided on the bench press, vertical jump and forty yard dash. Joe would do the first two inside before heading outside to the testing track. Despite having consented, all Mealey wanted was to get it over with so he could say his goodbyes and get on with his day. But Pollard watched with a curious eye as Joe finished a warm-up set on the bench press.

The first test required a straight bar be loaded to a total weight of 225 pounds. Joe would lay on his back, lower the bar to his chest, and then raise it until his arms locked out straight. His butt had to remain on the bench at all times, and the weight moved in a controlled manner. The team record was 39 repetitions, and Cooper was confident Joe would hit that mark.

Excusing himself from the group, Cooper walked up to Joe. Joe pulled a small speaker from his ear canal, and Cooper asked, "How you feel?"

"Good, what's the record?"

"Thirty-Nine."

"No." Joe shook his head and said, "If I'm going to do this, I might as well go all out."

Cooper turned to Mike and John. "What's the league record?"

Mealey rolled his eyes.

"Two years ago, at the combine," said Pollard. "a 345 pound nose guard did fifty-one reps."

Joe placed the ear bud back in his ear and loaded the bar with the appropriate weight. He sat on the end of the bench, and his head pulsed back and forth. Cooper wondered if it was driven by the music or something else. After three deep breaths, Joe closed his eyes and lay back, flat on the bench. Cooper stepped back, and Joe's body continued to rock ever so slightly as his hands found their grip. Pollard and Mealey took a spot on opposite sides of the steel bar, so they could offer assistance and re-rack the weight if need be. The rocking stopped, Joe grew perfectly still, exhaled, and hefted the cold steel. Inhaling, he lowered the weight to his chest, let it sit there for a beat, exhaled and pushed it toward the ceiling. When the bar reached its peak, he stopped and repeated the process.

Cooper counted off the reps; Mealey's scowl fade as the number climbed. Joe's pace remained steady, when he hit forty, Mike and John exchanged a look.

At forty-five Mealey heard himself say, "Push it, son." At forty-seven Joe's rhythm slowed but Mealey urged him to keep going. "Come on, don't stop … push it lets go."

Cooper called out, "fifty." Joe held the bar above his head for several seconds before lowering it to his chest. It lay there, frozen for a long moment, before slowly climbing upward.

"Fifty-one," Cooper called out.

His tone rung with new found respect when Mealey said, "Great job son." Assuming Joe couldn't possibly do another rep, he and Pollard reached for the bar.

"No!" Joe grunted.

Mealey glanced at Cooper.

"Let him go," Cooper said.

"Let's go," urged Pollard.

Again, Joe lowered the weight, and again it stuck to his chest. Mealey hollered, "Come on don't stop now!" Joe's thick arms trembled, and the bar broke free, Mealey yelled, "Yes … push it, kid!"

Joe's face burned with determination, and the bar rose until his elbows locked. Pollard and Mealey guided the weight as he re-racked it. Pollard wore a broad smile. Mealey wore a broad smile when Joe sat up. "Impressive," said the coach.

"Mike … you ain't seen anything yet," said Cooper.

Twenty minutes later Joe had not only bested the Freedom's team mark in the bench press, vertical-jump, and forty yard dash, he'd also beaten the WFL combine records. Like he had done on the bench, Joe's forty-six inch vertical had surpassed the old mark by one. If that hadn't sealed the deal for Philly's coach and GM, his forty time had. In 1990 the league began timing the forty electronically, removing the human error. Since then, no player had recorded a time better than 4.24. Many considered Bo Jackson's hand-timed 4.12 the fastest ever, Joe ran a 4.11. Insisting there must have been a mistake, Mealey and Pollard asked him to run it again so they could confirm the electronic time with a stopwatch. Happy to oblige, Joe ran a 4.09, which was confirmed by Pollard's handheld time. Cooper beamed with an *I told you so* grin.

"So?" Joe asked when he circled back.

Mealey stood slack jawed. Pollard shook his head in disbelief and said, "Young man, in 1935 Jesse Owens set three world records and tied a fourth at the Big Ten track and field championships. It's widely considered the greatest forty-five minutes in sports history. I believed it was, and I didn't think anything would ever compare … until today."

CHAPTER 22

Fairfield, Maine

When Cooper dropped Joe off, it was early evening, and Troy was out. It had been a long day, but Joe still had something he needed to do. He took a shower and headed back out. The low hanging sun burned the horizon and long shadows cut across the country road. The short walk was refreshing after such a long car ride. Before long he arrived at his destination and turned up the driveway.

AJ answered Joe's knock, surprised he said, "Oh hey, what's up?"

"How you doing AJ?" Joe extended his hand.

AJ shook it with a firm grip and said, "Good thanks."

"Is your dad around?"

"Yeah, he's out back we just got done eating. Follow me," AJ said, motioning Joe inside.

He led the way through a small but tidy ranch home. They went out a sliding door off the kitchen and stepped onto a deck. Becky Owad and an attractive woman, whom Joe guessed was her mom, were cleaning plates off a round patio table. Adam was in a chair, cutting a cigar. They all turned his way, and Joe said, "I hope I'm not intruding on dinner."

Standing, Adam said, "No we're finished. I know you've met AJ and Becky." Becky and Joe exchanged a smile. "This is my wife Beth, Beth this is Joe Blackstone."

Joe gave the Chief's wife a little nod and said, "Pleasure to meet you Mrs. Owad."

Beth set the plates down, walked up to Joe and threw her arms around him. She squeezed him as tight as she could. Joe's face turned red, and eye's shifted awkwardly to the rest of the family. Before releasing him, Beth whispered, "God bless you for sticking up for my little girl."

"You're welcome Ma'am."

"Please, Call me Beth."

"Have a seat," Adam said. He motioned toward an empty chair. "Can we get you a drink or something to eat? Beth's a great cook, and we've got a ton of leftovers."

Joe was starving but said, "No I'm okay, but thanks, Chief."

"Just Adam is fine."

"Yes, sir," Joe said.

Adam grinned, and Joe sat down. The rest of the family disappeared inside. "What can I do for you?" Asked Adam.

"Chi ... Adam, I know coach called you about me leaving the state, and you gave him the go ahead," — Joe still had a few days of probation, so Cooper had cleared their trip with Adam— "so first, I wanna thank you for that."

"No problem."

Before Joe could continue Beth emerged from the kitchen with a plate of barbecue chicken, corn on the cob, salad and a couple of beers. She placed the food in front of the Joe and set the two bottles on the table.

"Beth, you didn't—"

"Nonsense," she said. "Did you eat dinner yet?"

"No."

"Then eat, there's plenty more where that came from." She strode off.

The look on Adam's face suggested Joe do as she says. "Thank you," he called after her.

"You're welcome," replied Beth.

Adam pointed at Joe's plate. "Eat," he said, "then we can talk."

They sat under the porch lights while Joe ate. Starving, he made short work of the meal. "That was delicious," he said after clearing his plate.

"I told you she can cook," Adam said and took a sip of his beer. "So what's up?"

Joe told him about his trip to Philly with Cooper. He glossed over how we'll he'd done but shared his invite to camp.

"That's all great news Joe, your probation is about up, so there's no issue there. Plus I'm sure you can get transportation easily enough in the city until you get your license back."

"Oh yeah, none of that is an issue, that's not why I'm here."

Adam picked up the cigar he had prepared earlier and held it to a butane cigar lighter with a double flame. Once it lit, he took a couple puffs to ensure it stayed that way and said, "Okay, you've got me curious."

"I wanna train with your son, he's got a good arm, and I need someone to work with. I'm asking you first because I want you to know … I'm in a better place than I've been for a long time. Staying here was good for me, and I appreciate and respect how you handled things. If AJ wants to train with me, we'll work our asses off, but I'll take care of him and keep him safe."

Adam thought Joe's choice of words, 'keep him safe', were odd but let it go. "I appreciate you asking, and I'm sure he'd love to."

Adam called for his son, and when AJ appeared, Joe asked him what he'd come to ask.

AJ's jaw dropped. Finally, he said, "You want *me* to help *you* get ready for training camp with the Philadelphia Freedom?"

Joe grinned and said, "Yep … and I'll help you prepare for your season with the Dogs."

"Hell yeah," AJ shouted, and pulled out his cell phone. "I can't wait to tell the guys."

"Hey ... if they're up for it, we could use some extra guys from time to time."

"Holly Shi ... Crap, this is so cool, thanks, Joe." AJ was texting rapidly when he stepped back inside.

Adam held the cigar up. "I'd offer you one, but I guess that's not a good idea if you're in training."

"Thanks, anyway."

"How about another beer?"

"Sure," Joe said, "I can handle that."

An hour and several beers later they were still on the deck. With few homes in the area to mute the night sky, the stars shined bright overhead. They talked about Cooper's return to the sideline, and Joe told Adam how well he expected AJ to do under their former coach. They talked about Joe's chances of making the Freedom roster and Adam told Joe he expected nothing but greatness. *You damn right about that,* thought Joe.

Sometime around midnight, Joe stood. "Thanks for everything," he said "The food and beer hit the spot. I better get back, AJ and I have a lot of work to do tomorrow."

Joe extended his hand, Adam shook it and said, "Anytime Joe, you're always welcome here." Adam's eyes turned serious, and he continued to grip Joe's hand. "I'm sorry ... I'm sorry we never closed your dad's case."

Adam released his hand, and Joe turned toward the steps.

"Don't worry about it," said Joe as he stepped off the deck, "it's okay."

"I promise you I'll never stop trying."

Joe stopped in the shadows and glanced back. "It's already closed," he said.

Adam was surprised by his statement and unnerved by his tone, but the look on Joe's face sent a shiver down Adam's spine.

***

When Joe got home, Troy jumped off the couch so fast the bag of chips he was eating spilled across the floor. He rushed into the kitchen and asked, "So?"

A broad smile spread across Joe's face. "I'm going to camp."

"Yes," shouted Troy. "I knew you'd do it, this is awesome!"

"Hey relax I haven't done anything yet, half the guys they invite never make the team."

Troy rolled his eyes. "Dude, please … it's me you're talking to, I know you, and you don't need to pull that modest shit with me. Tell me you're gonna kick ass."

Joe's voice filled with conviction, and he said, "I've waited a long time for this, you best believe I am."

Troy bounced up and down. "Now that's more like it." He sat back down and asked, "What was Mealey like? What were the facilities like? What did they have you do for a tryout?"

Joe held up his hands. "I'll tell you all about it, but first I need to call Carrie."

"Oh God," said Troy, rolling his eyes. "Hurry up lover boy."

Joe disappeared down the hall, and Troy sat alone smiling. He could not have been happier for his friend or his sister.

Carrie answered on the second ring, her words jumped from the phone with excitement. "So what happened?"

Joe spent the next half hour telling Carrie about the trip. The more he shared, the more fulfilled he became, not in a boastful way, but sharing this step with her made for a better journey. She peppered him with questions. When he had answered them all, she said, "Baby, I'm so excited for you, you deserve this so much. I know you're gonna be great."

"Thanks, but enough about me. How'd your meeting go?"

"Oh my God, It went great. It's a dream role, and I got a good vibe from the producers and director. They offered me the part on the spot, and I took it"

"Congrats that's terrific."

"Thanks, I'm pumped. You won't believe this, they wanna pre-shoot some scenes here, then finish shooting in Atlantic City and the Philadelphia area. I'm gonna be stuck here for a while, but after, I'll be in the Philly area."

Joe hadn't given any thought to how Carrie's, and now his own, career could limit their time together. The next few weeks would be long without her but having her with him in Philly would be great. "Now I really can't wait to get to Philly," said Joe.

CHAPTER 23

As usual, Joe opened Champions on Monday. When the owner arrived, Joe informed him, he had to resign so he could concentrate on his training. The owner was understanding of the circumstances and even offered Joe continued use of the facilities at no charge.

Over the next five weeks, Joe and AJ trained hard in the gym and on the track. Often times, AJ's teammates joined them on the field for various drills. Coach Cooper was also a fixture during the field work, offering instruction to both his former and future players. AJ was shy at first, but once he got to know Joe he had become a great training partner. He couldn't physically match up with the older man, but he pushed Joe to compete against himself.

One afternoon Cooper noticed Joe wince while demonstrating proper throwing mechanics for AJ. When they took a water break, Cooper pulled Joe aside. "If it bothers you to throw the ball why don't you try left handed?"

Joe raised an eyebrow.

"Seriously," Cooper said, "didn't you pitch a baseball game left handed when you were in 8ᵗʰ grade?"

"Yeah, but it was because we were outta pitchers; I wasn't any good."

"Joe, your idea of *not any good* and everyone else's is a little different. If I recall you pitched a complete game and you guys won 4-2."

"I'm not sure coach."

"Well, I am," said Cooper. "I was there."

Joe put his hands up in surrender.

"all I'm saying is maybe you could try throwing left when you're working with AJ. Why kill yourself? It's not like you need to throw much, but when you want to show him something throw with your left, he's a lefty anyway."

When he was, younger Joe had been ambidextrous, the older he got, the more dominate his right hand had become. Figuring it wouldn't hurt to try Joe began throwing with his left, it didn't take long before he was throwing better than he could with his right. His passes were not the pinpoint rockets he had thrown in high school, but they jumped from his hand with a familiar zip.

***

A year ago, Joe had no one to call and no one he wished to hear from so he'd thrown his cell phone off a bridge, now he used his new phone to speak with Carrie two or three times a day. She was already in Atlantic City but would be shooting in Philadelphia within the next two days. The studio had rented her a home in the Blue Bell Country Club a few miles outside the city. It was a short commute, and Carrie had arranged to keep it until after football season.

Troy still had not replaced his Tahoe, so three days before he was supposed to drive Joe, and Joe's truck, to camp they went car shopping. Right as they crossed into Waterville on College Avenue, Joe pointed and said, "Pull in here ... right here."

Troy pulled into a boutique dealership they both knew specialized in Corvettes and muscle cars. By the time he parked Troy was already shaking his head. "Uh uh! No way, I'm not buying anything they have here."

Joe looked heavenward, and said, "Of course you're not you cheap bastard, you'd drive my truck forever if I weren't leaving."

"Then whatta we doin' here?" Troy asked, ignoring the barb.

Joe pointed out the front window to his left.

Troy followed his hand, his eyes bulged open. "No fuckin' way," he said.

They got out of the truck and approached a 1968 Dodge Charger RT. The sleek body lines shined beneath a mirror finish of black metallic paint, muted only by a flat black tail stripe. Red RT badges highlighted the black on black stripe and a peek-a-boo light cover on the driver's side. The entire chassis stood on Vector rims, and a four-speed Hurst shifter sat between black leather seats. The door was unlocked, so Joe opened and popped the hood.

"Holly Shit," Troy said.

The engine block was painted Mopar red. Matte black headers and braided hoses screamed performance. The much-coveted orange and black *HEMI HEAD 426* badge sat prominently on a chrome breather.

A salesman appeared at their side. "Good afternoon fellas, you got great taste, she's a beauty," he offered his hand and said, "I'm Travis."

They all shook as Joe and Troy introduced themselves.

"How much?" Joe asked, getting right to the point.

Joe and Travis had haggled for about two minutes before Travis accepted an amount Joe promised could be wired immediately. When the paperwork was completed Troy eased behind the wheel of Joe's new Charger. He ran a hand over the dash and said, "I can't believe you did that."

"Screw it, things are good ... we've gotta have some fun right."

Troy laughed and said, "I guess so brother ... I guess so."

"Now let's go get you some practical piece of shit with best in class gas mileage."

"Keep talking, I'll crash this thing like you did my wheels."

They both laughed.

***

Three days later, Troy helped Joe get settled at the team hotel three blocks from the stadium. Rookies like Joe were the first to report, veterans would arrive within the next 2 days. Since many of the players had flown in and were without a vehicle, shuttles were scheduled to run from the hotel to the training facility. But Troy drove Joe over so he could leave the Charger at the gated facility until he was legal to drive again.

Troy had plans to spend a few days in Philly with a friend from college before flying home. The two friends stood at the security gate waiting for her to pick him up. "Her she is," Troy said when her car pulled to the curb.

"Thanks again for the ride, and for everything else you've done."

"No thanks necessary, you do your thing." Troy thought for a moment and said, "Feel free to get me tickets, though."

"You got it."

They hugged goodbye, and Joe watched the car pull away. When it disappeared, he turned toward the main building and strode toward his dream with determination.

He was greeted in the lobby by an intern and asked to fill out some paperwork. Once that task was completed he was given an itinerary and facilities pass, which he hung from his neck. An intern escorted him to the auditorium. He was the first to arrive, and the intern suggested he make himself comfortable while he waited. On his previous tour of the facility, Joe thought the large hall resembled a movie theater built for giants, upon further reflection, Joe realized it was exactly that. He strolled down the gradual decline toward the front. Large pictures of past team greats adorned the walls. A center aisle cut horizontally across the oversized seating. The main stage consisted of a raised platform, like most theaters, it offered a variety of backgrounds and a giant screen. A room to the right of the stage was crammed full of audio and video equipment.

Joe settled himself in the front row and sat his duffel bag at his feet. After a quick review of the itinerary, he eased himself back into the plush leather seat. Closing his eyes, he pictured himself walking out of the tunnel and into the stadium for the first time. The image of Carrie looking on from the stands brought a smile to his face.

Soon the auditorium filled. The young faces surrounding him reminded Joe more of AJ and his teammates than the image he saw every day in the mirror. The other rookies sat scattered throughout the auditorium, several conversed amongst one another and a few crowed with false bravado. Unsure of what to make of the long haired man with serious eyes, they gave Joe a wide berth.

Mealey and a dozen other coaches entered through a side door. His assistants found seats and the head coach stepped to a podium at the center of the stage. Mealey glanced at his notes and addressed the team. "Good morning gentlemen and welcome to the Philadelphia Freedom Professional Football Team. You've all been given an itinerary so you should know we have a busy couple of days before we even start regular practices. If you need anything see one of the training staff or your position coach, if you want to speak with me directly my office door is always open. However, make no mistake, you are no longer in college. I'm not here to recruit, coddle or appease you, this is the WFL, and it's business." Mealey paused, searched each player's eyes for understanding and continued, "The environment here will be one of competition. Rookies, like yourselves, and veterans will all be fighting for roster spots. If you're not ready to compete, you should get up and leave right now." Again the coach stopped and took stock of the assembled players. "First, we'll get you situated with a locker and get your physicals completed. After that, you'll start the conditioning tests. Any questions?"

There were none.

"Good." Mealey pointed to the rear of the auditorium and said, "At the back of the room you'll see members of our training staff, follow them, and I'll see you all later today."

The group of twenty-eight rookies was shown to their lockers. Joe took a moment to soak in the Blackstone 86 above his before changing and reporting for his physical.

In the trainer's room, Joe stepped behind one of six temporary privacy curtains. A heavy-set man, of average height, and salty gray hair asked him to remove his shirt. The act attracted the cock-eyed stare he had received from his teammates moments ago. "Jesus, what happened to you?" asked the physician. "Were you in the service?"

In a light-tone, Joe said, "Just the wrong place at the wrong time Doc."

The doctor puckered his face but didn't push the issue. He recorded Joe's official height and weight at 6'5", 266 pounds and performed a quick examination. When he finished, he made a couple notations in Joe's file and said, "Alright Rambo, we're finished, beat it."

When the physicals were completed, everyone gathered outside. They were broken into three groups, each would be tested in a half dozen different speed and agility drills before lunch. The afternoon would be spent in the gym doing strength testing.

The players in each group all appeared to be of similar size, except Joe, who was by far the largest in his. Also, he and wide receiver Ryan Barrett, who was of Asian and Irish descent, were the only two players in their group who were not African-American. The forty yard dash would be their first test.

While they were stretching a 5'11", 190 cornerback started running his mouth. "In case you'll ain't figured it out, you'll fighting for second best in this one. Don't sweat it though it's just the way it is."

Joe knew all about Timmy Simms, he was a late round pick from Texas A&M, many of the draft experts said he lacked the toughness needed to compete at the pro level, no one doubted his speed. Simms had been an alternate on the Summer Olympic team and had dazzled at the combine, recording a class best 4.31.

"Wanna put a hundred on that?"

Everyone stopped and stared in Joe's direction. A chorus of laughter broke out. When they settled down, Simms said, "You are one stupid white boy but hey that's your problem, not mine, I'll take that bet."

When Simms lined up to run his 40, Barrett slid up beside Joe and asked, "Hey man ... you have any idea who that guy is? He'll be the fastest guy on this team rookie or veteran."

They turned and watched Simms sprint to a 4.28, his teammates hollered and celebrated the time, none more than Simms himself. Joe was up next.

With an edge to his voice, Joe said, "*Barrett* ... I've done my homework on all you guys, and I promise you he won't be the fastest guy on this team."

Joe walked away, leaving Barrett to wonder, *Who the hell is this guy?*

As he stepped to the starting line, Joe heard a snicker. "Cracker needs to get his ass over there with the lineman." The comment elicited another round of laughs.

Joe glanced to his right and spotted Mealey, player, and coach exchanged a look, and Joe readied himself. Long ago fate had altered his course, casting aside what appeared to be a golden journey. Instead, he'd found himself alone on a dark path, each turn leading to pain and guilt. At a time when he had lost his desire to moving forward, fate had once again intervened. This time bringing those who remembered him at his best back into his life, friends, and neighbors who saw in him what he no longer could. Their light had shone through the darkness which had shrouded him. The forty yards before him represented a new journey, Joe couldn't wait to take it and discover where it led.

He came off the line low and hard, eating up the track with powerful strides. Jeers turned to gaping stares when Joe crossed the line everyone in his group except Timmy Simms howled. The ruckus was so loud it drew the attention of the other two groups.

Joe's time flashed on the electronic timing device, and Barrett hooted and said, "Damn ... that boy can run!"

The entire group laughed, and when Joe jogged back, he was met with reverence. Forty yards had transformed him from an outsider to the alpha dog, a familiar label. The rest of the testing brought more of the same, he was faster and stronger than everyone there, same as he had always been. For the remainder of the day coaches engaged in animated conversations, unable to comprehend the physical gifts bestowed upon one player.

Curious, teammates asked where he went to college, Joe joked he wasn't smart enough. When asked where he was from, he said all over. An expert at hiding in plain sight, Joe quickly followed up with questions of his own, deftly steering one conversation after another in a different direction.

That evening while Joe was on the phone with Carrie many of his teammates were surfing the internet. Several found his name in the Maine State High School record books. Luckily Chief Owad had been able to keep his recent police records sealed, but the ones involving his father's murder were not. News quickly circulated and by breakfast the next morning his new nickname was already spreading.

On day two the rookies were given playbooks. They spent the day in meetings and on the practice field reviewing plays in t-shirts and shorts. The following day most members of the team made their way to the Sports Science Center after breakfast. It would be their last chance for a good workout before the pains of camp hindered the process. Like most of his teammates, Joe worked through his routine with his earbuds in. He acknowledged other players and exchanged a fist bump with a few of the rookies, but otherwise kept to himself. Despite his casual demeanor, stares from several of the veterans did not go unnoticed.

Joe was finishing a set of power cleans when a house of a man swaggered up to him. Rick Bell, a thirty-three-year-old defensive tackle, stood an inch taller and had 60 pounds on him. Bell's black head was shaved bald, and his yellow teeth were set in a snarl.

Joe removed his earbuds. "Hey man what's up?"

"You don't look like no legend to me, you just another punk ass rook."

"I'm Joe." He held his hand out, but Bell ignored it.

Loud enough to attract attention, Bell said, "I'm using this rack now punk so you best move along."

Joe put his hand down. "I've got two more sets," he said, "but you're welcome to work in."

Bell announced his intent with a slight shift in his weight and Joe read it like a book. When the bigger man lurched forward in an attempted shove, Joe slipped to the side and Bell came up with nothing but air. He added a push for good measure and Bell sailed over a bench and landed flat on his face.

Jeff Pergine watched with amusement as Bell hit the ground. The thug may not be much of a player anymore, but he was still one of the meanest and dirtiest guys in the league. The Rookie's career was about to end before it even got started. Bell sprung to his feet like the former first-round pick he was and was on the long-haired hillbilly in a flash. His big paw reared back, and Bell launched a haymaker, but it passed harmlessly by the Rookie's head. In a flash, Hillbilly had Bell's wrist and massive arm pinned behind his back. The rook gripped Bell in a headlock while applying pressure to his arm, dropping him to a knee. Even from a distance, Pergine could see the violence in the Rookie's eyes, it was unlike any he had seen before. Without a word, he released Bell and stood his ground. Bell rose to his feet and pivoted to face the Rookie.

"Are we done here?" The warning in Joe's voice was clear to all those in earshot.

His scowl withered and whatever bravado Bell had left drained from his posture. Deflated, he turned trudged away without another word.

Someone said, "Legend is a baaad man." Laughter drained the tension from the room.

Joe pushed the buds back into his ears and resumed his workout. The rest of the players did the same, but one pair of eyes were still stuck on Joe. Pickell scrutinized the Rookie from a balcony overlooking the weight room. Even more impressive than the way he'd handled the altercation, he was unfazed by it.

AC/DC's *It's a long way to the top*, pulsed in Joe's ears as he added weight for his next set. He couldn't help but wonder what would have happened had Bell confronted him a year ago. As violent a thought it was, Joe took comfort in the hope he'd changed; maybe he did deserve a second chance.

CHAPTER 24

By the time the team hit the field for their first full practice, news of Philadelphia's twenty-eight-year-old rookie phenom had spread like wildfire. Reporters lined the fence to get a look at the workout sensation. Longtime beat writer Bud Perkins was first to get the scoop, a source within the training staff had given Perkins a heads-up on Blackstone's unprecedented test scores. The veterans hadn't been there and were generally guarded where rookies were concerned, so Perkins had pressed those who'd witnessed it for more information on Blackstone. In doing so, he was able to confirm what his source had given him and learned the younger players had begun referring to him as Legend. After countless phone calls, Perkins had done a Google search, hoping to fill in some of the many blanks in his story. But all it revealed was decade old news of high school glory and a father's murder.

Under the watchful eye of Perkins and the rest of the local media, the Philadelphia Freedom trotted onto the field for their first full practice of camp. Perkins had half expected the Rookie to be wearing a red S instead of the #86. While tall and broad shouldered Blackstone wasn't the biggest of his teammates. And despite all the hype, Bud doubted he was faster or quicker than the marque veterans who filled the skilled positions. Sure, he may be more athletic than the other rookies, but maybe they sucked. As far as his outrageous 40-time went   Bud chalked it up to human error.

The morning practice deemed to be uneventful. The players wore helmets, shoulder pads with shorts. They ran drills and a few plays but at no time did they go live. Blackstone was in great shape, there was no denying that. While other players wilted under the hot summer sun, he seemed unaffected. He wasn't the only athlete who had reported to camp in shape. Wide receiver Dwayne Wilmot, running back Kirk Matthieu, and safety Gino Mays were a few of the veterans who appeared to be in peak condition.

Perkins caught up with Philly's star quarterback as he left the field following the early session and asked, "Jeff, how's it feel to start camp?"

Pergine flashed his All-American smile and said, "Great, I'm excited about the season, and I can't wait to give our great fans something to cheer about."

What a phony, thought Perkins, but instead asked, "What can you tell me about the twenty-eight-year-old rookie sensation I've been hearing about?"

Perkins noticed a flash of ire in the quarterback's eyes. It quickly disappeared, but it hadn't gone unnoticed.

"He seems like a solid athlete but let's give the guy a break, it's pretty tough to go from high school to the pro's so we should all temper our expectations." Jeff jogged away before Bud could follow up.

That afternoon, for the first time in a decade, Joe took the field wearing a complete football uniform. He felt great. Practice started the same as the earlier one had, with players running through easy drills to loosen up. But when the air horn sounded, signaling the next phase of practice, it represented the first contact session of camp. It wouldn't be full live, like a game environment, but it would be the first time Joe got to compete physically against professional athletes.

Joe's group, consisting of tight ends and fullbacks, matched up against the linebackers. The first drill called for the offensive players to pass-block the linebackers. This was a tough assignment for the tight ends who were seldom asked to block one on one on pass plays.

One member of each group lined up opposite the other. A coach knelt, down the line from the opposing players. He held a ball to the ground, barking out signals. Each time he jerked the ball off the field the players sprang into action. The offensive players defended a cone, which represented the quarterback, while the linebackers attacked it. Each group shouted for their member to pummel the others. Coaches berated the first three offensive players when they were bested by the linebackers.

When it was Joe's turn, he stepped forward and squared off against John Atkins, one of Philadelphia's only returning linebackers. The two men were comparable in size if nothing else. On the coach's signal, Atkins used a speed move, and tried to race past Joe to the outside; Joe was too quick, he cut him off with his first step and made contact with his second. Joe's hands struck the front of Atkins shoulder pads and jolted him backward. A final burst left Atkins on his back gasping for air. Joe hustled back in line amidst praise from his fellow tight ends. He loved it.

Lafond and Mealey observed the interval from the middle of the field. It lasted sixteen minutes, and Joe went seven times. Each time the commotion grew as he faced off against a new opponent and each time ended the same. With a beaten defender on his back and the offensive unit in an uproar. Pickell had gravitated toward his fledgling linebackers, launching into a tirade and questioning the talent, heart, and sexuality of each man Joe pummeled. Wide-eyed on the far sideline, Bud Perkins took notice.

Again, the air horn sounded signaling the next interval. The offensive and defensive units gathered separately in preparation for a scrimmage session. No one was permitted to touch the quarterback and defenders were not allowed to bring ball carriers to the ground. Everything else was live.

Joe stood with the backups while the starters took the field. Pergine led the offense on a couple of scoring drives before both starting units were replaced by the second string. Again, Joe waited on the sideline. The second team defense dominated its counterpart on the first series. Joe was growing frustrated when Lafond called out, "Blackstone … tight end." *About time*, he thought and dashed onto the field.

Brett Hopewell's days as a starting quarterback were behind him, but he was a solid backup. Never the most durable, he did provide talent and experience off the bench. When Joe stepped into the huddle, the veteran signal caller looked to him and said, "'Kay Rook, let's see whatcha got, Scat Left Y Post Z 63 curl, on two."

They broke the huddle and hustled to the ball. Joe lined up in a three-point stance on the left side of the formation. The play called for him to run eight yards straight down the field, and break to the middle. Ideally, he'd run toward the goal post between the two safeties. Joe noticed, the starting free safety, Gino Sayers, had reentered the scrimmage. He was aligned right in the middle of the field, exactly where Joe needed to go. Strong side linebacker Boyd Reed, one of the several players Joe had embarrassed earlier, was lined up over him.

Before the snap, Reed taunted, "It's my turn bitch, this ain't no drill now Smalltown."

" —Hut,HUT" Barked Hopewell.

Reed's Popeye-like forearm wound up to deliver a blow the instant the ball was snapped. Before it landed, Joe's left hand shot forward and snatched the top of Reed's pads. He yanked the 250 pound Reed with all his strength, launching himself forward. Reed's arms flailed, and he stumbled forward as Joe jetted past him.

When Joe broke free off the line, he drew Sayers attention. At eight yards Joe made his move. The lowering of the hips and tilt of the head would have gone unnoticed to all but the most seasoned of veterans. Gino shifted his hips and broke on the outside pass route. When he did, Joe planted his outside foot and cut to the center of the field, opposite the direction he had faked. Sayers had surrendered his advantage but was not yet beat, he recovered and ran with Joe stride for stride.

Hopewell had recognized the coverage as soon as they lined up. To get open, the Rookie would have to beat a linebacker and a safety, who happened to be Philly's best defender. Assuming Joe had no chance of getting open, Hopewell set up in the pocket and looked at his outside receiver first. He was covered, so Hopewell glanced back to the middle. Despite his surprise, instinct took over, and he threw the ball deep down the middle.

The ball arced high out of Hopewell's hand. Lafond thought it had been overthrown, but Blackstone pulled away from Sayers and raced under it as it fell. Lafond wiped his forehead. "Holy shit," he said.

Joe was eight yards behind Sayers when the ball dropped into his outstretched hands. The all-pro pulled up and gaped; Joe jogged into the end-zone. "Muthafucka," said Sayers.

Lafond looked at Mealey and asked, "Is this kid for real?"

"God I hope so," said Mealey

Pickell screamed at Sayers and the media watched with wonder. A few teammates shook their heads in disbelief while others shouted approval. All in attendance were starting to believe the hype. Standing by himself on the sideline, Pergine's face filled with disdain over all the attention Blackstone received.

For the remainder of practice, Joe run through, over and around defenders. When it was over, he was swarmed by reporters on his way to the locker room. One shouted, "Joe how come you never played in college?"

Another asked, "What have you been doing since high school?"

If you only knew, Joe thought.

Bud Perkins worked his way to Joe's side and asked, "Why now kid? After ten years, why'd you decide to play again?"

Joe kept walking but glanced in Perkins direction. "As a kid, I dreamed of playing pro ball." He waved his arm across the field toward his scattered teammates. "No different from them I suppose. I had some bad luck, and I guess I lost my way, but some good friends helped me find it again. So, I'm here now, and it'd take an army to drag me away. I'm here to stay."

Joe was thankful for the reprieve when he reached the locker room, which was closed to media. After a shower, he headed to the cafeteria. He loaded a tray with grilled chicken, salad, and pasta, grabbed two bottles of water, and found an open seat at an occupied table.

Outside Linebacker, JJ "Clubber" Lang stopped eating, looked at Joe and said, "Goddamn Legend, I thought you broke my rib."

Joe shrugged. "Sorry man, I'm full go or no go, don't know any other way."

Corner Timmy Simms was sitting across from Joe and asked, "You a big cat and all, but how's a white boy like you that much faster and stronger than the rest of us? Seriously? Every muthafucka here was *The Man* in college, and you didn't even play college ball, what's up with that?"

"Yeah … what's up with that Rook?"

Joe, Lang, and Simms pivoted and saw Wilmot hovering at their table. The veteran receiver motioned to an open chair. Joe threw a thumb at it and said, "Have a seat."

Wilmot set his tray on the table, sat and waited.

Three sets of eyes waited on Joe's answer. He stopped eating, took a sip of water and said, "You guys are all world class athletes' right?" They all nodded in agreement. "As good as you were in college, and even high school, I'm sure you had a rival. You know, someone who pushed you, challenged you." Joe looked directly at Wilmot, "Maybe it was a teammate or an opponent, but you had that guy right?"

"Yeah," said Wilmot.

Joe shook his head and said, "I never did." *At least not in football*, he thought.

His teammates waited for Joe to explain, but he had nothing else to say and resumed eating.

Wilmot was the first to speak. "Well Legend, I'm glad you're on our team."

At sunup the following day, Joe jogged to the training facility. He was inside the Sports Science Center when he spotted activity outside on the practice field, Wilmot was running routes with a young coach. Joe moved toward the back door, which was propped open. Leaning on the frame he watched, appreciating the precision with which Wilmot practiced. Every movement planned and rehearsed to perfection.

As the coach tired, the ball fluttered. "Sorry Dwayne my arm's shot," he said after several wobbly passes.

"Come on Ricky, a couple more," urged Wilmot.

"No can do man," replied Ricky.

Joe called out, "I can toss a few."

Wilmot hadn't noticed Joe standing in the doorway, he looked, pointed Joe's way and said, "You're up, thanks, man."

Joe jogged onto the field.

Wilmot tossed him a ball and asked, "You need to warm up?"

"Yeah, let me throw a couple." Like he had with AJ, Joe threw left-handed. After a few tosses, he said, "I'm loose, what do you wanna run?"

"I'd like to run some deep out's, but I know that's a tough throw. I could run slants if that easier?"

"The outs are good, I can get it there," Joe said, wondering if he could.

He stood in the middle of the field with Wilmot to his right. The route called for Wilmot to run straight down the field for fifteen yards and take a ninety-degree turn to his right, toward the sideline. It was a long throw and had to be thrown with velocity.

Joe tapped the ball and said, "Set … go."

Wilmot shot down the field, and Joe dropped back. When the receiver reached fourteen yards, Joe hurled the ball to his outside. Wilmot broke right at fifteen yards, before finishing his second step toward the sideline he stretched up and snagged the ball above his head.

Joe threw to him for half an hour. Afterward, they went inside to lift. There were only a dozen players present but soon, the gym filled with activity as others arrived.

While he was spotting Joe during a set of shoulder presses, Wilmot noticed the scar on Joe's right shoulder. When Joe racked the weight, he pointed at the wound and said, "That looks nasty."

Joe put his hand on it "Yeah, it was."

"Doesn't bother you when you play?"

"It gets stiff from time to time, but they did a good job patching me up. The biggest issue was nerve damage, I don't have a lot of feeling in it, except when I throw and that ain't so great, can't throw for shit."

Wilmot laughed and said, "People do tend to struggle throwing with their off-hand."

"My left is my off-hand."

"Wait." Wilmot shook his head. "Are you telling me you were throwing those bullets left handed and you're a righty?"

"Yeah, that's why my accuracy sucked, gets worse if I'm moving but I was always a bit ambidextrous, so I'm okay if I'm stationary. The more I move, the more my mechanics break down."

Wilmot stared wide-eyed. "Unbelievable," he said, "I guess you better spend some time in the simulator and fix that accuracy, God forbid you're not perfect at everything."

Joe chuckled, and thought, *thanks, Dwayne, good idea.*

CHAPTER 25

By mid-August Cooper and his Bulldogs had also begun camp. Joe checked in with his former coach and AJ as often as possible. He was pleased, but not surprised, to hear both player and coach had exceeded the others' expectations. Troy texted regularly, assuring Joe he'd be back in Philly soon. After dropping Joe off, Troy had spent a couple of hedonistic days with his college *friend* and was looking forward to round two. Troy planned to be back for the home opener. And in his typical ball-busting fashion, he informed Joe, he expected him to take care of the tickets, whether or not he made the team.

For most players training camp is a month-long grind, which pushed players to the brink of physical and mental exhaustion. For Joe, it was a resurrection. Every morning he rose with renewed enthusiasm, as eager to distance himself from his past as he was to pursue lost dreams. But the highlight of each day came later, after practice when Joe spoke with Carrie. She shared the events of her day on the set, and he shared his. Separately they were each living a dream, but together it was more. For Joe, his day was incomplete until he shared it with Carrie. She had expressed similar feelings, telling Joe, '*The best part of my day is sharing it with you.*'

Having climbed to the top of the depth chart, Joe and other key players, saw limited playing time in four meaningless preseason games. But when Joe and the other starters did play, he was unstoppable. By the time the preseason was over Joe Blackstone had become the biggest story in pro football. Local and national media couldn't mention the Philadelphia Freedom, if not the WFL, without referring to the superhuman rookie. The Philadelphia coaching staff celebrated their good fortune while opposing teams fretted over how to contain the phenome.

Philly fans were filled with excitement as the opener neared. Yet an entirely different emotion consumed Jeff Pergine. While the preseason had been a rebirth for Blackstone, it was like death for Pergine. Ever since high school he'd been the focal point of his team. Although still relevant, Pergine was no longer the main attraction and found himself answering questions about Blackstone. Having lost the spotlight, Pergine longed to regain it, the need akin to an addict's desire for a fix.

After practice and the regular meetings, Pergine tried to watch game film. But his mind was elsewhere and he gave up trying after an hour. They opened in Detroit in less than a week, Pergine knew he needed to focus on his assignments, but he couldn't think of anything but Blackstone. Adding insult to injury, Lafond's game plan revolved around the Hillbilly more than any other player. *A fucking tight end,* thought Pergine.

When he got to the parking lot, he was surprised Blackstone's car was still in there. Eyeing the dated hunk of metal, Pergine's face twisted into a frown. He couldn't imagine why someone would want to drive a forty-year-old car. Remembering Mealey drove an old Pontiac, Pergine shook his head in disgust. He slid behind the wheel of his Ferrari and tore out of the compound. Soon he was off Broad Street and on I76, but no matter the distance he put between himself and Joe Blackstone, the man consumed him. Overcome with frustration, Pergine picked up his phone and hit speed dial.

Harvey Litt answered on the third ring. "Hi, Jeff, what's up?"

Skipping the pleasantries, Jeff said, "I've got a job for you."

Un-phased Harvey replied, "Shoot."

"I need all the background info you can get on Joe Blackstone."

"Jeff the media's been all over him, they haven't found shit. One day he's a high school kid with a murdered father, and ten years later he's in the WFL."

Pergine's knuckles turned white as he squeezed the steering wheel. "You're not the fucking media. If you can't dig up more than those blowhards what the hell do I need you for?"

"Easy now … I didn't say I couldn't dig deeper. I'm saying it would help if I knew why or what I'm digging for."

"Anything!" said Jeff. He took a deep breath and lowered his voice. "Anything I can use to get rid of that motherfucker."

Litt suspected such but wanted to confirm it. Blackstone could help put Philly over the top, get them to the championship, maybe even win it, but Pergine wasn't willing to sacrifice his ego. Litt didn't care, he wanted to be clear on the objectives. "I'll do some digging," he promised. "You worry about Detroit, and I'll worry about Blackstone."

"Call me as soon as you have something." Pergine hit end and killed the call. A sense of accomplishment comforted him. Easing back in his seat he accelerated, weaving through traffic on the Schuylkill Expressway, as the narrow road snaked along the river and climbed out of the city.

***

The lights in the SSC had been turned down for the night. As Pickell approached the door, Blackstone plowed through it and almost knocked him over. Unfazed, Pickell asked, "What the fuck are you doing in there? I've been looking for you."

"Getting some extra work in, what's up?" Asked Joe.

"Not here," replied Pickell. "Follow me."

Pickell led the way to his office, once there he motioned Joe to a chair across from his desk while he closed the door. When Pickell settled into his seat, he locked eyes with Joe and asked, "What's your deal?"

"Excuse me?" Joe asked.

"You're the best athlete on this team if not the league, you're a fucking monster at tight end, yet every chance you get you're throwing the goddamn ball."

"Coach look—"

"Don't bullshit me," said Pickell. "I've seen you throwing to Wilmot, and everything you do in the simulators is on camera. So, I ask again, what's the deal?" Joe was silent, so Pickell continued, "Listen if you don't wanna tell me, fine. But you do know Ms. Taylor pays Pergine a hell of a lot more money than she does you, or me, right? Personally, the guy rubs me the wrong way, but then again, most quarterbacks do. Still, the boss likes him so no matter what you might be thinking … it's not going to happen."

Joe sprung to his feet and said, "Great talk coach but it's been a long day, so I'm gonna head out."

Pickell motioned him to sit back down and said, "Please … humor me." Joe eased himself back into the chair. "You do what you want, I'm not judging, I'm just curious, I've had crazy ideas since before you were born. And, I've got another one I'd like to share with you if you can keep your mouth shut?"

"Not a problem," Joe said. When Pickell explained what he had in mind, Joe couldn't help but smile. "That's nuts, I love it."

CHAPTER 26

The night before the team traveled to Detroit, Joe and Carrie went to Trinacria for dinner. It was one of the few places outside the city where beautiful hostesses in evening gowns escorted you to tables covered in white linens. Tuxedo-clad waiter's poured wine from an extensive list and served authentic Italian dishes. An L-shaped cherry wood bar was the focal point of the main room. Behind it, matching cabinets stocked high-end liquor bottles; which were neatly displayed with accent lighting. Two separate dining areas were decorated with crimson curtains and ornate wallpaper. The experience came at a cost, a typical dinner for two at Trinacria cost over four hundred dollars if you were frugal with your wine selection. Neither Joe nor Carrie cared, it was less than a mile from the country club, they were lucky enough to afford it, and the food was the best either had ever had.

They were seated at a small table in the back dining room. Both enjoyed a three-course meal which the chef had recommended. With his first pro game on the horizon, Joe refrained from indulging in the 2012 Sassicaia Carrie had ordered. When they had finished their meal, and their empty plates were cleared, Joe said, "Why don't we grab a seat at the bar, I'll get a cappuccino, and you can finish the wine, it would be a shame to waste it."

Carrie giggled and said, "I'm not sure I should finish it, but I'm not ready to give up yet."

There were four people sitting at the bar when they walked in, but Joe centered his attention on one. Jeff Pergine saw him approach and waved. "Hey buddy, I thought that was your car out front."

Joe had yet to build any bond with his quarterback. Pergine was blessed with an abundance of talent. He said all the right things and put plenty of work in, yet Joe still had his reservations. At first, he thought it was because Pergine spent no time with his teammates off the field, but Joe had to admit he was not the most sociable guy either. Self-aware, Joe knew he resented Pergine because he held the job Joe coveted most. Still, there was something else he didn't like, but he hadn't put his finger on it yet.

Joe forced a smile, stepped forward and extended his hand. "Hi, Jeff how you doing?"

Jeff stood and shook Joe's hand. "Great man, I love this place," —he pointed a thumb at the chubby guy beside him— "so I made my manager take me, Joe meet Harvey, Harvey meet Joe."

Joe shook Harvey's hand. "Nice to meet you," he said and introduced Carrie.

Carrie smiled and shook with Harvey. But Jeff held her offered hand a tad too long before he bent at the waist and kissed the top of it. Her face flushed and Joe's burned.

Jeff looked at Joe and said, "My … my Blackstone you're sure full of surprises." He turned to Carrie and added, "I'm a huge fan, how on earth did you two meet up, no offense Blackstone."

"None taken," said Joe, but an edge in his voice said otherwise.

"We've known each other since we were kids."

"No shit?" Jeff said.

"Yep, grew up in the same small town."

Jeff gestured toward a couple open seats and said, "Please join us I have a million questions."

Before Joe could come up with an excuse to leave Carrie hopped on the open seat beside Jeff. Joe set her wine on the bar and slid onto a stool. Jeff smothered Carrie with questions, and they dominated the conversation. They spoke playfully, bordering on flirtatious at times but Carrie seemed to be enjoying herself, so Joe held his temper in check. On more than one occasion Joe had caught Harvey staring at him. Stares had become commonplace since joining the Freedom, but there was something odd in his beady eyes. Joe couldn't put his finger on it, but he didn't like it.

Carrie finished the Sassicaia and had two glasses of lemoncello before the evening wound down. They all left together, and when they got to the parking lot, Jeff gave Carrie a hug, which lingered too long for Joe's taste.

Harvey and Jeff bid Joe goodbye and turned toward Harveys Mercedes. But right before Jeff's face disappeared from Joe's view he saw something. Most people would not have caught it, but Joe had. In a flash, Jeff's charming smile had vanished. Joe was no stranger to what it revealed.

Joe was quiet during the short ride, pondering what he'd seen. Carrie chatted about how much fun she'd had and how interesting Joe's *friend* was. When they got home, Joe went upstairs to pack for his trip to Detroit.

Carrie joined him in their room and sat on the bed. "What's the matter?"

"Nothing."

"Nothing? Yeah right? You haven't said two words since we left Trinacria?"

"I didn't say two words at the bar either, you didn't seem bothered then."

Carrie's eyes narrowed. "You've got to be kidding me … you're jealous!"

"I'm not fucking jealous," said Joe, not believing his words. "The guy's an asshole, I can't believe you don't see it."

Carrie glared at the back of Joe's head while he continued to pack. Her frustration boiled into a strangled, "Pff." She exploded off the bed and marched out of the room.
***

Litt was lounging on Pergine's eight-thousand dollar Natuzzi couch while Pergine paced the hardwood floor in his living room. The fixer's calm exterior added angst to each step echoing off the high ceiling.

On the far side of the room, Pergine came to a sudden stop and wheeled around. "So now you've met the guy, are you going to tell me what the hell you've dug up or not?"

As if he hadn't a care in the world, Litt placed his hands on his lap and said, "I found nothing after the Fall of his senior year in high school until last winter, it's like he disappeared."

"What fucking good does that do us then?"

Unfazed, Litt continued, "No one is that far off the grid unless they're hiding or have something to hide. I was able to dig up a few interesting pieces of information from before he went dark. His mother was killed in a car accident when Blackstone was six. Apparently, she was alone in the middle of the night and twice the legal limit when her car struck a tree. What's odd is, every person interviewed after the crash said Mrs. Blackstone never drank. And not a single person could explain why she had been on the road at such a late hour. Now, everyone knows Joe walked in on his father's murder when he was in high school, it's been all over the news. It's rumored he killed one of the assailants, so I dug into that. I had to burn through some serious favors because a lot of information involving the case, disappeared. But I confirmed it, the rumors are true, he beat the guy and stabbed him with his own fucking knife … but that's not the interesting part."

Pergine threw his hands up and said, "So what is?"

"The guy he killed was an Ex-Army Ranger … he was a mercenary."

"So?"

"Wait, there's more. Blackstone showed up in Maine a few months back and got into a scuffle with two guys at a truck stop. Do you know who Anthony Calabrese is?"

"The New York mobster?"

Litt nodded. "The one and only. One of the guys Blackstone got into it with was his son and the other his nephew. Neither one is a big player in the family business, more like wannabes. But both are tough as nails with the records to prove it. I tracked down a truck driver who was there, and he claims Blackstone cut through them in seconds. It turns out, these guys had some cluster fuck drug operation going on, and their car was loaded with the shit. Both were looking at serious time thanks to Blackstone, but it looks like old man Calabrese pulled some strings and got them out.

"Why haven't I heard any of this on the news?"

"Because Blackstone's a hero there and the local cops buried it. I only got wind of it through a contact in the Maine State Police."

"Okay, but I still don't know what all this means."

"What it means is … Joe Blackstone is someone we do not want to underestimate. From what I've gathered it's pretty clear, bad things happen to people who fuck with him. We have a move here, but we'll be operating on a higher ledge than we ever have before. And if things go wrong there may be no coming back from it. Not to mention the cost, it's going to be expensive … very expensive." Litt slowed down and asked a question he already knew the answer to but was not about to avoid. "Are you one-hundred percent certain you're prepared to do this."

"Whatever it takes," Pergine said, "I'm in."

CHAPTER 27

Detroit

Carrie and Joe had barely spoken before he left for the airport. That night he was in his hotel room staring at the ceiling when she sent him a text, "GOOD LUCK."

He wanted to call but followed her lead and typed his reply, "SORRY ABOUT LAST NIGHT, I'LL MAKE IT UP TO YOU WHEN I GET BACK." His response had gone unanswered. Hoping to clear the air, Joe sent two more texts messages and left a voicemail. But they had all gone unanswered, and his misgivings over an argument were turning into concern.

As the game drew near, Joe pushed all other thoughts to the back of his mind. It was time to focus on the first game of his professional football career. For the first time since his sophomore year in high school, Joe had butterflies. He walked the field before the stadium filled, alone with AC/DC and his thoughts. His mind's eye ran through each assignment, his pulse quickened, and he urged each stubborn minute to pass. Time dragged, but the pre-game activities came and went, and Philadelphia took the field moments before kick-off. Electricity from sixty-five thousand fans surged through Joe as soon as his cleats hit the turf. It didn't matter they booed him and his teammates, if anything, it added to the jolt.

Philly won the toss. After a decent return, they started 1ˢᵗ and 10 from their own 27. The first play was a run to Joe's side. His assignment was to block the outside linebacker, and he did. On the snap, he fired off the ball at #57, who was lined up on his outside shoulder. The defender reacted quickly and set his feet, attempting to hold his ground. Joe's palms shot out and battered the man's chest, jarring him back on his heels. Off-balance he was helpless as Joe thundered through him, drove him to the sideline and launched him out of bounds. Detroit coaches, players, and fans cried out in protest, demanding a penalty. Joe's sideline was every bit as vocal in its support.

Joe's block sprung Matthieu for a twenty-three yard gain, setting Philly up at midfield. The next play was a pass Joe drew double coverage in the middle of the field, which left a single defender trailing Wilmot down the Philly sideline. Pergine hit him in stride for an early lead.

Philly's initial excitement fizzled when Detroit tie the game 7-7 three plays later. On their second series, Joe picked up where he left off, dominating defenders in the run game, and drawing two defenders every time Pergine dropped back to pass. They moved the ball past midfield. But after a six yard run gave Philly a 1st down at the Detroit 38, Matthieu remained on the turf.

With Philly's star running back on the sideline, Detroit focused on stopping the pass. They abandoned their base defense, shifting exclusively to nickel and dime packages. These packages replaced one or two run stopping linebackers with smaller and more athletic defensive backs. This strategy lessened a team's ability to defend the run but added men to the secondary, which strengthened their pass defense. With the extra pass defenders, Detroit could double both Blackstone and Wilmot.

Lafond stuck with the run, attacking Detroit's weakened front. But a holding penalty on Schank and a bobbled handoff forced Philly to pass. On 3rd and 27, Joe beat the double team, but Pergine threw in Wilmot's direction. Two defenders had him bracketed and knocked the ball out of play. Philly was forced to punt.

Detroit chewed up the remainder of the quarter with a twelve play touchdown drive and took a lead 14-7. By halftime, they had increased their advantage to 28-10.

Joe had yet to see a pass thrown in his direction. Costly fumbles by Matthieu's backup had ended two long drives, but he had been diagnosed with a sprained ankle and was doubtful to return. In the visiting locker room, frustrated players migrated into offensive and defensive units.

On one side of the room, Pickell berated his players for their inability to generate a pass rush. Detroit's quarterback had picked the Freedom defense apart and moved the ball at will.

Struggling to be heard over Pickell's rant, Lafond addressed his unit. "Our O-line is shredding their front, but you backs need to step it up. The protection's been good when we've thrown, but we need to spread the ball around." Lafond looked at Pergine and said, "You need to get the ball to Blackstone."

"Coach he's doubled on every play, so I've..."

Lafond cut him off. "I don't give a shit if they have the entire National Guard on him. Throw the fucking ball."

Pergine glared daggers at Lafond and gritted teeth. "Yes, Coach."

On the opening drive of the second half, Detroit went eighty yards in seven plays, extending their lead to 35-10. They kicked the ball out of the end-zone, and Philly took over eighty yards from paydirt.

When Philly lined up for their first play of the second half, Pergine smiled inwardly when he saw the alignment of Detroit's hard hitting safety. He recognized the scheme and knew the outside receivers would be covered one on one, and only Blackstone would be doubled. Detroit's safety was free to roam the middle of the field, even if Blackstone did beat the two defenders assigned to cover him, he had no chance. It was a simple play for the defense to read, and Safety would pummel Blackstone if the ball were thrown his way. The correct decision was to throw to an outside receiver, but Lafond wanted Jeff to throw to Blackstone, so that's exactly what he was going to do.

Pergine stood in the shotgun. "Green 23 — Green 23 — Hut, HUT." He caught the snap and glanced at Wilmot out of habit. The corner slipped, rendering any catchable pass to his wide receiver a sure touchdown. But Pergine pivoted and found Blackstone's, who had beaten the double team the same as he'd done the entire first half. This time, Pergine threw the ball in his direction. A perfect spiral sailed high in the air toward Detroit's 235 pound safety. Self-satisfied, Pergine couldn't help but smile.

Joe tracked the ball with long strides and bound off the turf. He knew he was going to get hit, there was nothing he could do to protect himself, so he didn't try. At the peak of his jump, Joe stretched skyward for the ball. The safety hit him at a dead run. Having leaped into the air, most of Joe's forward momentum was lost. A stationary target, he absorbed the entire force of the blow and was hurled into a helicopter like spin.

When he crashed to the turf, his teammates froze with dread. Detroit players looked on with concern, and a hush filled the stands. A yellow flag sat by the safety, who was climbing to his feet. The rest of the stadium was still until Blackstone, who was still on the ground, raised the ball in the air. The official signaled it was a catch and murmurs of disbelief rippled through the stadium. The Freedom bench erupted, and his teammates swarmed as Joe got to his feet. The sixteen yard reception and a penalty for hitting a defenseless receiver netted Philly a thirty-one yard gain.

In the huddle, Joe fixed Pergine with an icy stare and said, "Nice pass." Pergine ignored the remark and avoided eye contact.

Two plays later Pergine hit Joe on a deep flag route for a touchdown. Philly still trailed by eighteen but two things had happened, the offense was back on track, and Joe Blackstone was pissed off.

Joe was standing beside Pickell when the defense took the field. He tried to ignore the determination on Joe's face, but the unspoken request was unavoidable. Setting aside a dozen reasons why he shouldn't do what he was about to, Pickell scratched his head and said, "You know, if you fuck this up it's both our asses?"

"I'm pretty sure this was your idea coach … besides, do I look like I'm gonna fuck this up?"

Pickell was confident in Blackstone as an athlete and even more so as a man. And Blackstone was right it had been his idea. The night he had called Joe into his office, Pickell had laid out his plan to incorporate him on defense. He had given Joe the defensive playbook and continued reviewing schemes with him in private. Pickell had intended to create some practice drills, which would highlight Joe's potential as a defender. Once the rest of the staff witnessed Joe's potential, he would approach Mealey with the idea. Regardless of when Pickell brought the plan to Mealey, he'd told Joe they'd wait until late in the season or the playoffs before implementing it. Pickell believed the new wrinkle could give Philly a fresh push toward a championship run and Joe had agreed. But Pickell knew Joe had no intention of waiting, he would want to go in at the first sign of trouble. Pickell respected that about the kid. Still, what they were about to do was so unorthodox even Pickell feared he might be losing it.

The crowd cheered, and the officials signal another first down for Detroit. "Fuck this … get in there for Lincoln," Pickell commanded.

Mealey was standing ten feet away when Blackstone jogged onto the field. "What the hell?" He stepped forward, and hollered, "Blackstone, BLACKSTONE!"

Knowing what was going to come next, Pickell said, "Coach, It's okay, I got it … I sent him in."

Mealey swung his head in Pickell's direction. "You sent him in? Have you lost your fucking mind?"

"Coach I—"

"Damn it," —Mealey threw his hat on the ground— "I can't waste a timeout on this shit, but you better have someone in for him on the next play."

Pickell focused on the field and thought, *come on kid make a play.*

The defensive was so battered from the ass kicking they were receiving, Joe's appearance on the field didn't draw a second glance. But as the *JACK* linebacker, whose job was to rush the quarterback, he would change that.

Detroit broke the huddle and Orlando Green, Detroit's left tackle, shuffled to the line. Although a couple years past his prime, the 6'7" 345 pound behemoth was still considered one of the top left tackles in the league. With size, strength and a notorious mean streak, he was a formidable opponent. When he saw the Philly tight end aligned as the outside linebacker on his side, Green took it as an insult. He crouched into his stance determined to punish the smaller man.

Coiled in a three-point stance, Joe ignored the offenses cadence. Instead, he focused on the ball, and he sprung forward as soon as the center's hand twitched. The big tackle lurched forward, and the collision reverberated throughout the stadium.

When Blackstone charged straight at him, Green blessed his good fortune and hit him harder than he had hit anyone all day. In an instant, his forward momentum jolted to a stop and was reversed. His head snapped forward and pain radiated throughout his body as he toppled backward.

Joe had heard Mealey and Pickell's heated exchange and knew he needed to make a play. As he had done many times before, Joe tapped into the anger he fought to control. He blasted through the bigger man and thrust him into the backfield. Joe gave him a final heave when he saw Detroit's quarterback extend the ball to their back. Green slammed into his teammates and knocked the ball free. Rookie linebacker Tony Nicks recovered it for Philadelphia.

On the sideline, Pickell glanced in Mealey's direction, the head coach was rigid, staring wide-eyed at the field. Pickell hollered, "Coach you still want me to take Blackstone out? Cause … ah … we're on offense now."

Mealey turned to Pickell's and shook his head. "Play the kid."

Philly rolled the rest of the way winning 45-35. Pergine ended the game with four-hundred-sixty-five yards passing, and 5 touchdown passes. But all the press cared about was Joe's one-hundred-sixty-eight yards receiving, 3 touchdowns, 3 sacks and 1 forced fumble. Professional football hadn't seen such a dominating two-way performance in over fifty years.

A horde of reporters gathered at Joe's locker and peppered him with questions. He cited the coach's game plan and the team's execution as the reasons for their success. Although Joe was unwilling to take credit for a tremendous individual performance, his teammates were not bashful about tossing praise in his direction.

Wilmot referred to Blackstone as, "A man amongst boys."

Defensive leader Gino Sayers said, "Blackstone is the most physical player I've ever seen … And I mean EVER."

Clowning around, injured running back Kirk Matthieu added, "I guarantee I'll be ready next week, no way I'm letting Legend have a crack at my spot."

The only player refrained in his adoration was Pergine. While his teammates celebrated and the media swarmed, he sat alone, content knowing something none of them did.

CHAPTER 28

As Joe was boarding the bus to the airport his phone buzzed. He pulled it from his pocket and was relieved to see the call was from Carrie. "Hey there," he answered while taking a seat.

"Oh … my … God, you were incredible! It's all anyone has been talking about on the set. I'm so happy for you Joe."

Joe laughed. "And here I thought you'd been blowing me off all weekend."

"Oh baby, I'm sorry, I broke my phone, and we got called in for an unexpected shoot. We got an opening to film a restaurant scene at La Famiglia in the city, but we had to do it over the weekend. It's been nonstop work, but we got it done, and it's going to be great. I sent an assistant out to get me a new phone, so I'm back in touch now. Sorry I couldn't get back to you sooner."

"I'm just glad you're okay, I was worried something happened. Do me a favor, send me someone else's contact info. That way I can call them to check in on you if something like this happens again."

There was a long pause before Carrie responded, "You wanna *check in on me*?"

"Bad things happen to all kinds of people Carrie … every day."

Suddenly conscious of Joe's past, Carrie said, "You're right, I'll text you some numbers, I should have done it sooner."

"Perfect, will you be home when I get back?

"You bet I will, and you better sleep on the plane because you won't be doing much resting when you get home."

Joe smiled into the phone. "Promise."

"I heard what everyone's been calling you, you think you can live up to it … Legend?"

"Ohh … you can count on it."

***

After the flight home, Mealey invited his two coordinators for a drink in his office. The head coach retrieved beers from his mini refrigerator and opened one for himself and Lafond, who was the first to arrive.

Pickell strolled in a moment later with three tumblers and a bottle of bourbon. He poured them each a glass and joined the other two coaches at Mealey's conference table. Pickell held his glass up and said, "To 1-0 … it's a hell of a lot better than 0-1." Mealey and Lafond chuckled, and all three took a sip.

The Glenfiddich 18 lingered on Mealey's taste buds like smooth jazz. He tipped his glass to Pickell and said, "Good stuff Pick, you don't mess around, I could get used to this."

"Yeah this is nice," Lafond added.

Pickell tilted his head. "It doesn't suck that's for sure."

Still focused on Pickell, Mealey raised a brow and addressed the elephant in the room. "So … Coach, did you ever consider working Blackstone in on D during practice or are you more from the Allen Iverson camp?"

"Practice? You talkin' about PRACTICE!" said Pickell, mimicking the infamous rant.

The other two coaches laughed, and Mealey said, "Seriously, it was a brilliant out of the box idea, but we need to communicate as a staff."

Pickell's expression turned serious, and he said, "I agree. The truth is, the kid was never supposed to do that today."

"Are you trying to say that was improvised, 'cause, I ain't buying."

"No not improvised, I've been working with Blackstone for a few weeks, going over schemes. He picks up everything, and I mean everything. I tested him a couple times, gave him conflicting assignments for the identical situation, and he called me on it each time. Like everything else, his football IQ is off the charts."

"He's right," said Lafond. "Blackstone knows every assignment on every play, He could play any position except quarterback."

Pickell shook his head. "I wouldn't be so quick to exclude QB."

"What do you mean?" asked Mealey.

"My plan was to slide Joe into some drills," Pickell said and pointed to Mealey, "and show you his potential on defense. He's that special player who can make any defense great. I figured once you got a glimpse, it'd be any easy sell."

"And if I didn't agree?"

"I'd have done it anyway." Mealey rolled his eyes and Pickell continued, "I've been thinking about this since day one, so I've been watching the kid like a hawk. I wanted to know if he was for real, if he got along with his teammates or if he's an ass-hole. As we can all see he's the real deal, he's one of the first two or three guys in the building every day and always the last to leave. Do you know what he's been doing with all the extra time?"

"He's a monster," said Lafond. "I'm sure he's in the gym."

"Nope," Pickell said. "He works out as hard as anyone on the team, more even, but he hasn't been spending any more time in the weight room than anyone else."

"So what the hell is he doing ... watching film?" asked Mealey.

"Some but that ain't it." Satisfied their interest was piqued Pickell said, "Kids been throwing."

"Throwing?" asked the two other coaches.

"Yep, with Dwayne, and afternoons in the simulator."

Mealey waved his hands in the air, and said, "Wait a minute that makes no sense, his arm was all fucked up from the shit that went down when he was in high school, you've seen the scar. I've seen him toss the ball at practice, I bet he can't throw forty yards. Why would he or Wilmot waste their time?"

A sly grin spread across Pickell's face, he tossed back the remainder of his bourbon and said, "I've seen the scar, big old fucker on his right shoulder. But I never did see one on his left."

In a voice thick with doubt, Lafond asked, "Do you expect us to believe, he's spending all that time learning how to throw left handed?"

Pickell locked eyes with his offensive counterpart and asked, "How would you rate Pergine's arm against other QB's in the league?"

Lafond considered his response and replied, "Top three."

Still grinning, Pickell said, "That's fair, I'd say top four or five, but it's close. But then again I have the advantage of knowing Pergine has the second-best arm on our team."

CHAPTER 29

That week on their day off, Joe met Dwayne at the practice facility for an extra workout. His arm strength was better than his right had ever been and his accuracy much improved. When they were walking off the field, Dwayne commented on Joe's progress. "Jesus man, you were throwing laser beams out there."

"Arms feelin' pretty good, I guess I'm gettin' the hang of this whole lefty thing," Joe replied.

"*That's* an understatement," Dwayne said, chuckling. "You have plans for lunch?"

"Yeah I do, I'm picking a friend up at the airport."

On the short ride from the Freedom complex to Philly International, Joe pondered his situation. He had no doubt Mealey would continue to play him at tight end and linebacker, but quarterback was a different story. How could he even broach the subject, '*Hey coach, now that I'm a two-way player I think I'd like to play QB too, you don't mind, do you?'* Doubtful that would fly, Joe considered pummeling Pergine in practice, *that would be fun.* He shook his head at that thought, certain it wouldn't be perceived well by the staff or Ms. Taylor.

"Fuck it, I'll worry about it later," he said aloud and trained his thoughts on spending some time with Troy.
***

That afternoon Dwayne and his agent met with John Pollard. The GM's office contrasted with both his image and Ms. Taylor's office. Where Pollard projected a calm exterior and his boss decorated her office with sparse elegance, his office was loud and stimulating. Autographed AC/DC albums hung on the walls, and an 80's era electric football game sat on a coffee table. Pictures of Pollard's wife and two daughters could be found on nearly every surface. Eight feet from a vintage Pac-man game, Dwayne sat at a round table, having signed a five-year extension. Pollard had been negotiating with Dwayne's agent since June and was happy to close the deal. As the meeting was wrapping up, Mealey knocked on the door and let himself in. Everyone stood to greet him.

"So, we're good to go for five more years?" Mealey asked.

Dwayne smiled. "Yes, sir, I couldn't imagine playing anywhere else."

"Great, we're excited to have you. So … I know there's some media downstairs, but before we head down," Mealey glanced at Dwayne's agent and said, "John and I would like to talk with you alone for a minute."

His only concern, the three percent commission he'd earned, the agent said, "No problem gentlemen I'll meet you downstairs."

When the door closed, they all sat back down. Dwayne glanced at Pollard, and the pair exchanged a private thought. Dwayne worried he'd missed something in his new contract.

Pollard was the first to speak. "We heard you've been working out with Blackstone."

Dwayne relaxed and said, "Could you think of a better workout partner? The guys an animal."

"We're interested in the early morning workouts, like the one today … when he's throwing." Mealey clarified.

"From up here in the cheap seats," Pollard said and motioned toward his window overlooking the practice field, "he looks pretty good, and the extra work has paid off for you. I also pulled film of him in the simulator and was pretty impressed. What we're asking here Dwayne is your opinion."

Dwayne drummed his finger on the table and glanced out the window. When he turned back, he said, "I'd prefer this doesn't get back to Jeff, we're not close to begin with, and I don't want to give him something to be pissed about."

"Stay's here," Mealey said.

"Joe has the best arm I've ever seen ... the guy has a cannon. When we first started, he struggled with his accuracy but the improvement in only a few weeks has been incredible. Like I said the guys an animal."

Mealey stood signaling an end to the meeting. "Thanks, Dwayne, we appreciate your input."

The other two men rose, and Pollard said, "Dwayne, if you don't mind, could you give us a minute? Wait for us outside, we'll walk down to greet the media with you."

"No problem."

Alone with the head coach, Pollard asked, "Can you name a single guy on the team Pergine's close with?"

"No, I can't."

"Me either, I find it strange the face of our franchise for the past few seasons has no off field relationships with his teammates. That's something I need to look into. Now that you've got further confirmation on this Blackstone thing, what's your plan? Despite his quirks, it seems to me we already have a good QB and Blackstone can't play every position, as nice as it would be."

Mealey walked to the window and stared out over the field. "You can never have too much talent, especially at quarterback. The first thing I'm going to do is check Blackstone out myself. But Pergine is and will be our guy for the foreseeable future. We haven't even seen Blackstone take a practice rep ... Although something tells me there ain't nothing the kid can't do."

***

Pergine spent his day off at home. Usually, he would indulge himself with one of the local trophy wives or a couple of college girls, but things were far from normal. The local media was so focused on Blackstone they had all but forgotten about him. To make matters worse, Litt had informed him the endorsement deals were on hold. Both apparel companies wanted to *explore other options.*

Aware of his client's instability, Litt suggested Pergine remain at home as much as possible until things were worked out. With no appetite for his usual distractions, Pergine relented. But twenty-four hours of solitude had him bouncing off the walls, so he decided to go out for dinner.

He avoided Trinacria, least he run into Blackstone, and decided on the William Penn Inn. The historical Inn offered a wide menu of American cuisine and was less than three miles from his home. Multiple dining rooms and two separate bars could serve hundreds of patrons at a time. Pergine requested a table in one of the smaller rooms upstairs, where he could dine in relative privacy. He selected the oyster appetizer and filet with garlic mashed potatoes from the menu. Having enjoyed his neighbor's wine, Pergine washed his meal down with a bottle of 2013 Chimney Rock Cabernet. He was finally relaxed when his waiter approached.

The *kid* was only three or four years younger than Pergine was, but it might as well have been decades. The server had recognized Philly's QB as soon as he'd been seated. But had kept to himself. Now emboldened with a small level of familiarity, he wanted to have a conversation. "Mr. Pergine, can I get you anything else this evening?" asked the waiter.

"Just the check, thanks."

"That sure was a heck of a game last weekend."

Pergine held his practiced smile.

"I bet you're happy we got Joe Blackstone, he's amazing."

Pergine's smile faded, and his eyes turned venomous.

The young waiter hurried off.

Pergine chastised himself for losing his composure. It was imperative he keep his emotions in check, especially with what Litt was planning. When his server returned, Pergine had re-applied his smiling mask. Having glimpsed behind the curtain, the young man dropped the check and hurried off.

Despite his error, Pergine took pleasure in the fear he saw on the waiter's face. *Fuck him,* he thought, *Philadelphia's my team, and I've heard enough talk about Joe fucking Blackstone to last a lifetime.*

Pergine left cash on the table for his bill, but no tip. Downstairs, he crossed the main lobby, toward the exit.

Two young boys, about nine and eleven years old, jumped in front of their parents in a race for the door and arrived at it with Pergine. The younger of the two recognized him and asked, "Are you Jeff Pergine?"

"Yep, that's me kid."

Pergine was smiling at the mother when the other boy said, "Do you know Joe Blackstone? My dad says he's gonna be the best player in the league this year."

Wild-eyed, Pergine glared at the boy. He bent down and brought his face an inch from the child and said, "Guess what? Your dads a fucking idiot!"

The mother gasped, and the father stepped in front of his boys. Pergine pushed the older man aside and flung the door open. His car was parked at the curb, by the front door where he had left it. As he approached, a Valet opened the door and handed him the keys. Before starting the car, Pergine pulled his phone out and hit speed dial for Litt.

"Hi, Jeff, how are ..."

"Shut the fuck up Harvey and listen, I'm done waiting, do what you need to do, spend whatever it takes, but do it right fucking now. Get this shit done or I'll find someone who will. Am I clear?"

"Crystal ... I'll take care of it."

CHAPTER 30

Joe and Carrie spent as much time with Troy as their schedules allowed. Every night at dinner, they reminisced about old times and caught up on events in the WFL, movie business and Fairfield, Maine. All three were happy, and things were good. Saturday, Joe said his goodbyes. After a walkthrough and meetings at the practice facility, he and the rest of the team would check into a hotel for the night.

Troy had not seen his college *friend*, Shelly Marino, all week because she'd been traveling for work. Although they had never dated, their friendship had developed *benefits*. Since she was joining Troy and Carrie for Joe's home opener, Carrie suggested he invite her to dinner.

When Shelly arrived, Troy answered the door. She was holding a bottle of wine, but he didn't notice. He was too busy drinking in her sinful figure, which she had poured into a faded jeans and a v-neck top. "Holy shit," Troy said, "look at you, I didn't know you were bringing desert."

Shelly cocked her head to the side, "Funny, are you gonna let me in or stand there with your tongue out all night."

Troy stepped aside and held his arm out toward the kitchen. Shelly glided in and led the way as he followed with his eyes glued to her backside.

Carrie slid from behind the center island and extended her hand when Shelly walked in. "Hi, I'm Carrie."

"Hi Carrie, I'm Shelly thanks for the invite."

Carrie tossed her thumb over her shoulder and said, "Ahh ... Romeo, why don't you get the steaks ready while I get our guest a drink."

Troy gave his sister a mock salute and did as he was told. It was a warm night, so the girls joined him outside while he grilled. They hit it off well, sharing stories about him, each trying to embarrass him in front of the other.

The stone patio offered plenty of privacy and a beautiful view of the golf course. They stayed there after dinner, sipping wine and enjoying each other's company. Eventually, the sky turned orange and faded to black as the sun fell behind a small rise on the course.

Troy went inside to turn on the patio lights and grab more wine. He found a bottle and was searching for a corkscrew when he heard a noise behind him. As Troy spun toward the source, a sharp pain stabbed the back of his head. He dropped to his knees and the bottle smashed against the marble floor. An expanding pool of red filled his clouded vision. He heard a distant scream before a second blow sent him crashing to the floor and everything went black.
***

Joe first spied Pergine staring at him on Thursday. Several times Joe had locked eyes with him, and each time Pergine would smile and turn away, only to resume gawking shortly after. They had not spoken since their encounter at Trinacria, until Wednesday, when Pergine chatted Joe up like they were best friends. He had asked how Joe likes living in Blue Bell and how Carrie was doing. Joe had responded with one-word answers. Undeterred, Pergine pressed on, eventually asking if Carrie had anything fun planned for Saturday night. Joe had walked away without a reply. The next day, Pergine returned to his reclusive self, but the staring had started.

Short on patience, Joe was relieved to distance himself from Pergine when the evening meeting ended. He and Dwayne, whom he was rooming with, went straight to their room and settled in for the night. Joe called Carrie, but she didn't answer, so he tried Troy. When he didn't answer, Joe texted them both, thirty minutes later neither had replied. Joe texted Carrie's friends on the production crew, thinking a last-minute set had become available and she was called into work. Three separate friends confirmed that was not the case.

Lying in darkness, Joe was surrounded by familiar demons. Intimate with horrors only the cursed have seen, he stirred throughout the night. Each time he checked his phone, he tried to convince himself there was nothing to worry about, each time there was no word from Carrie he worried there was. He needed to believe everything was okay, but as the night crept by, he knew it wasn't. Like the bond between twins, he sensed the devil's work … always had.

When Dwayne woke, Joe was dressed and packing his overnight bag. He rubbed the sleep from his eyes and asked, "What time is it … you didn't let me oversleep did you?"

"It's six, you're fine." Joe slung his bag over his shoulder and pivoted toward the door.

"Hey man, where you going?" asked Dwayne.

Joe ignored him.

Suddenly wide awake, Dwayne jumped from his bed. "Hey Legend, what the hell? What's going on?"

Joe stopped but kept his hand on the door. "Sorry," he said, glancing back. "But I gotta go."

"Go where? What the hell are you talking about?"

"Something's wrong at home, I'm not sure what, but something's not right, I have to go." Joe pulled the door open.

Dwayne waved his hands in the air and said, "Hold on man, hold on. Listen, I don't know what's going on, but you're in the WFL now, you can't be taking off on game day because you have a feeling."

Joe hesitated in the open doorway.

"You don't even have a car here, it's back at the facility, so let's chill for a second, okay?" Joe's expression remained rigid, but he stepped back into the room and closed the door. Dwayne backed off and said, "Alright ... good, here's what you're going to do ... call the local police and have them check things out for you. I'm sure everything is fine, but if there is a problem, they can get there a lot faster than you can."

"Okay," Joe said, conceding the point, "you're right, I'll call the cops."

Officer Brian Leary was walking across the parking lot at Wawa on the corner of Germantown and Skippack Pike when his radio squawked. He set his coffee and breakfast sandwich on the roof of his cruiser and acknowledged the call. "Unit ten, Leary here, over."

The monotone voice of his dispatcher replied, "We've got a report of possible suspicious activity in the Blue Bell Country Club on Bayhill Drive."

"Roger that, I'm two minutes out."

The dispatcher gave him the house number, and Leary slid into the front seat. As he started the car, Leary pictured the million dollar homes bordering the eighteen-hole course. *Possible suspicious activity in the Blue Bell Country Club, what the hell does mean?* Leary shook his head at the thought. Maybe some prick got pissed because a landscaper parked his pickup in front of the wrong house? God forbid anybody is caught with less than a 3-series BMW in their driveway. Leary had been on the force for three years. During which, he had learned the definition of suspicious activity, was altogether different in the Blue Bell Country Club, than almost anywhere else.

Leary pulled to a stopped at the gatehouse and waved to the lone security guard. The orange and white bar rose above his car, and he glided into the upscale community. Leary cruised the main drive, passed a manicured fairway and turned left after the clubhouse. Four-hundred yards later he took another left onto Bayhill. He found the address and a Mercedes in the driveway. Leary drew the cruiser to the curb, walked climbed the short driveway and followed a stone walkway to the front door. He rang the doorbell and waited. Two more attempts with the bell went unanswered, so Leary decided to walk the perimeter.

He strolled back toward the garage and peered through a window. Except for a few boxes, all three bays were empty. He followed the driveway, toward the rear of the property, and was about to turn the corner when he heard laughter. Leary glanced back toward the street, a pair of MILF's were gossiping while out for a morning walk. With his eyes fastened on the two women, he backed around the corner, stumbled on the patio step and fell on his ass. "Motherfucker," said Leary. He hauled himself up and brushed off the seat of his pants. When Leary finally turned his attention to the patio, he froze in his tracks. A couple of birds were perched on a glass table, picking at the remains of a meal, which had been left out overnight. One of the surrounding chairs was tipped over, and a shattered wine glass had been left unattended.

Leary drew his weapon and scurried to the far side of the patio entrance. He pressed his back against the stucco, reached out, and pushed on the sliding door, it moved. Hesitant he edged toward the opening and called out, "Police … anybody home." He pushed through the dangling blinds.

The house was silent, but a rancid odor assaulted his senses. He yanked his t-shirt from beneath his vest and pulled it over his nose. His heart raced as he angled toward the kitchen. Cherry wood cabinets, stainless steel appliances, and granite tops filled the space. A large island with a built-in sink sat in the middle of the room. Moving to his left, Leary slid around the island, he stopped when he spotted the red liquid spilled across the floor. Recognizing it for what it was when he saw the broken bottle, he continued circling the island. He was careful not to step in the wine, but someone else had.

The trail led to an arched doorway at the back of the kitchen. Leary inched forward and leaned against the door frame. He held his breath and spun through the opening with his gun extended in both hands. Rocked by the carnage he gasped and staggered back. His legs wobbled, and he groped at the wall in search of something to steady himself. When he finally gathered himself, Leary pushed off the wall, pulled the t-shirt back over his nose and turned toward the doorway. He made it two steps before vomiting down the front of his chest.

CHAPTER 31

Joe was pacing the floor when he got the call. Dwayne rose from the edge of his bed, and Joe answered on the first sound. "Blackstone."

"Mr. Blackstone this is Detective Porter with the Blue Bell Police, you spoke to my dispatcher officer a few minutes ago."

Joe's stomach sank, *a detective, not good.* "What happened?" he asked.

"It would be best if you came to the station, I'd like to ask—"

"Detective," said Joe, out of patience. "What the hell happened?"

There was a long pause before Porter answered, "We found a body."

The words cut deep, Joe's head sagged, and he lowered the phone; and Porter's voice to his side.

"What Joe ... what is it?" asked Dwayne.

Joe ignored him, his chest ached and his vision blurred.

Dwayne moved in front of him. "Joe ... JOE ... LOOK AT ME!" Joe lifted his head, the turmoil Dwayne saw caused his voice to crack. "What happened Joe?"

Joe opened his mouth to speak but stopped and raised the cell to his ear. Porter was mid-sentence. "—know this can be difficult—"

"Detective," said Joe, interrupting him. "You said you found a body ... one body?"

"Yes, we found a young female. I know this is difficult, but it's imperative I see you right away."

"I'll meet you at the house in forty minutes."

"No, it's best …"

Joe ended the call and silenced the detective. A muscle twitched in his jaw. "They killed her Dwayne, they killed her."

Dwayne shook his head. "What? Carrie? Who … who would do that?"

Joe's only response was a transformation.

Eyes which seemed lifeless a moment ago burned with fury. A chill ran down Dwayne's spine, he no longer recognized the man in front him. Having been raised in the projects, he had spent his youth avoiding eyes like the ones he saw now. They were the eyes of a vicious man, evil to the core. Dwayne's talent had been his ticket out, but he never forgot those eyes or the demons within. Frightened his friend had joined their ranks, his blood ran cold, and he wondered, *who the hell are you?*

Releasing Dwayne from his stare, Joe turned and grabbed his bag off the bed. He stormed out. Nearly taking the door off its hinges in the process.

Joe marched into the banquet room where the team breakfast was set up. Being early, few players were there yet, but Joe found Pergine on the far side of the room with Lafond.

A chair toppled over, and Pergine looked up. He spotted Joe, and a sly grin spread across his face. He masked it before Joe got to his table and greeted him in a friendly tone. "Morning Joe."

Lafond glanced at Joe to acknowledge his presence. Had he not been preoccupied, he may have noticed the look in Joe's eyes and asked what was wrong. But he didn't notice and instead asked, "Hey Joe, ready to have a big game, Joe?" He continued pouring over the papers in front of him without a second thought.

Joe said nothing; the muscles twitched in his jaw.

The odd silence was lost on Lafond, but the grinding teeth were not. He looked back at Joe, startled, he asked, "What's wrong … what is it?"

Joe's eyes narrowed on Pergine, who seemed neither fazed nor surprised. "Did you have anything to do with it?" he asked, rage spilling from every word.

Lafond opened his mouth to say something, but nothing came out. He ran his hand through his hair and waited for Pergine's response.

Turning his back on Joe to retrieve his phone, Pergine replied, "Do with what?"

Joe dropped his bag and stepped forward. Pergine scrambled from his chair and jumped back.

"Hey … take it easy guys, let's calm down," Lafond said, hurrying to his feet.

"I asked you a fucking question," —Joe's nails dug into his palm— "did you," —veins bulged in his forearm— "have anything to do with it."

All eyes were on Joe when Dwayne entered the room, *oh shit,* he thought and pushed through the growing crowd.

"Listen, man," said Pergine with his hands raised. "I don't know what's going on, but you need to chill."

Joe searched Pergine for any hint of dishonesty. The grin he had seen earlier was gone, but he wasn't fooled. Instincts that had always served him well were screaming now.

Dwayne tried to grab his arm, but he was too late; Joe sprung forward, latched onto Pergine and mauled him.

Pergine slammed into Lafond, knocking him over their table. He plowed through a half-dozen chairs, tumbled over another table and crashed to the floor. Still clinging to Pergine's tattered shirt, Blackstone's fist rained down, thumping against his face. He was unconscious by the time Dwayne and a dozen teammates managed to pull Blackstone off. A team trainer, who had witnessed the scene, attended to Pergine, while everyone else struggled to restrain Blackstone.

Hotel security rushed in, and a dozen men surrounded Joe. Still, he gave no sign of surrender.

"Joe please," said Dwayne, pleading. "This isn't helping. You need to calm down, this isn't what Carrie would have wanted."

The use of Carrie's name rocked Joe, he snapped his head toward Dwayne and froze.

Right then, Mealey walked in. Assessing the scene he hollered, "What the hell is going on here?"

CHAPTER 32

After being suspended and escorted from the hotel, Joe took a cab to the training facility. Again, security guards accompanied him to his car and off the property. He raced out of the City and up the expressway, arriving in Blue Bell, the passenger of a sinking ship. Drowning in despair with no hope of escape, the man he had become fell into the abyss. An altogether different man drove his Charger into the Country Club.

Law Enforcement vehicles clogged the narrow street and residents stood behind yellow tape, watching the spectacle from afar. Eight houses away from his own, Joe stopped in the middle of the street and killed the engine. He continued on foot, pushed between his curious neighbors and ducked under the yellow tape.

A young officer cut Joe off as he neared the house and said, "You can't go up there without proper ID." His sullen expression and soiled shirt spoke volumes about the scene inside.

"My name's Joe Blackstone, I live here."

"I'm sorry, but I can't let you in there."

"I'm supposed to be meeting Detective Porter here, call him."

The officers face twisted in thought, he came to a quick conclusion lifted his radio and said, "This is Leary out front, does anyone have eyes on Porter? I've got Joe Blackstone out here, he says Porter's expecting him."

They waited a moment, and Leary's radio squawked. "He's coming out."

Porter emerged from the front door a beat later. Slim and of average height, he wore dress pants with a collared shirt and jacket but no tie. He descended the gradual slope of the lawn at a brisk pace, extended a hand and said, "I'm Chuck Porter, sorry to be meeting you under these circumstances." Joe shook his hand but didn't speak, so Porter continued, "Let's take a ride over to the station. I need to get some background information and a statement."

Joe shook his head. "I'm going inside."

"Sorry that's against procedure, this is a crime scene, and I can't allow any unauthorized personnel inside." Joe had his phone out before Porter had finished his statement. He was dialing a number from memory when the Detective asked, "What are you doing?"

Joe hit send, cast a cold stare at Porter and said, "Getting authorized."

Irritated by Joe's lack of respect, Porter opened his mouth to say something. But a flare in Joe's ice blue eyes seized his voice.

Joe's call was answered on the fourth ring. "By God, Joe Blackstone, how are you? I've been following you on the news, sorry I haven't had a chance to call."

"Hello Sir," Joe said. "I'm sorry to bother you, but I need a favor."

The direct request conveyed more to the person at the other end of the call than his words. It wasn't the tone, it was the man. He knew Joe Blackstone in a way few others did. And one thing he knew to be true, was Joe Blackstone seldom asked anybody for anything, but if he does, it would be ill-advised to deny him. "Tell me what you need Joe."

"Thank you, Sir, I can't get into all the details right now, but I'm in Blue Bell, Pennsylvania. Someone I love was murdered in the house we've been living in, and I need to examine the scene. There's a Detective Porter here from the Blue Bell police department who says I can't go inside … I am … going inside Sir."

"Joe … I'm so sorry … I don't know what to say … Give me a minute, and I'll get you in there. And if you need anything else, and I mean ANYTHING, you let me know."

"Thank you." Joe ended the call, tipped his phone at Porter and said, "Pull your cell out."

Porter shook his head and said, "Listen, Mr. Blackstone, I know who you are, but it doesn't matter, you're not stepping foot into my crime scene, we're wasting time here, let's take a ride over to the station."

"Wait," said Joe. The single word and his set jaw indicated he was done debating the matter.

Porter checked his watch and glanced down the street. The crowd of spectators had grown which added to his concern, *how the hell am I going to get this monster away from here without causing a scene?* He was searching for the answer when his phone buzzed. His eyes shot from the caller ID to Joe … it was his boss's boss. "Detective Porter," he answered.

The detective was singing a chorus of *yes sir* and *no sir*, so Joe started toward the door. He was on the steps when Porter ended his call and hollered, "Blackstone … hold up." Joe stopped and waited on the steps. Porter hustled up the lawn. "Who the hell did you call?"

"A friend."

Porter raised a brow and turned to the door.

Joe followed the Detective into the kitchen. Technicians from the crime lab were dusting for prints and photographing every surface. Porter was talking, but Joe wasn't listening, his mind was busy cataloging ... like he'd done so many times before. There was activity throughout the house, but even if his sense of smell had failed him, sheer numbers indicated the body was in the dining room.

He nudged between a pair of technicians and, to their chagrin, stepped over the wine. His heart stopped as he continued into the dining room and forced his eyes upon the scene.

She was stripped naked and bent over the formal dining table, each ankle was secured to a table leg with duct tape. Her arms were splayed forward, and steak knives had been driven through the back of each hand securing her to the wooden surface. Blood scabbed over the top of each wound, and a large pool had leaked from a slash across her carotid artery. Blonde hair and blood molded together, forming a grisly bonnet, and obscuring her face.

The scene would have been gruesome by any standards had that been the whole of it, but it wasn't. A message had been left, *FOR YOU JOE* was etched into the middle of her back. The amount of blood surrounding the wounds told Joe, she had been alive when the words were carved.

Joe's eye's narrowed, he'd almost missed it, hidden beneath the blood, but there it was, a small butterfly tattoo on her lower back. He pushed his way to the other side of the table, drawing the ire of everyone in his path. But his scowl and size kept them silent as they cleared a path.

The girl's face still wasn't visible from his new vantage point, so Joe eased her head off the table.

Porter groaned and said, "Oh Jesus, Blackstone you're contaminating the scene."

Every eye in the room was on Joe; every face frozen with horror. To the assembled professionals, his actions were nearly as horrific as the crime itself.

The girl's face was too battered to identify. Her lifeless blue eyes held his attention exactly as his fathers had a decade earlier, He offered a silent promise, *your revenge will be mine,* and gently brushed a hand across her eyelids. The gesture brought another chorus of moans from the room. Joe didn't care, their job was to preserve evidence to use in a trial, neither preserving evidence nor trials had ever concerned him.

Eager for his departure, the gathered personnel stepped aside, and Joe walked unimpeded from the room. He skirted around the island, tracing the path Leary had taken earlier. Out on the patio, he wasn't surprised to see three table settings. Joe went back inside and briskly surveyed the remainder of the house with Porter in his wake.

The Detective had given up trying to communicate with Blackstone. He wasn't even sure his questions had been heard, what he did know, was the big man was no stranger to death. He had not flinched at the visual horrors or acknowledged the pungent odor. Porter watched as Blackstone's eyes darted across each room, scanning and absorbing every detail. He recognized the skill-set because he did the same thing, only Blackstone did it faster.

Finished his search, Blackstone was in the den, staring at the fireplace. Porter stood behind him, contemplating Blackstone's behavior, waiting for him to speak. What stood out the most, was the intimacy he shared with the violence, which had occurred. Not as the perpetrator, but as an observer. It was like watching a painter browse through another's gallery. Unnerved, Porter repeated the thought he'd had since they'd met, *who the hell is this guy?*

"That's not Carrie," said Joe.

"Are you sure? asked Porter, "We found Ms. Hill's ID and —"

"I'm sure," Joe said. "Carrie doesn't have a tattoo on her lower back, and her eyes are green, that girl's eyes are blue."

Embarrassed by the oversight Porter relented. "Alright … what else can you tell me?"

"There were at least two men."

Porter raised a brow. "How can you be so sure?"

"There were three people here, one male, who could handle himself, and two females. It would've been difficult for one person to control all three of them. Plus." Joe pointed toward the dining room. "The girl in there doesn't have any defensive wounds, and there's no sign of skin under her fingernails. No way a single person could control both her arms and drive those knife's through her hands hard enough to impale her on the table."

Porter couldn't argue with the logic. "We found a wallet and ID for a Troy Hill, we ran it, and it looks like he's Ms. Hill's brother, is that correct?"

"Yes, most likely the girl on the table is a friend of his, a Ms. Marino, first name Shelly or Michelle."

"Mr. Blackstone, clearly whoever did this wanted to send you a message. Is there anyone who would want to do you or your friend's harm?"

Joe shook his head. The answer was much more complicated than Porter realized. Joe still suspected Pergine's involvement, but this seemed beyond his scope. If Pergine was involved, he had hired professionals, if so, why kill the girl? They couldn't have known she was going to be present, he hadn't. And why leave a message? The act seemed spontaneous but the message was personal, it made no sense. He set the thought aside and asked, "Have you canvassed the neighborhood for security footage?"

"I've got a half-dozen officers doing it now."

"Email me everything you get as soon as you get it."

"Listen Blackstone I can't be sending evidence to you this is —" Porter stopped when Joe reached for his phone. "Okay, okay, I'll do it, but you need to let us handle this."

"I'll text you my email address," Joe said, heading for the door.

"Blackstone … you need to stay out of this, it's not your job."

Joe stopped, wheeled around and locked eyes with Porter. "Don't fuck with me, you just send whatever you get."

Joe's tone matched his glare, both struck Porter with more force than his words. Resigned to meet Joe's request, the Detective watched him leave, unaware of the storm he was about to unleash.

CHAPTER 33

Carrie and Troy were imprisoned in what would normally serve as a small bedroom. Exposed logs formed two exterior walls, each with a boarded-up window. Thin rays of light sliced through the gaps, carving beams of clarity into the darkness.

Troy had been in and out of consciousness since their captures had left them. His face was battered, and he had a large knot on the back of his head. His sister was positive he had suffered a couple of broken ribs.

Carrie's upper lip was swollen and the side of her face tender. The taste of copper lingered. Terrified and with no one to talk too, Carrie kept replaying the nightmare. Their jeers echoed with the vulgar images she could not escape. Every time she had looked away the bald man had done something to cause Shelly more pain, sometimes it was a punch, sometimes worse. So Carrie had watched the horror, witnessed the cruelty and pleaded for them to stop.
***

Carrie's sobs were muted by Shelly's screams. Troy woke and struggled against his restraints. Unable to free himself, he rolled across the floor in a desperate attempt to quell Shelly's beating. His captors laughed at the effort and pummeled him until he lay motionless. The taller man brandished a knife, bent and lifted Troy's limp head by the hair.

Carrie's lower lip trembled. "Oh, God please no."

He put the blade to Troy's throat.

Her eyes spilled with despair, and she pleaded with the Monster. After what seemed like days, but was only a few seconds, he removed the blade from Troy's neck and let her brother's head fall to the floor.

Carrie's relief was short lived, he turned and sunk his blade into Shelly's back. She withered as he pulled the steel through her flesh. When he was done, he lifted Carrie to her feet so she could see the gruesome wound. He held his face to her's, leaned over Shelly's mutilated form and said, "Don't get jealous it'll be your turn soon enough."

She struggled to pull away, but he slammed her face against the table. Pain erupted from her nose and mouth.

The bald man held his hand out and said, "Okay Benny, enough fun, we need to go."

Benny handed his knife to the bald man, strengthened his hold and pulled Carrie's back into his chest. He yanked her hair and his hot breath assaulted her when he whispered, "You better watch this or Sleeping Beauty's next."

Carrie trembled but looked on as the bald man flicked the blade across Shelly's neck. A steady stream poured from the wound and whatever life remained with it. Paralyzed with horror, her eyes lingered on the knife as Shelly's forearm was used to clean it.

***

Try as she might, Carrie could not stop reliving the heinous events. As much as those images haunted her, she was equally repulsed by her own failure. She and her brother had been shoved into two giant cases and wheeled from her home. *Why didn't I call out?* She kept asking herself.

The fact that she'd been in shock offered no solace. Now, sitting helplessly in an empty room, her brother seriously injured, she loathed herself for her failure. She was certain, had she died trying, it would have been a better fate than what lies ahead.

Carrie thought they had been loaded into a van or similar vehicle. After three, maybe four hours of driving they had stopped and been unloaded. Her case was pulled over a rough surface, up several steps and across what she guessed was a porch. She heard keys and the squeal of unoiled hinges before the threshold bounce beneath her, and the case came to rest.

Blinded by the sudden light when the case was opened, Carrie was unable to see much before being shoved into the empty room. For the remainder of the night, she sat in the dark and tears ran from her eyes while she cradled her brother in her lap.

Carrie heard three separate vehicles arrive during the night, and was certain none had left. Shortly after sunrise, the drone of small boat carried across the water confirming they were on a lake. Every so often, she heard the boards creak as someone walked past her door. And she heard voices on two occasions, but not well enough to listen in on the conversation.

Emotionally and physically Carrie was beaten, but she steeled herself for a fight. She pushed past her fear and willed herself to focus on an escape.
***

Joe left the country club, resigned to his course of action. His journey, once again altered by evil, had awakened a part of himself he'd fought to suppress. A calm blanketed him, and his mind focused on the singular purpose of finding Carrie and Troy. While considering how best to accomplish the task, he recalled all the things he'd done, which prepared him for this moment. Despite all the violence, he had rained upon his enemies, Joe had always fought to restrain his rage. He had never set it free. He feared, once it was loose, he may never regain control. But that didn't matter now.

Joe recalled a number he'd sworn never to use again. He took a hard right onto Morris Road and punched the digits into his phone.

A series of electronic squeals chirped in his ear, and an unidentified voice answered, "Odin Group."

"Support," Joe replied.

After another chorus of electronics, a second voice answered, "Support, user account please."

"Tango, Whisky, Roger, Foxtrot, Alpha, Tango, Niner, Zulu."

The voice on the other end of the line repeated the code, while rapidly typing it into a terminal. The typing stopped, after a long pause the voice responded, "ID confirmed … uh … I'm sorry sir, but the director has frozen all support on this account."

"Patch me through to him."

"Sir … I'm sorry, but that's against protocol."

"Do you recognize the name on your screen?"

"Ye … Yes," said the voice, stuttering.

The name on the monitor was not Joe Blackstone, it was a call sign. Only five people on the planet knew whom the call sign belonged to, but everyone at Odin knew of it and had heard the legend.

"So we're clear, the stories you've heard are bullshit. They're fucking lullabies compared to the shit I've done … don't make me ask again."

"Hold sir."

A moment later a deep voice said, "I thought you were out? I could have sworn you told me you wanted nothing to do with us?"

"Edward I don't have time to fuck around, I need your help, and I need it now."

Edward Hughes was one of the few people who did know Joe by his call sign.

Hughes let out a sigh and said, "Joseph I didn't want you to leave, but you did. Now I see you on TV living the American dream, congratulations. I'm sorry, but we aren't social services, you wanted out, you're out."

Joe paused a beat. His tone cut with a sharp edge when he replied, "Edward, the two people I care for more than anything have been taken. The motherfuckers who abducted them, raped, beat, and mutilated a woman just to send me a message. If anything happens to my friends … my family … that could have been avoided with Odin's assistance, I will consider you, and everyone else at Odin, every bit as responsible as those who took them."

"I don't think threats are necessary."

Joe was silent.

Hughes was pissed, but he knew what Joe had done to earn his call sign, he was after all the person who gave it to him.

"Okay … what do you need?"

"I need a complete fit out," said Joe, "including safe house and I'll need the support group to work on some security footage."

"Where are you?" asked Hughes.

"Fort Washington, Pennsylvania approaching the turnpike."

"I'll call you back at this number in five minutes." Hughes ended the call.

***

Mealey had issued a gag order concerning the altercation between Blackstone and Pergine; nonetheless, rumors were widespread. News of Blackstone's suspension added fuel to the fire. In addition to a mild concussion, Pergine's lip was split, his eye was swollen and the side of his face discolored. Team doctors would not clear him to play but, in a move of gamesmanship, Mealey had not immediately scratched his quarterback. Amidst the turmoil, his team needed any edge they could get going into their game against division rival Dallas. Technically it was against league rules to conceal an injury, but he was willing to risk a fine if it prevented his opponent from adjusting their game plan.

True to form, Pergine was deftly playing the victim. The team rallied around their battered quarterback voicing support. The only player to refrain was Wilmot, who, like Joe, had noticed Pergine's odd behavior, and heard him reference Carrie Hill on multiple occasions during the week. In the aftermath, the veteran had voiced his concerns to Mealey, but the head coach had chastised him for it.

Unbeknownst to Dwayne, seconds after Mealey had told him to, *"Drop the subject and focus on the fucking game,"* the coach dialed his GM.

When Pollard answered Mealey said, "John, I've got no clue what's going on, but I heard something you should know. Wilmot told me Joe's girlfriend was murdered last night, that's what set him off. Apparently, Pergine was asking a lot of questions about her this week, and Blackstone thinks he's involved. I can't imagine there's any truth to it but if something did happen ..."

"Jesus ... no wonder Blackstone went nuts, I'll check this out."

"Listen ... I sent the kid packing. If something happened to his girl ..." Mealey's voice was thick with concern.

"Don't worry Mike, I'll find him."

CHAPTER 34

Las Vegas
Eight Years Ago

A growing pool of blood crept over the Italian marble, the man at its center supplying a constant stream. Naked and taped to a chair, his face was beaten and disfigured. But it was the ten toes and ten fingers scattered across the soiled floor which had broken him.

His tormentor could see, he had broken the man, after removing his first toe and cauterizing the wound with a hot iron. But that hadn't stopped him from repeating the process nineteen more times. He could rationalize, he was being thorough, but it would be a lie, he enjoyed it. His victim's fear was his joy, their pain his narcotic.

The man in the chair was "Tiny" Carlo Gonzalez. Standing 6'4", and weighing well over 260 pounds Tiny was a lot of things, but tiny wasn't one of them. He was the owner of Gonzalez Logistics, which ran container ships out of ports in Texas and Louisiana. Gonzalez Logistics had been a small player in maritime transport until Tiny forged an alliance with a group from the Middle East and a South American drug cartel. That both organizations had been linked to numerous terrorist acts were of no concern to Tiny. His only interest was self-interest.

Texas District Attorney, Mitchell Flynn, had targeted Gonzalez's illegal activities as soon as he took office. Tiny and his associates, retaliated by kidnapping Flynn's eleven-year-old daughter, Lindsey. It was a bold and costly move, but the young girl's abduction had gone off without a hitch. Tiny's sources confirmed Flynn had followed their instructions and not gone to the authorities. But less than twenty-four hours after they had taken the girl, Tiny had lost contact with his man running the operation. He'd sent people to the location where she was being kept, but all they had found was bodies, and the girl was gone.

Tiny had fled Texas, flown to Las Vegas, and checked into a posh Casino; secretly controlled by the cartel. Monitoring the news from his villa, his angst grew as each hour passed without word of Lindsey Flynn's safe return.

There had been those around him who'd advised against the kidnapping, warning, Flynn wasn't like other politicians, he was a man of action, unafraid to fight fire with fire. Failing to heed their advice, Tiny now knew fear. It was not the way he'd been manhandled or how he'd been disfigured. Above the pain, pulsing through every fiber in his body, and behind eyes, which were swollen shut, he could still see his attacker's eyes. Calm violent eyes, void of all emotion, they were the eyes of a predator. When Tiny woke, taped to a chair, and met their gaze, he had known his fate.

His tormentor stood in front and asked, "Is there anything else you want to tell me before I go?" His tone carried the same urgency one would use to ask directions at a grocery store.

Tiny's head sagged lifelessly. Only the bloody bubbles forming around his mouth and a fatal wheeze gave evidence he was still alive.

I'm going to need an answer. I know it's been a rough night for you, but it can get worse … much … much worse."

A fresh wave of fear surged through him, and his head rolled to the side. "I … I told you everything," he managed before choking on his own blood.

The man waited patiently as Tiny's body shook from a fit of coughs. When they subsided, he said, "Tiny … I believe you've told me everything, so it's time for me to go now, but it's the end of the line for you. If it's any consolation, I'll be visiting each and every one of your associates, and we'll have similar conversations. They'll all be joining you soon."

He reached behind his back and removed a light weight carbon steel knife from its sheath. The flat black blade was almost invisible in the low light.

As the man stepped behind him, Tiny summoned the last of his strength and said, "Wait—" Was all he managed to say before his head was yanked back. Tiny never felt the blade slice across his neck, but when he tried to breathe his lungs were filled with his own blood, panicked seized him; he shuddered against his restraints.

Lifted by a weightless sensation, the man circled in front of Tiny. He watched death arrive for the fourteenth time tonight, savoring his atrocity. When it left, he followed and disappeared into the night.

Tiny had given him five names. Over the next three months, Odin Group tracked those men to four countries on three continents. Each time, the same man was sent to terminate the targets. The collateral damage was unlike anything Director Hughes had ever seen. His operators were precision instruments and the new man, their youngest ever, possessed unparalleled abilities. But where his peers struck with surgical precision, leaving little to no sign of their involvement, he rained down on his targets like the Angel of Death. In the wake of his actions in Texas and Las Vegas, the Director had given him a verbal reprimand. But it had fallen on deaf ears.

Odin Group operated covertly outside the confines of the law and within the best interest of the United States. They were formed independent of the U.S. Government, but two-thirds of their assignments were for various government branches. With intercept capabilities rivaling the NSA and no congressional oversight, Odin Group was the last and best option for locating anyone or thing on the planet. Once located, one of their elite operators could be called upon to *resolve* most any issue.

Hughes' new operator had killed more people in his first three months than all of Odin Group had in a decade. While his wrath was appreciated by their client, Mitchell Flynn, Hughes was troubled by the attention it would draw. Eager to retain such a skilled operator, Hughes summoned him to a private meeting and said, "You could be the best damn operator we've ever had, but if you keep stirring up all hell, you could expose us. Every one of my guys, except you, knows the routine. When they're in the field, they do what they've been trained to do, accomplish the mission, and get the fuck out. But not you, you're like the fucking Grim Reaper killing everything you see. We don't need that kind of attention. If people find out about us, it will be a damn witch hunt, and they'll shut us down. I can't let that happen."

The young man didn't flinch. "Have I killed anyone who didn't deserve it?" he asked.

"No, but that's not the point."

"Have we been on the news?"

"Goddammit, no, but it doesn't mean people in certain circles haven't taken notice."

"Exactly."

"'Exactly', what?" Hughes asked, slamming his desk. "What the hell are you talking about?"

"You do what you need to do, but if you send me on an assignment, I'm not fucking around. There are sick people out there; monsters who think they're untouchable, I've seen them. But they're wrong," —His ice blue eyes sparkled with excitement— "I'm the real fucking monster. I want them to know I'm out there, to know they're being hunted, and experience that fear. So you're right, there will be people who know what I've done. But it may save lives."

I never want to be alone in a room with this man again, thought Hughes. After a moment he cleared his throat and said, "Okay, we'll try it your way."

"Good," Joe said and headed for the door.

"One last thing."

Joe stopped and said, "What's that?"

"Your new call sign is Reaper."

Known only as Reaper, to all but the most informed people within Odin, Joe Blackstone quickly built a reputation for violence and efficiency. While his identity was unknown, his exploits were; rumors of missions circulated in clandestine circles. Knowledge of his existence was a great comfort to some, to others, he was the nightmare that kept them awake.

CHAPTER 35

Hughes called Joe back and directed him to a farmhouse in Bucks County. With more than two hundred acres of private property and close proximity to the North-East Philadelphia Airfield, the farm was a perfect staging ground for Odin operators. Joe had used the location on two previous occasions. Typically reserved for the highest priority missions, Joe was grateful for Hughes cooperation.

During the drive, Detective Porter had sent Joe three video files from the country club. Joe had forwarded those to the secure link Hughes had provided and was now waiting on the techs from Odin's support group. He was confident they would locate the individuals who had taken Carrie and Troy, his concern was whether or not they would be in time.

Clouds churned in the sky by the time Joe arrived at the private sanctuary. He bypassed the house and went straight to the old barn adjacent to it. To the untrained eye, both structures were weathered and in need of repair. They did indeed need fresh paint, but beneath the flaking boards, lay a sturdy frame and exterior walls reinforced with steel. All windows were bulletproof, and each structure had secure satellite communications. A hidden vault, containing firearms and tactical gear, was located in each building. The larger selection, stored under the barn floor, was what drew Joe's attention.

He rotated a false board on the side of the barn giving access to a keypad. After entering the appropriate code, hydraulics hissed as the door lock disengaged and the barn doors swept open. Inside he found a similar keypad and closed the doors behind him. In contrast to the structure's exterior, the interior was modern and well organized. LED lights lit the space from high above and orderly workstations lined the walls where stalls had once been. A Tahoe, Ducati, ATV vehicle, and Zodiac were all stored in the center of the barn. Behind them sat a large desk, computer station and a wall of monitors. Six different forty-inch screens, rotated real time video, from two dozen cameras located around the farm and barn. Two additional screens displayed the status of motion, infrared and pressure sensors employed throughout the property.

At the computer terminal, Joe logged on and typed a command. To his right, a large section of floor opened revealing a staircase. He descended into the opening and entered the vault. Automatic lights came on overhead, illuminating the twenty by the forty-foot armory. Three aisles stretched the length of the space, each lined with tactical gear, guns, munitions and communication equipment. Joe grabbed a canvas bag off the wall and filled it with gear. Satisfied he had everything he needed, Joe climbed the steps out of the vault.

After a trip to the gun range, located in an old gravel pit six-hundred yards from the farm, Joe was cleaning his newly sighted weapons when his phone buzzed. There was no caller ID available, but he answered assuming the call was from Odin Group. "Go."

"Joe? John Pollard, I'm glad I got you."

Joe said nothing. He'd ignored a half dozen calls from Pollard, but this time, the GM had blocked his number and Joe had answered thinking it was Odin.

"We heard what happened at your house. Dwayne talked to coach earlier, and the media just broke the story. Have the police located Carrie or her brother yet?"

"No."

"I want you to know we're here to help in any way we can. I don't know what happened between you and Jeff, but I'm sure he had nothing to do with this, even so, we'll do everything we can to alleviate your concerns. You have my word."

"Maybe Jeff didn't have anything to do with this, if so, I'll apologize to him, Ms. Taylor and the entire organization and accept the consequences."

For the first time all day, John was hopeful. "Good, I'm sure we can work through this."

"There's just one thing."

"Which is?"

"I'm a lot better at finding people and solving these kinds of problems than I've ever been at football. I *will* get to the bottom of this … you have my word."

The connection went dead, and John thought, *this is going to end badly.*

CHAPTER 36

Ms. Taylor had spent the afternoon watching her team get slaughtered by Dallas. When her GM called to request a meeting, the urgency in his voice announced her day was about to get worse. Waiting for Pollard to arrive, she took the liberty of pouring him a scotch and a second for herself.

Pollard was shown to Ms. Taylor's library, where his boss greeted him with a drink. The lavish room was the size of a basketball court. Floor to ceiling bookcases covered three of the four walls, and a massive stone fireplace dominated the fourth. The bookcases were constructed from dark cherry wood. A matching ladder hung from a brass rail and gave access to the top shelves.

They sat at the owner's desk. The strain on Pollard's face spoke volumes as he relayed his conversation with Blackstone. When he was done bringing Ms. Taylor up to speed, Pollard expressed his concerns. "The way I see it, we need to find out more about Joe. I knew there was something strange about his past when we researched him. It was like a black hole, we let it slide, but now I don't know. I'm nervous, he went ballistic with Pergine, but on the phone he was different."

Sky Marie swirled the amber liquid in her glass and asked, "Different how?"

"I expected him to be a mess, but he spoke with poise. His words were clear and calculated like he knew exactly what he was doing. To be honest, it creeped me out."

"So ... what do you think?"

Pollard sagged in his chair. "I don't know what to think. But no matter what happens, this is going to receive a ton of press. Joe was the biggest story in the league. Now he beats up our QB because he thinks the guy's involved in this. Plus, one of the missing people is Joe's girlfriend, who's a freaking movie star and this has media storm written all over it. So far, the press hasn't gotten confirmation on what happened between Jeff and Joe, but they will. The police confirmed, it is Carrie and her brother who are missing. It won't take long for the press to connect dots between fighting teammates, murder and kidnapping. When they do, every media outlet in the world will be all over this. God help us if anything in Blackstone's past can bite us in the ass." Pollard took a long pull from his drink. The liquid warmed his throat as he willed it to calm his nerves.

Ms. Taylor mirrored his actions and lifted her glass. When she sat her drink back down, her eyes met Pollard's, and she said, "You forget something."

"What?"

"Pergine."

"You don't seriously believe Pergine had anything to do with a murder and kidnapping do you?"

Ms. Taylor raised an eyebrow and said, "You've said it before John, Pergine's an oddball. Would you suggest, we sit back and assume Blackstone is our only potential problem?"

Pollard scratched the late day stubble on his chin and admitted, "You have a point.

***

While Pollard and Ms. Taylor were planning a course of action, Blackstone received a call. "Go," he answered.

"We were able to pull some information off of the files you sent," said Hughes.

Joe was surprised to hear Hughes voice. Typically the director wasn't involved at this level of mission planning. His involvement highlighted how unusual this situation was.

"We identified the vehicle and tracked it with local cameras. We also signaled out two cell phones, which made outgoing calls along the route. We lost visual contact once they left the main roads but we're still tracking the phones, they're on a lake in upstate New York. I'm sending you coordinates and satellite imagery of the region. Do you need anything else?" Hughes asked.

"No Edward, I have everything I need, thanks, I owe you one."

"No," Hughes said. "You don't, I shouldn't have been a prick before, but I guess I'm still pissed you left us. Do what you do and go get your friends." Hughes broke the connection.

Joe lowered the phone and said, "You can count on it."

CHAPTER 37

In contrast to their last meeting, Litt paced the floor while Pergine sat comfortably on his couch. Philadelphia had gotten destroyed without him, Blackstone was suspended, and his teammates had rallied to his side. Not even his battered face could dampen his spirits. "Jesus Harvey, will you relax? It was a great day, we win, Blackstone is history."

Litt gnawed away on manicured nails and continued to waddle around the room.

Pergine rolled his eyes and hollered, "Harvey!"

Finally, Litt stopped and looked at Pergine. "What?"

"Relax man you did it."

Litt shook his head and said, "I told you, something isn't right. I have a source who swears they let Blackstone examine the crime scene."

"So what? Who cares? Let's celebrate."

"Jeff you're not listening," Litt said. "My guy says they let him in and he was examining the fucking scene. That's not right, no way should they have let him in there. What the hell does he know about crime scenes?"

Pergine waved a dismissive hand and said, "They probably let him in as a courtesy because he's a celebrity."

"No way, that's not how it works, we're missing something big."

"Whatever, you keep worrying, but I'm gonna celebrate." Pergine stood and fixed himself a drink, while Litt continued to pace.
※※※

News of Joe's suspension and Carrie's kidnapping was already snowballing when Bud Perkins linked the stories together. He appeared on both local and national media channels, unleashing a landslide of inquiries and speculation. One of the most ridiculous, and therefore popular, theories had Blackstone perpetrating the crimes in Blue Bell, out of jealousy, over an affair Hill was having with Pergine. The media descended upon Blue Bell like an invading army. At the same time, interview requests lit the phones at Philadelphia's practice facility.

***

Darkness fell, and Troy had not regained consciousness. Carrie's concern grew with each labored breath he took. She had called out to their captors and asked for help, but the cabin was silent, and her pleas had gone unanswered. Finally, she heard a door, and footsteps, somewhere in the cabin. "Hey … somebody, please help us. Please … my brother needs help. He's hurt bad." Carrie felt her way to the door, pounding on it, she hollered, "Please, please help us."

Before long, Carrie's hands throbbed and her words scratched at her dry throat. But she ignored the pain and continued her assault on the door.

A mix of relief and fear billowed in her stomach when Carrie heard someone approach. She stepped back, and her heart raced as the door was unlocked. As it swung open, she raised her arm to help shield her eyes from the light. A large shadow filled the door. Without warning, a vicious blow stung the side of her face and knocked her off her feet. Awake, but not conscious, she registered a distant laugh. Pain on her face and skull radiated through her fog loud and clear.

Before she could recover, Carrie was dragged by her foot. The rough surface burned her skin until she was yanked from the floor and tossed onto a table. A split second floating sensation, ended with a fresh jolt of pain before she faded into darkness.

CHAPTER 38

Joe was five miles from the camp Odin Group had located when his phone rang. Since leaving the farm, Joe had received calls and texts from every person he considered a friend, he'd ignored them all. Focused on the mission at hand, he had intended to do the same this time until he saw Carrie's name. Joe opened the phone and clicked on the text. A single image of Carrie naked and tied to a table appeared on his phone. Even on the small display, he could see her face was swollen and discolored. Her eyes were closed and blood leaked from a split lip.

For as long as Joe could remember, rage burned in his soul. He had learned how to use it at a young age, calling on it in extreme circumstances. But each time it was summoned he had to fight to keep it in check. The tiny image caused his rage to burn out of control … Joe was thankful.

In his previous occupation, Joe had always fought on two fronts, attacking one monster while suppressing one within. Of most concern, was his internal battle, least he becomes what he despised. His Odin Group file would suggest it had already happened. Nonetheless, Joe had never surrendered to the rage, until now. Unified within himself, he set aside all worries of self-control and concentrated on the task at hand.

A mile from his destination Joe pulled off the road and backed the Charger behind a line of bushes. After killing the engine, he called Carrie's number, it was answered on the fourth ring.

"Hey there superstar." The voice was vaguely familiar, but the laugh that followed was unforgettable.

"Benny Calabrese."

Worried about who else might be listening, Calabrese replied, "I have no idea who that is, but I'm sure he'd be moved to know you're thinking of him." Again the laugh boomed. "I'll tell you what though, your woman is one fine piece of ass. My friends and I have been resting all day, dreaming of the shit we're gonna do to her tonight."

Joe remained silent.

***

In the cabin, Benny was grinning ear-to-ear. "What's the matter superstar, you got nothing to say?"

"I was just dreaming of the shit I'm gonna do to you."

The tone on the other end of the line caused the blood to drain from Benny's face. The line went dead, and he stared at the phone in his hand.

"What?" Asked Junior.

Regaining his bravado, Benny said. "Fucking guy hung up on me, can you believe that shit?" No sooner had the words left his mouth, than another ring captured their attention.

Junior snatched the phone from Benny's hand and answered, "Listen motherfucker... Huh? Oh .... Never mind, what?" Confusion painted Benny's face as watched his cousin. "I got it ... goddammit, I said I got it."

Junior ended the call and turned to Benny. "That was the Jew, Litt, he says to get rid of these two. "

"He said we could use the broad to get Blackstone to fix a game?"

Junior shook his head and said, "He's pissed we killed the girl, says it's too hot now, shit ... maybe he's right."

Benny threw his hands in the air. "What the fuck ... we haven't even had fun with this broad. And what about the extra money? We'd clean house on a rigged game."

"He's gonna double our fee." Knowing his cousin's real concern, a sadistic thought curled Junior's mouth, and he said, "How the hell is he going to know when we dump this bitch?"

Benny looked at Carrie's with wild eyes and said, "I'll pull the brother out so he can watch."

***

As soon as Joe hung up, he got out of the car and retrieved his gear from the trunk. He shrugged into a tactical vest and secured grenades, flashbangs and extra ammo to it. He placed a pistol in the holster built into his pants and slung a rifle over his shoulder. The last piece of gear was a strange looking helmet which Joe placed atop his head and strapped to his chin. It resembled a motorcycle helmet, except a single hinge attached four optical cylinders to the front of it. The alien looking optics were panoramic night vision goggles. Ready, Reaper flipped the NVG's over his eyes and melted into the woods.

The forty-acre property was more compound than camp. Hughes email said it was owned by a wealthy developer with connections to the Calabrese crime family. Seven buildings were stood on a central clearing along the water. Satellite photos and thermal imaging showed the Calabrese's had brought friends. Joe had noted four vehicles and at least six sentries spread across the property.

His goggles illuminated the forest floor in a collage of greens. Like a grizzly tracking its prey, Joe raced through the woods with surprising stealth. When he drew close to his planned point of entry, Joe lowered himself and crept toward the edge of the clearing. He found the first three sentries right where surveillance images had shown. Two were stationed at the wood line, and a third was seated behind a horse stable.

The inner man had chosen his position poorly. The building obstructed his view, and left no sightline to the water or guard closest to it. Had he picked a spot on the opposite side of the building, he could have kept watch over half the compound. The long structure would have given him cover, a view of the lake and both perimeter guards. Adding to his blunder, he was smoking, ensuring his night vision would be poor at best.

The guard nearest Joe had the best field of vision. Able to see his counterpart near the water and behind the stable, he posed the biggest threat.

Joe slid back into the woods and blended into the night. Circling toward his first victim, he synced each step, and each breath, with the light breeze and rustling leaves. What little sound he made was masked.

The guard was looking to his right, toward the lake, when Joe seized his head. Joe's left hand engulfed the top of his skull, while the right gripped the bottom of his chin. He barely had time to flinch before Joe's hands exploded in opposite directions. One thrust down and to the side; the other ripped up and out, snapping the guard's neck like a twig.

Joe caught the limp body and froze, listening for any reaction. When none came, he pulled the corpse into the trees. The only communication equipment he found on the dead man was a cell phone, so he doubted the guards had any scheduled check in. Joe was pleased, whatever professionalism the Calabrese's had shown in Blue Bell had not carried over into their security.

A scream from somewhere in the compound broke the silence. The guard at the stable turned an ear toward the sound. Joe drew his pistol, the matte black suppressor on his Nighthawk 9mm led the way when he broke from cover. He sprinted away from the stables and down a shallow incline.

The guard at the tree line, near the water, spun toward Joe and went for his gun. His finger never touched the trigger. Three silent rounds destroyed his head, and his lifeless form toppled back into the water.

The lower portion of the compound offered a clear view from one side to the other, but no cover. The dead man's splash would draw attention, so Joe angled back toward the stable. He hurried along the wall until he reached the end, where heavy footsteps announced the guard's approach. Joe wheeled around the corner with his gun raised. A single 9mm slug traveled ten feet and pierced the center of the man's forehead. Joe continued moving and stepped over the body. Had he bothered to look, Joe would have seen surprise frozen on the dead man's face.

At the other end of the stable, Joe peered around the corner toward the center of the compound. Men were pouring out from two nearby cabins. Their rally point was an illuminated area beside a small utility shed. A large cylinder beside the small structure forced Joe's mouth into a wicked grin.

He removed the 300 Win Mag sniper rifle from his back and flipped the NVG optics up, out of the way. When all the men had gathered, Joe tucked the stock against his shoulder. Looking through the scope, he took aim, when the crosshairs centered on the target he exhaled, froze, and touched the trigger.

The shot reverberated across the lake. Joe's high-powered round obliterated the regulator attached to the compounds natural gas supply. The ground shook, and flames filled the sky. Two men had survived the blast but not the inferno. Their screams warmed Joe as much as the blaze. He let them burn, skirted the fire and ducked back into the shadows.

Three cars and a van were parked in front of a large camp at the center of the property. Joe swept the area for more guards, found none and descended upon his primary target. He was close enough to hear shouting inside when the lights went out.

***

Like his sister, Troy was dragged into the main room. His arms, ankles, knees and thighs had been bound with duct tape again; he was still unconscious. Benny propped him against the back of a couch, which faced the other half of the cabin.

When Benny finished positioning Troy, Junior poured a bucket of ice water over his head.

The cold water stabbed his skin and invaded his lungs. Troy coughed, gagged and fought for air. The effort sent lasers of pain through his broken ribs. When his misery subsided enough so he could focus, Troy's heart sank. The sight of his sister splayed across the table was far more painful than anything he had ever endured.

Junior knelt beside him and said, "We're gonna let you watch us, I hear some brothers get off on that shit."

Fire filled Troy's eyes. "I'll fucking kill you. You touch her, and I'll fucking kill you."

"The more trouble you cause, the more painful this'll be for her." Junior winked. "I'll show you what I mean … Benny, get her attention."

Carrie was back in a foggy state, when Benny treated her to the same experience as her brother, dousing her with freezing water. When her coughing faded, and the Calabrese's amusement with it, Junior signaled his cousin.

Benny cut Carrie's right hand free from the rope of duct tape restraining it. A portrait of Shelly's fate assaulted her memory. Panic stricken, she tried to pull her hand back, but Junior snatched her forearm.

"Please don't … please, let us go, please." Caries words trailed off as fear seized her voice.

Ignoring the pain, Troy thrashed against the couch. "Don't do it you piece of shit … LET HER GO!"

Benny stepped away from the table and leaned toward the counter.

When he turned around, Carrie's eyes went wide. "No, no, no, please no."

Back at the table, Benny held his hands in the air, showing Troy the hunting knife and meat cleaver that had added to his sister's nightmare.

Junior addressed Carrie with the sincerity of a game show host. "The choice is yours, Carrie. The knife will hurt … a lot I'd imagine, but it'll heal if we decide to let you live. On the other *hand*." his cousin found the choice of words amusing. "If Benny cuts your hand off … I doubt it'll grow back." Carrie's tears filled Junior with excitement, "What'll it be?" he asked.

Troy stared wild-eyed at Junior, and his sister fought back sobs, but neither said a word.

Junior pointed to his cousin and said, "You decide Benny."

Fear shattered her voice as Carrie cried out. "Wait." Her body trembled, and she looked at the knife.

"So there's no confusion," said Junior, tormenting her with a broad smile, "I'm gonna need to hear you say it."

Carrie forced herself to look Junior in the eye and said, "Use the knife."

"Excellent, see that wasn't so hard. Now lay your hand flat on the table. If you don't do as I say or if you move your hand and it doesn't go through on the first try, Benny's gonna use the cleaver, you get what I'm sayin'?"

"Yes." Carrie opened her fist and set her palm on the pine surface.

"Good girl." Junior kept her forearm pinned with one hand and yanked her hair back with the other. "This is too exciting to look away, so keep your eyes open and watch." He leaned down and whispered, "Don't worry … I promise this won't be the most painful thing you ever feel."

Fear spilled from Carrie's soul, not because she was going to die, but how. Junior yanked her head back again, and Benny lifted the Blade high in the air. The steel glistened in Carrie's wet eyes. She heard sobs but was unsure if they were Troy's or her own. She realized it was both of them and Benny thrust the blade downward. It sliced through her hand and burrowed into the table. A nauseating light blinded her, and a wave of agony swept her breath away. When it returned, her pain rang out across the compound.

Helpless, Troy cried with his sister as the Calabrese's laughed.

Carrie stiffened when Junior grabbed her shoulder. Her skin crawled as he slid his hand down her back and cupped her ass. His touch lingered, and she lay frozen until he slapped her exposed skin. The entire table lurched forward. She gritted her teeth and held back another scream, but her tears continued to flow.

Carrie turned her head when Junior resumed groping her. Facing her brother, she searched for hope and strength, but his eyes couldn't lie.

Benny looked on with hungry eyes.

Junior took his time and circled the table. He stopped between the siblings and unbuttoned his shirt. "I can't tell you how happy Benny and I are to have you two as our guest. Imagine my surprise, when I got a call, telling me the hillbilly fuck who jumped us was none other than WFL superstar Joe Blackstone. The Jew prick even offered us money, can you believe that? We would have paid for this, it's fun, right Benny?"

"You bet cuz, nothing better."

"How's superstar gonna like it when we send him pictures of this? Maybe even some memorabilia." Junior retrieved a knife identical to the one staked through Carrie's hand, looked at his cousin and said, "Cut her other hand free, it's my turn."

Benny moved to cut her free, but a fat man burst through the door and interrupted him.

Junior's stare stopped the man in his tracks. "What the fuck Paulie? I told you guys to stay the fuck outta here."

Paulie leaned over and put his hands on his thighs. Sweat poured from his brow, and his jowls shook when he said, "Mr. Calabrese I'm sorry, but something's wrong. I saw Johnny fall in the lake and someone was running across the lawn." His words trailed off, and his chest heaved. "Dino and Billy ain't answering their phones … I sent Sal to get the rest of the guys."

"Slow down." Confused, Junior shook his head and said, "What do you mean, Johnny fell in the lake?"

"I think someone shot him, like with a silencer or something," Paulie said.

Benny waved the notion away and said, "No way, no one even knows we're here. Who could have shot him? You came up here so you could get something to eat you fat fuck."

Junior removed his phone from his pocket and pulled up Sal's number. When he hit, send an explosion rocked the cabin. All three men jumped back. Benny and Paulie clamored toward the front of the cabin and gawked out at the fire. Junior panned the room for his gun, retrieved it and hollered, "Hey … HEY, get away from the windows."

Benny retreated from the fiery view with Paulie on his heels. The high both he and his cousin had shared moments ago was gone. "Whatta we gonna do? Urged Benny. "Junior … what'da we do?"

Junior ignored his cousin. He loved the man like a brother, but Benny was no leader, didn't have the mind for it. Junior's father had ordered them to keep a low profile and stay out of trouble. The incident in Maine had cost the man a tremendous amount of cash and favors. Senior had made it clear, it would not happen again. Junior was fairly confident he could survive another regretful incident but doubted Benny would receive the same leniency, nephew or not. It would be easier to make a run for it without the Hills, but that wasn't an option. The camp belonged to a business associate of his father. If the movie star and her brother were found there, it would attract a mountain of unwanted press. Junior feared such an event would seal his cousin's fate and possibly his own.

Benny followed Junior into the hall and continued his rant. Junior opened the breaker panel and killed the power. When they got back to the kitchen, Paulie joined them, and they knelt bellow the counter. Bennie waved his gun at Carrie and said, "We need to kill these two and get outta here right fucking now."

Junior shook his head. "No, we have to take them with us, we can't leave'em here." Junior looked at Paulie and said, "Back your car by the front steps and pop the trunk."

The fat man's face swelled with fear, but he didn't move. "Boss, I'm not sure —"

"Now!" Junior yelled.

Paulie hefted himself up and waddled toward the door. His hand trembled as he reached for the knob. He glanced over his shoulder, hoping to get a reprieve, but none came, and he pulled it open.

Outlined by fire, Paulie's silhouette filled the doorway. Behind him, the Calabrese's raised their guns. Like a frightened child darting through a dark hall, he lunged forward. As soon as he crossed the threshold, his head jerked to the side, and he toppled over onto the porch.

Before Junior and Benny had processed Paulie's execution, a small canister skidded across the floor. Both men were staring at it when a paralyzing storm of noise, light, and smoke filled the cabin.

***

Joe rushed through the door behind the flash bangs detonation. Scanning right to left he located the cousins and fired one shot each, in their direction. He followed his shots and found Benny laying half on top of Junior. Their blood spilled onto the floor. Both men were gravely, but not fatally, wounded. That would change. He kicked their guns across the floor and raised his goggles. Joe stood above his prey and relished the look in their eyes, he'd seen it many times before. But it had never brought him more solace … or pleasure. Their bravado was gone, only fear and empty words remained as they begged for their life.

Their pleas fell on deaf ears, the only sounds Joe registered were the rage spurned voices in his head. His furry was so focused on killing these men, he forgot about Troy and Carrie's presence. Joe yearned to visit evil with its superior. It was a familiar thirst, he had quenched it many times and on each occasion, his soul sunk to the depths of hell. Yet, he never lost sight of the light, and it had always guided him back. But now he turned away from it, welcomed the darkness and searched for vengeance.

Like a rag doll, Benny was ripped him off the floor by his neck. His feet dangled, and his lungs burned. He tugged at Joe's grip, but his efforts were futile. Pain stabbed his throat and panic seized his face when his larynx collapsed.

Benny's throat popped, and Joe slammed him against the wall. He held his face inches from the dying man while life drained from Benny's eyes. When the last flicker was snuffed out, Joe released his grip and the dead mobster crumbled to the floor.

Blackstone turned his wrath on Junior, latched onto his wounded arm and yanked him to his feet. A wave of pain caused the room to spin, and Junior staggered. When he steadied himself, he looked death in the eye and pleaded, "Please man, things got outta hand, but we never wanted to hurt anyone. I can get you money, lots of money."

Junior's mouth was moving, but Joe wasn't listening. He scanned the room and found what he was looking for on the counter. Despite the blood leaking from his shoulder, Junior raised his hands to shield himself when Joe grabbed the cleaver. Joe struck like a rattlesnake and snagged Junior's left wrist from the air. In one violent motion, he twisted it behind Junior's back and slammed him over the table Carrie was still secured to.

The table shook and a fresh jolt of pain shot through Carrie's hand. Her senses had recovered from the flash bang, and she was aware of Junior's presence. She craned her neck and looked forward. His face was inches from her own, snot bubbled from his nose and spittle dripped from his trembling mouth. He looked at her with tear-filled eyes. In them, she recognized the despair he had recently shown her. A sharp crack rang out, like a bat crushing a ball, and the table vibrated. Junior's head rocked in an unnatural way, and the table shuddered when something crashed to the floor. Carrie screamed.

Fiery shadows danced across Junior's face as it swayed atop the table, frozen in terror for all eternity. The corners of Joe's mouth pulled tight, into a satisfied grin.

For the first time since breaching the cabin, Joe fixed his gaze on Carrie. She stared back at him with fear in her eyes. Joe removed his knife from its sheath and took hold of the tape around her left hand. She flinched and fought against her restraints. "Carrie, it's me, Joe, I'm not going to hurt you. You're safe now."

She stopped squirming, but her eyes were still cautious. Joe cut her hand loose and circled behind her to free her ankles. Carrie twisted to keep him in sight, but her staked hand restricted her movement.

"I'll be right back," Joe said. He needed to check on Troy before addressing the knife in Carrie's hand. He placed two fingers on his friend's neck and was relieved to find a pulse, albeit a weak one.

Despite being free from the duct tape, Carrie was still trapped in a similar position as she had been, when Joe got back to her. "Listen this is going to hurt, but you're going to be okay." He gripped the hilt of the knife with his right hand and placed his left palm flat on the table. "There aren't many ways to do this, but we don't have time to mess around. We need to get Troy to a doctor right away, are you ready?"

Carrie nodded as best she could and said, "Yes." Without further warning, Joe yanked the knife out, she stifled a scream and jerked her hand back. She staggered and nearly fell as she tried to stand. Joe caught her in his arms, but as soon as Carrie regained her balance, she recoiled from his touch. Clutching her hand, which was bleeding badly, Carrie backed away from Joe, hurried to Troy, and tried to lift him with her good hand.

Joe picked a blanket off the couch and draped it over Carrie's shoulders. He rummaged through the kitchen cabinets and returned with a dish towel. Carrie's blanket had fallen to the floor, and she was still struggling to lift her brother. Joe reached for her injured hand, but she pulled away again. "Carrie please," he said, "you're losing a lot of blood, I need to wrap your hand."

Slowly, Carrie extended her hand but she avoided eye contact while Joe attended to her wound. He secured the towel with duct tape, picked the blanket off the floor, and placed it over her shoulders again. Carrie clasped it around her neck with her good hand and sobbed.

Joe searched the fat man's pockets and found a set of keys. He hefted Troy over his shoulder and lugged him outside. Carrie stood frozen in place until Joe called out to her from the steps. "Come on, we need to get Troy to a hospital."

Carrie sat in the back and held her brother's head on the way to the hospital. Joe told her he was going to leave them at the ER and implored her not to mention his name to the police or anyone else. But she refused to meet his eyes in the mirror, and he wasn't sure she had heard a word he said.

When they arrived, Joe got out and opened Carrie's door. He offered his hand, but she leaned away from him, so he pulled it back and said, "I have to leave, but you need to go inside and get help for Troy. Remember what I told you."

Carrie hauled herself from the backseat, turned toward the hospital and walked off like a zombie.

Joe looked down at Troy and said, "I'm sorry brother … I'm so sorry." He grabbed his gear from the front seat and slipped into the night.

CHAPTER 39

By daybreak, Carrie Hill's kidnapping, and mysterious reappearance was the lead on every major news network. Talk show hosts found her ordeal irresistible. And a wide range of speculation colored reports about the Hill's reappearance.

Initially overshadowed by the Hill story, reports of mass murder in upstate New York began to surface. An explosion, and fire, at a lakeside property owned by real-estate mogul John Mitchell, had prompted neighbors to call 911. When authorities responded, they discovered fourteen bodies at Mitchell's compound and were seeking him for questioning. The massacre's proximity to the hospital where the Hills resurfaced caused a swell of media unseen since the OJ Simpson trial.

That evening Ms. Taylor arrived at the most famous residence on the planet. When she was shown into her host office, he stood and scooted from behind his desk to greet her. "Good evening Sky, thank you for coming down on such short notice."

"Good evening to you Mr. President, it's always a pleasure to be in your company."

President Mitchell Flynn and Sky Marie Taylor had become acquainted through her late husband. The former Texas Governor was often criticized for his lack of decorum, but Ms. Taylor found his candor and no-nonsense approach refreshing. When Flynn had announced his campaign for President, Ms. Taylor had been one of his most outspoken supporters. While not always in agreement on every political point, they had tremendous respect for one another. It spoke volumes of their friendship that Ms. Taylor not only allowed Flynn to call her by her childhood name but took comfort in it.

"Damn Sky it's been too long." Flynn kissed her on the cheek, and they exchanged a hug. He motioned toward a pair of couches in the center of the room, and said, "Please have a seat." She did, and he asked, "Can I get you anything to drink?"

"Whatever you're having would be perfect."

The President retreated to a silver tray beside his desk and poured from a crystal decanter. He returned and held the amber-orange liquid out for Ms. Taylor. "Kentucky's finest."

The two clicked their glasses together and enjoyed a sip. "Very nice," Ms. Taylor said with an appreciative smile.

"Pappy Van Winkle Family Reserve, I requested it for you."

"Always the gentleman."

The President glanced at his drink, took a long pull and fastened his attention on Ms. Taylor. A firm jaw replaced his easy smile. "So I hear you've been looking for background on Joe Blackstone."

Ms. Taylor experienced the unfamiliar sensation of having been caught off guard. She could list a half dozen reasons why the President would summon her, but Joe Blackstone was not one of them. In typical fashion, she recovered in a flash and said, "I had no idea you were a fan of my team, I assumed your loyalties lay here in Washington or in your home state of Texas."

The Presidents mouth set in a hard line, emphasizing the serious nature of his question.

Ms. Taylor sighed. "Ah ... well, I don't see how it would be worthy of your attention, but yes, given recent events, I've put some feelers out."

"Yeah, I've heard." Flynn knew Sky had the resources and will to uncover anomalies in Joe's background. When she did, she'd double her effort, which would shed lite where it wasn't needed nor wanted. "I asked you here, so I share some information with you. But what you're about to hear cannot leave this office. There's no room for interpretation, under no circumstances can you repeat any of this"

Ms. Taylor's expression mirrored the President when she replied, "Of course, you have my word."

"Back when I was a DA, some people I was trying to put in jail kidnapped my little girl." Surprise shined in Ms. Taylor's eyes. "I was fortunate to have a connection with a unique and discreet organization. Their first objective is information gathering and tracking. They don't operate within the boundaries of the constitution. But if you're trying to track or locate someone, they're more effective than the CIA."

"And you're offering to put me in touch with these people to find information on Blackstone?" Asked Ms. Taylor.

The President shook his head no. "Their second directive is action oriented. They did more than find my daughter, they brought her back. Their efficiency matches or exceeds the most elite combat teams within the U.S. military." Seeing the confusion on Sky's face, he explained, "When these people take action, they do so without the burden of the law, they don't collect evidence, and they don't make arrests. They're a different breed, the kind you wouldn't want to cross. The man they sent to get my little girl is the most lethal operator in the history of this organization. He saved her life, and I'm eternally grateful." Flynn paused and considered his next words carefully. "He also visited every single man who was involved in Lindsey's abduction, for which, I'm grateful."

"I understand."

"I hope you do," said Flynn. "A few years back a consortium of Italian, Russian, and South American crime families posted a fifty-million-dollar bounty on his head. They didn't know his identity, only his call sign, Reaper."

"That's a lot of money, what happened?"

"Officially nothing, I spoke to my contact there, and he told me his organization didn't do anything."

Ms. Taylor cocked her head, "Unofficially?"

"A lot of Italian, Russian and South American criminals were assassinated. The survivors didn't want to be next, so they revoked the bounty, and the killing stopped."

Ms. Taylor took a moment to process what she'd heard and asked, "Are you telling me ..." Unable to finish the sentence she stopped and stared at President Flynn.

"Yes, Joe Blackstone is Reaper. He's my friend and based on what I know; the deadliest man on the planet."

"My God." Ms. Taylor gasped, still trying to grasp what the President had said when another realization hit her. "Wait, do you think Blackstone was involved in the thing at the lake?"

The President raised an eyebrow and said, "Sky … when they took my daughter, whom Joe had no personal connection to, he killed thirty-seven people. These idiots kidnapped his girlfriend and his best friend, two people he's known since childhood. There's no doubt in my mind; Reaper took those guys out. It won't surprise me if he's not done."

"What do you mean not done? The Hills are safe, and the men responsible are dead."

"All of them?"

CHAPTER 40

After retrieving his car, Joe spent the night at a hotel near the hospital. First thing in the morning, he went to check on his friends, but Carrie asked him to leave. He went back to his hotel and repeated the process for two days, each time he got the same results. Carrie did not want to talk to him, and she didn't want him around.

Wednesday, when Joe left the hospital, he got in his Charger and started driving. The rumbling engine helped him think as it ate up the asphalt. He'd been wrong about Pergine and reacted badly. He'd blown a second chance at his dream and a regular life. Mostly he thought about Troy and Carrie and the harm his actions had caused them.

Mentally and physically, Troy was in for a long recovery. The injuries to Carrie's hand and face would heal, but Joe wasn't sure her emotional ones would.

Try as he may, Joe couldn't forget the horror in Carrie's eyes when she'd looked at him. She'd seen the other side of him, and he couldn't take it back. What made it worse, was knowing he hadn't even fought to contain it, he let it consume him.

At the hospital, Carrie had avoided eye contact. The one time she had glanced in his direction, it was clear she was repulsed by his presence. It was an image Joe would never forget.

Another concern arose before Joe like a mountain on the horizon. For the first time in his life, he had surrendered to his rage. He didn't try to harness it; he let it flow. The surge of adrenalin was like nothing he had ever experienced, and he longed for more. The desire caused Joe to fear two different things with equal and grave concern. What the hell would he get himself into next that would elicit a similar reaction? And, would he ever again be able to suppress his bloodlust?

Time and time again, Joe had gone looking for monsters, and each time he had delivered them to hell. He had no illusions about whom he was or what he had done. But he worried his time with demons had turned him into one.

Embattled by his struggle for self-preservation, Joe was unaware of his destination until he saw the sign for Fairfield. He veered off 95 and glided to a stop at the top of the ramp. There was no traffic in sight, but Joe sat there for a solid minute before cranking the wheel to the right. Less than a mile later he took another right.

The Charger crept up a slight rise and bounced over a speed bump. The middle school sat on a hill to the left and trail on the right led to the old little league field. Both flooded Joe with memories of a simpler time. When he crested the hill, he couldn't help but smile. Eight trucks and a pair of cars lined the right side of the road. Fathers were gathered in a group, discussing their sons, the team, and next week's opponent. Below them, Cooper and his assistants were leading the Bulldogs through practice.

Heads turned in Joe's direction as he rolled by and pulled over. He killed the ignition and got out. Stretching his legs, Joe walked down the hill and stood beneath a large pine tree at the edge of the field. By doing so, he avoided the spectators and the questions they were sure to ask. For the next hour, Joe lost himself watching many of the same drills he'd done, while playing for the same coach, on the same field. He took note of AJ's progress, true to Cooper's word's the kid was a player and had made great strides.

When practice ended, the boys headed in Joe's direction. AJ was the first to greet him. "Hey Joe, whatta you doin' here? I've been keeping tabs on you; you were tearing it up. How come you missed the game Sunday?"

Joe hid the sting of AJ's words and forced a smile. "I've been keeping tabs on you guys too, 2-0 with a big win at Bangor last Friday night, impressive keep it up."

The kids gathered around the famous alum. Having become acquainted with many of them over the summer, Joe and the boys talked easily about Maine High School Football and life in the WFL. After dodging a few questions about his suspension, Joe promised he'd try and catch tomorrow's practice and suggested they hit the showers. Cooper's staff had been hanging back and joined him when the kids cleared the field. He recognized most of the faces, and they all knew him.

The assistant coaches took a moment to catch up with Joe before excusing themselves. Once they were alone, Cooper asked, "How are Carrie and Troy?"

Joe dropped his head. "I wish I knew coach … I wish I knew."

"You haven't been able to see them?"

"I tried, but Carrie doesn't wanna see me."

Sensing there was a whole lot more to the story Cooper said, "Listen … let me get changed up, then how about you and I head back to my house for some dinner?"

"No thank you, coach, I don't wanna impose, I should get going anyway."

"Nonsense, Mary would love to see you, join us for dinner then you can go."

Joe relented and said, "Okay, thanks."

Cooper called his wife on the way home and gave her a heads-up. He and Mary kept the topics of conversation lite over dinner, but Joe hardly said a word. When they were through eating, Cooper stood and said, "Come on Joe, it's a nice night, let's have a seat on the porch."

Joe pushed his chair away from the table and said, "Dinner was great Mrs. Cooper, thank you."

"You're welcome," Mary said. "You know our door's always open."

Outside, a cool breeze rustled trees, and street lamps cast a yellow hue over the neighborhood. They enjoyed the quiet for a while before Cooper asked, "What happened Joe?"

It took a moment for Joe to speak, when he did his voice was detached and clinical. He told Cooper about the murder at his house, the Hills kidnapping, his initial suspicions concerning Pergine and their altercation.

When Joe finished Cooper said, "The media's been all over this. Did you know they released the names of the guys suspected of taking Carrie and Troy? They're the same guys who were killed at the lake in New York. No one seems to have a clue what went down there, but you know what's strange?" Cooper looked at Joe but didn't wait for his response, "I got a call from Chief Owad before practice, and he recognized two of those names." Joe turned to face him, but the eyes he saw were those of a stranger. The man he knew was gone, and the predator on his porch confirmed what he had suspected. Cooper looked away, but he still sensed Joe's stare.

Joe stood and said, "I should leave."His voice clipped and filled with a dark edge.

Cooper grabbed his arm. "No, stay ... please."

Joe glared at his coach's hand.

"It was you," Cooper said and released his arm. "At the lake."

Joe's conscience won out, he lowered himself back into the chair and confirmed Cooper's suspicion. "Yes."

"How? I don't understand," asked Cooper. But as soon as the words left his mouth, he realized he did.

"It's what I do," Joe admitted, his jaw clenched, and nostrils flared. "I hunt bad people who do bad things. Ever wonder if monsters have nightmares?" Joe looked Cooper dead in the eye. "I can assure you ... they do when they think of me."

The hairs bristled on the back of Cooper's neck. He didn't know what to say, but it didn't matter. Something within Joe had broken open, and he kept talking. Cooper listened for hours while Joe shared the burden of his past, each revelation, a much-needed cleansing of his soul. He spared Cooper the details, but Joe was as honest with the man as he had ever been with himself.

By the time Joe finished it was late, so Cooper insisted he stay the night. Joe slept in and went for a run. Later, he caught practice and joined the team afterward for their traditional Thursday night dinner. Watching him interact with the kids, Cooper marveled at his ability to bury the things he had seen and mask what he had done.

Friday night, Lawrence played host to the Mt. Blue Cougars. The crowd arrived early. Cars stretched a half mile down Savage Street and clogged every cross street within two blocks of Keyes Field. Reminiscent of another era, a constant flow of fans passed through all three gates in anticipation of a classic. To no one's surprise, Cooper's return had elevated Lawrence from the bottom of the division. Encouraged by the improvement, the entire community was anxious to see how their boys measured up against the defending state champs.

As was his ritual, Joe walked the field hours before kickoff, except this time he wasn't alone. AJ strode beside him, seemingly without a care in the world. Joe had watched video of the team's first two games and AJ's performance at QB had been impressive. But Joe wasn't surprised, he had seen the talent during their workouts. What was surprising, was the kid's physicality on defense. Lacking depth, Cooper had been forced to use his star player on both sides of the ball and AJ had delivered. After two games, the kid with the goofy grin was leading the conference in tackles and forced fumbles.

They were tossing a football when AJ asked, "Are you going back to the WFL?"

Joe had avoided asking himself the same question. "I'm not sure AJ, I don't even know if it's an option."

"I hope you do because I can't wait to see you kick Deavers' ass."

"Who the hell is that?"

AJ scrunched his face. "You don't watch much TV do you?" Joe shook his head no. "Lucius Deavers is a rookie defensive end for Dallas, and he's been all over the news. He dismantled Philadelphia last week. The guy's been running his mouth about kicking your ass."

Joe grinned and said, "If he's such a bad ass I'm surprised none of my teammates were talking about him last week."

"He's a rookie. The guy was in all kinds of trouble in college. Got expelled from school and had to sit out a year before he was eligible for the draft. Dallas took him with their first pick last spring, but he held, just signed his contract last week." Curious why Joe was unbothered, AJ asked, "Doesn't it piss you off? A guy talking smack like that?"

Joe caught a pass from AJ and held the ball. "Someone's always talking smack. All you can do is take care of your own business. Who knows, maybe Deavers and I will bump heads, and we'll see what happens. Either way, I'm not gonna lose any sleep over something the guy says."

Pregame came and went, and both teams returned to their locker rooms. It was there Cooper gathered his team and the young men took a knee. Standing outside their circle, Joe recalled a similar gathering after a less than inspiring week of practice. In an attempt to wake his team, Cooper had delivered a forearm to one of the lockers. The damage had been so severe a school janitor had to cut it open so Joe's teammate could retrieve his belongings after the game.

Since then, the locker room had changed, but the passion in Cooper's words remained the same. "You're playing the defending champs tonight … they have swagger, and they have confidence. What they don't have is respect for you. To them, you're just a team they beat by thirty last year. Well, this ain't last year." Cooper swept his gaze across the room, magically making eye contact with every player in a matter of seconds. "You all know your assignments, no matter what happens, focus on 'em and do your job. If you do, YOU WILL beat these guys. They've scouted us, and they think we're gonna run *blue I 632* on the first play … so on the first play … we're gonna run *blue I 632*," —teeth grit and nostrils flared, Cooper's words were like a shot of adrenaline— "then we're going to line up and run it again."

His players exploded to their feet in a frenzy, even Joe felt the hair stand up on the back of his neck. No one had ever motivated him like Pete Cooper, it was comforting to know he still did it better than anyone.

CHAPTER 41

Carrie stayed at Troy's side while he recovered, avoiding the police and press as much as possible. Her official statement was, she had no recollection of the events which had freed them or how they'd arrived at the hospital. Carrie had been diagnosed with a severe concussion, which gave credence to her fabrication.

When Troy finally regained consciousness, Carrie had been there to offer support and collaborate their stories. In truth, he didn't remember much; he knew it was Joe who'd come for them but couldn't recall the details. When Troy asked Carrie about Joe, all his sister had said was she didn't want him around right now. Groggy and confused, Troy had initially dropped the subject, but by Friday he wanted an explanation.

Having grown tired of Carrie's inability to explain herself, Troy sat up in his hospital bed and asked, "So let me get this straight ... Joe saves our ass from these fuck heads and HE'S the bad guy?"

Carrie hurried to the door and stuck her head in the hall. She closed it and snapped around. "Jesus Troy, keep your voice down."

"Screw that, you need to explain to me what your problem is."

"This was all his fault, they did this to us because of him." Carrie leaned in close to her brother and whispered loudly, "They killed your friend."

Frustrated, Troy tried to take a deep breath, but a jolt from his broken ribs stopped him. He winced and looked at his sister with heated eyes. "Yeah Shelly's dead but so are the pieces of shit who killed her. It doesn't bring her back, but at least those two assholes are gone, thanks to Joe. And don't tell me this was his fault, that's bullshit and you know it. He can't control what some psycho does any more than you can."

Tears shimmered in Carrie's eyes. "You didn't see it, he was ... he was, a monster." Her voice trembled and she said, "The things he did, they were awful, but it was the look on his face, his eyes ... he liked it."

"Come here." Troy reached for his sister's hand and said, "He loves you, Carrie, he loves us both, we're all the family he's got. He'd die before he'd let anything happen to either one of us."

***

King of Prussia, PA

Pergine and Litt were seated in the *library* at Sullivan's Steak House. Dark paneling, books, and wine bottles decorated the restaurant's most requested dining room, but neither man cared. Litt was trying to get Pergine's attention, but he was busy flirting with another patron's wife.

"Damn it, Jeff, are you listening to me?"

Pergine looked at Harvey and narrowed his eyes. "You better watch your tone."

"Tone ... Tone? Fuck my tone." Litt lowered his voice and leaned across the table. "If you want to end up in jail or worse be my guest, but it's not what I signed up for." Litt hefted himself out of his chair.

Pergine slammed his hand on the table and said, "Sit down Harvey." Heads turned in their direction.

Litt sat but retained his resolve. "We're in trouble. You need to take this seriously."

"You've been saying that all week but nothing's happened, we're fine."

"Jeff my sources think it might be one guy who took out Calabrese's crew, one fucking guy. To make matters worse, someone high on the food chain has all but ordered law enforcement to stand down."

"What do you mean?" Pergine asked with genuine interest.

"Someone," Litt said, drawing the word out to emphasize his point, "called off the dogs. The Hills were kidnapped and taken across state lines, the Feds have jurisdiction over this all the way, yet they're pulling their resources. My guy on the ground there says everything their reporting is complete bullshit, all the real investigators are already gone, anyone left is for show."

Pergine took a minute to consider this and shrugged and said, "Who cares, doesn't change anything for us." Vexed, Litt shook his head, but Pergine ignored him. "There's no way one dude did all that. Those grease balls got cleaned by some other crew, it was dumb luck, bad luck for the Calabrese's." Satisfied with his conclusions, Pergine cut into his steak.

The lady Pergine had been flirting with got up from her table. A black dress clung to her hourglass figure. She glanced at Pergine and drew her bottom lip between her teeth as she glided by. Litt wanted to argue his point, but the look on his clients face confirmed it was a lost cause. On cue, Pergine set his silverware down and gave chase.

CHAPTER 42

The lights above Keyes field illuminated pleasant memories from Joe's past, providing a rare and welcome distraction. He enjoyed the game as Lawrence routed Mt. Blue 36-12, the outcome never in question.

Except for AJ, Mt. Blue had better athletes, but it didn't matter. Cooper's team was well prepared and highly motivated. Their near flawless team effort beat the Cougars in every phase of the game.

For as long as Joe could remember a sign hung in the coach's office, it read, *"It's not the size of the dog in the fight, but the size of the fight in the dog."* The slogan personified Pete Cooper and his football teams.

Leaving the field, Joe watched players, parents and loved ones celebrate the win, fondly recalling a similar experience with his dad. So lost in the memory, Joe walked right by her on his way to the locker room.

"I like the helmets," she said.

The familiar voice was unexpected in the current setting and stopped Joe in his tracks. He did a 180, and Sky Marie Taylor's hazel eyes were smiling at him. The billionaire had her hair in a ponytail and was wearing jeans with a Lawrence Football sweatshirt. She couldn't have blended any better with the crowd.

Shocked, and unwilling to believe his eyes, Joe asked, "Ms. Taylor?"

"I heard it was supposed to be a good game," she said and motioned toward the visiting sideline. "I guess Mt. Blue didn't get the message."

"I like your sweatshirt," Joe said, it was all he could come up with.

"Thank you, I was raised a southern girl. I know all about Friday night games under the lights, the cold not so much."

"Give it a few weeks," Joe said, "you'll need a lot more than a sweatshirt."

"I bet." Ms. Taylors face turned serious. "Joseph, can we talk privately for a minute?"

Joe smiled at the use of his full name. "Sure if it's not too cold for you we could take a walk?"

"Lead the way."

Joe led Ms. Taylor through the front gate, across West Street, and up Summit.

When they were clear of the dispersing crowd Ms. Taylor said, "Until recently I didn't know we had a common friend."

"Oh, Who?"

She twisted to see Joe's reaction and said, "President Flynn."

Shadows hardened on Joe's face.

"He speaks highly of you," said Ms. Taylor, "and he shared some information with me."

"Like what?" asked Joe, his tone cooler than the fall air.

"It's okay, I'll never repeat a word, the President was trying to help."

They turned right at the corner and continued in silence. Several blocks later they passed a church and took another right. A little ways up the sidewalk, Joe stopped. He pointed at a dilapidated structure and said, "There used to be a basketball hoop on the side of that building, below the spotlight. A bunch of us would come here after school to play; it didn't matter if it was a shitty nine-foot rim nailed to a piece of plywood or that the court was dirt, it was all we had, and it was fun. So, one day there were six of us here, playing. I was twelve, everyone else was a year or two older. Anyway, this car pulls up, and four high school kids get out. None of us recognized them, but they grab my friend, Teddy Gant. Teddy had it rough, no dad, his mom was a drunk, a little slow but a good kid. These guys beat him into a coma, and the rest of us stood there and did nothing. I found out afterward, they thought he stole some weed from them. He hadn't though, his older brother had. None the less, Teddy spent four weeks in the hospital, but he was never the same afterward. He died when we were in high school, got hammered and wrapped his brother's car around a telephone pole." Joe looked at Ms. Taylor and his voice filled with shame. "I've done a lot of bad things, but not helping Teddy was the worst, I swore I'd never let it happen again."

"Joseph, you needn't explain yourself to me. I'm many things, but blind isn't one of them, I can see the good in you." Joe averted his gaze, and she said, "Please … humor an old woman and look at me." Joe turned and met her motherly pose. "You're a good man, I know you've done unpleasant things, but if history has taught us anything, it's that even the purest of souls must rise up and defeat evil from time to time. Now … if I may be so bold, you've done your share … let others bear the cross."

"My parents would have liked you," Joe said, his voice cracking.

Ms. Taylor gave him a warm smile. "I wish I could have met them."

They started walking again and rounded the corner onto West Street, the school was visible in the distance. "What are my options?" Joe asked.

"I know people look at me as a hard ass bitch, and most of the time they're probably right. But I came here to tell you, you have my support with whatever you want to do. If you want to play football, great, we want you back. If you want to walk away, fine, tell me what I can do to help, and it's done. No string attached."

"Why are you doing this?"

"Because you deserve it and I can." She placed her hand on Joe's arm, and he stopped. "Also, because the President told me what you did to the monsters who took his little girl."

The President knew bits and pieces but not the details. Joe wondered how she'd feel if she knew the terror he'd inflicted on those men. "Thank you," he said in a half-whisper. The lights on Keyes field went out behind him. Joe swung around and stared into the void. "When I played here, people from all over the state came to watch, ten, twelve-thousand people at every game. I could do whatever I wanted, and I knew I had something special in me. I was still a kid, but I was in control. Everything was so simple and pure, then one day it was gone. Despite everything, I still love the game. To me, it's still simple and pure, but I'm not a kid anymore; or the same person. I'm … different, the things I've done, they change you. What if I can't leave that person behind … what if it's who I am now?"

Ms. Taylor took Joe's hand and said, "We're all changing all the time. We never stay the same. The person you are right now will grow, and he'll change. How … will depend on the path, you chose from this point forward. I can't pretend to understand your past but I know this, you have a lot of people who want to be part of your future, whatever it holds."

CHAPTER 43

Saturday, Mealey met with his two coordinators to discuss their upcoming game with Oakland. Pergine was cleared to play, but they were concerned with the hole left by Blackstone's absence. Mealey was ready to end the unproductive meeting when someone knocked. "Come in," he hollered through the door.

Ms. Taylor walked in but left the door ajar. "I hope I'm not disturbing you, gentlemen?" she asked.

All three coaches stood, and Mealey said, "No of course not, to what do we owe the pleasure?"

"Please sit," — the owner motioned toward their chairs — "I brought someone with me who'd like to speak with you."

Blackstone filled the doorway and approached the coaches. He turned at Lafond first and said, "Coach I'm sorry about what happened, I was outta line, and it won't happen again." He looked back and forth between Pickell and Mealey. "I wanna apologize to all of you, and if it's alright, to the team also."

"I appreciate it, Joe, apology accepted," said Lafond. "I heard what happened and I hope your friends are doing okay."

Joe gave Lafond a grateful nod and said, "Thanks, coach."

"Yes Joe, apology accepted, damn glad to see you, we were all worried," Mealey added.

Joe looked in Pickell's direction, and the coach said, "What? You think I care about one of my guys beating the shit outta some pretty boy quarterback? Still, maybe you can do it to someone on a different team next time, you think you can handle that?"

The corners of Joe's mouth turned up. "Yeah … I think so."

***

The first thing Joe did when he walked in the locker room, was look for Pergine. He found him in the trainer's room getting his ankle taped. Joe saw Pergine's surprise from across the room.

When he got to the table, Joe tapped the trainer on the shoulder and said, "Can you give us a second?"

The trainer looked up with concern. Pergine signaled it was okay and the man retreated to the other side of the room.

"I apologize for what happened. I thought you were mixed up in the shit that went down with my friends. But it's no excuse for the way I acted. I was outta line, and I'm sorry?" Joe held his hand out.

Pergine blinked a couple times, shook Joe's hand and said, "No man I get it, it's cool."

After an awkward silence, Joe said, "Thanks, Jeff, I appreciate your understanding."

Joe headed back the way he'd come and Pergine called out, "Hey, why'd those guys take your girl?"

Joe stopped. It wasn't the question, which caused alarms to go off, but the way Pergine asked it.

"You can't turn the news on without hearing about this," Pergine said. "I'm curious if you know why it happened?"

Joe ignored what he saw on Pergine's face. "No," he said. "No idea."

Lots of sick people in this world, I'm glad everything worked out."

"Yeah me too." Trying not to repeat his mistakes, Joe brushed his concern aside and left without another word.
***

Later, at the team hotel, Joe was waiting for the elevator when his phone buzzed. He saw Carrie's name and angled toward the lobby. "Hello?" His chest tightened.

"Hi, Joe."

"How are you?" Joe asked as he walked outside. "How's Troy."

"We're good, Troy's doing much better. We're both going to be okay."

Tension drained from Joe's body. "I can't tell you how glad I am to hear that."

"I'm sorry I didn't call sooner," Carrie said, her voice low and uncertain. "I'm … I'm not sure what else to say, I just wanted you to know we're okay."

"You don't need to say anything. I love you both, you're okay, and nothing else matters."

"They're gonna let Troy out in a few days. I'm going back to Maine with him for a while."

"Why don't you bring him here? We don't have to go back to the Country Club. I'll get a new place, and Troy can stay until he gets sick of us."

There was a long pause before Carrie said, "I need some time Joe, you saved us, and I'll never be able to repay you for it, but … I'm not sure where we go from here, I have to go, bye Joe."

"Carrie wait —" Joe said, but it was too late, she was gone.

CHAPTER 44

Philadelphia rolled over Oakland 38-14. The win ignited a ten-game win streak, which brought their record to 11-1. Only their next opponent, divisional rival Dallas, had a better record at 12-0.

The Freedom air attack, featuring Pergine, Blackstone, Wilmot and Matthieu's out of the backfield, topped the league in every major passing category. Pickell's defensive unit was much improved but relied heavily on Blackstone, who was fifth in the league in sacks. Although not as dominant as he had been in the opener, Blackstone was having a solid season. Philadelphia's success hinged on his performance. Conversely, Dallas featured a balanced offensive, led by a future hall of fame quarterback Hayes Nolte. But the strength of their team was a defense many experts touted as the best of all time. Flush with all-pros and led by rookie sensation Lucius Deavers, Dallas' defense had been near impenetrable. Deavers, the league leader in sacks, had knocked six opposing QB's out of the game and mauled the shorthanded Philadelphia offense in week two.

Of all the possible headlines, which could be written about the rematch, none were more prominent than Deavers versus Blackstone. Not only were they the league's top two rookies, but they were also candidates to win the MVP award. Even though Blackstone's play lacked the passion he displayed the first week of the season, he was still the league's only true two-way player in fifty years.

Deavers had established himself as the WFL's most physical player. At 6' 7", 315 pounds he was one of the biggest men ever to play linebacker. Dallas deployed their most devastating weapon in a multitude of ways. Deavers was often used to pressure the quarterback but was equally effective as a run stopper or cover man. With the quickness, size and speed to cover running backs, tight ends and wide receivers there was nothing he couldn't do on defense. The addition of a world-class mouth to his freakish talent made Deavers the most talked about player in the game.

Thursday, Dwayne was on his way to the morning meeting when Joe arrived. He grabbed Joe in the hallway as they crossed paths and asked, "Hey man where you been?"

Joe looked at Dwayne with bloodshot eyes and said, "Late night, I went out with a couple of the guys, and we ended up at Del Frisco's. After the bar closed, Richie the GM, took us to an after-hours club."

Shortly after rejoining the team, Joe had moved out of Blue Bell and into a Center City loft. As the wins and his personal stats had piled up, so had his need to indulge in the spoils of fame and the Novocain it provided.

Dwayne's disapproval was etched to his face. "You've been late for every one of our workouts for the past month, now you're blowing them off? Not to mention we've got Dallas this week and you roll in late for the team meeting because you're hung over. What the hell's the matter with you?"

"Relax mother, you're already the best wide receiver in the league, and they're never gonna play me at quarterback anyway so who gives a shit about our workouts?" Joe stepped by and headed to the locker room.

Dwayne twisted around and watched Joe walk off. After a minute, he continued on his way and wondered, *what the hell happened to you, Joe?*

During practice, Joe had already dropped two catchable balls and gone, when he dropped a third, Pergine hollered, "Let's go, Blackstone, sharpen this shit up."

"Fuck you, pretty boy." Joe snapped back.

The two locked eyes as Joe trudged back to the huddle. The tension between them, while always present, was at its highest since their week 2 altercation. On-field success had done nothing to mend the fracture between Philadelphia's two most important players. That Philly's offense had flourished, in spite of this divide, spoke volumes of the job Lafond had done.

After practice and meetings were done for the day, Joe was the first player to leave the facility. Ms. Taylor watched from her office. When the Charger disappeared down the street, she turned from the window and returned to her desk, her face tight with concern.

***

A door slammed and woke Joe from his slumber. He was in a hotel, after a moment it dawned on him, He was in Dallas, and it was game day. He stared at the alarm clock and struggled to bring into focus. When he did, Joe saw he had less than forty minutes to shower and grab something to eat. Tired from a string of late nights, he'd overslept. He contemplated skipping breakfast but decided against it and hauled himself out of bed.

Downstairs, Joe fixed himself a plate of food and a cup of coffee. He spotted Dwayne on the left side of the dining room and headed over.

Dwayne stood and greeted Joe with a cold shoulder.

"Where're you going?" Joe asked.

"Meeting," Dwayne replied as he brushed past.

Joe set his plate on the table. "Hey Dwayne," he said as his roommate walked away, "thanks for waking me up."

Without looking back, Dwayne hollered, "I'm not your fucking mother."

"Dick," Joe mumbled and planted himself in a chair at the empty table.

"I see you're still making friends?" Pickell said from two tables away.

Joe looked. "Whatever."

Pickell gathered the notes he'd been reviewing, grabbed his coffee and joined Joe. He waited silently for the other players to leave while Joe ate. When those nearest them had, Pickell sat his cup on the table and asked, "What the fuck is your problem Blackstone?" Joe ignored the remark and continued eating. "What the hell happened to you? You've got all the talent in the world, but your attitude is for shit lately. In this league, that's not unusual, but you weren't like that. I thought you might be one of the greats, but it looks like I was wrong."

Finished eating, Joe set his fork down, wiped his mouth and said, "I had no idea I was such a disappointment, maybe I should stick to offense then." Sarcasm laced his words.

"Yeah maybe, but why stop there? Why not skip the fucking game and stick to partying all week with your practice squad pals."

"Fuck this, I don't need to listen to your shit." Joe reared up and knocked his chair over.

Pickell sprang from his chair and was in Joe's face in an instant. Everyone left in the room looked in their direction. "You can run away or do whatever the fuck you want," —his tone walked the line between bitterness and disbelief— "but you are going to hear what I've got to say. Your attitude sucks, your preparation sucks and your effort sucks. Sure, we've been winning, but not because of you, because other guys on this team are putting in the time and getting the job done. But not you, you're cheating yourself, and you're cheating this team. The guy who was in camp, the guy I first met, he'd be leading the league in sacks, I don't even recognize you. I'll tell you this, though; you better be ready today because Deavers is the real fucking deal and unlike you, he gets better every week."

"Nice speech old man." Joe sidestepped Pickell and walked off with disinterest plastered across his face.

Philly received the kickoff and returned it to the 21-yard line. On first down, they ran a wheel route to Matthieu, who gained four. A pass to Wilmot fell incomplete on 2nd down.

On 3rd and 6, Deavers lined up on Joe's outside shoulder, four yards from the line of scrimmage. The Dallas linebacker shot forward on the snap and bludgeoned Joe with a forearm to his chest. Failing to anticipate the big man's quickness, Joe was caught off guard. The blow knocked the air from Joe's lungs and took him off his feet. He landed hard on his back, and his head bounced off the turf.

With his primary receiver knocked on his ass, Pergine scrambled to his right in search of a target. He spotted Wilmot streaking across the middle of the field and fired the ball back across his body. Dallas cornerback, *Showtime* Lloyd, intercepted the ill-advised pass and raced down the sideline untouched for six points.

Joe fought for air as he crawled to a knee. A shadow fell over him, and he looked up. Deavers was looking down at him, a wide grin exposed a row of gold teeth.

266

Deavers wagged a figure at Joe and said, "Your ass is mine son, you might as well stay down, cause you gonna be there all day muthafucka." He turned and bounced in celebration all the way to his sideline.

Joe hauled himself up and hobbled over to his.

Raucous fans rocked the cavernous stadium. Dallas had landed a crippling physiological blow on the first series, and the home crowd knew it. Philadelphia was stunned, not by the sudden deficit, but by the sight of their fallen hero. Deavers had manhandled Blackstone and set the tone of the game.

Trailing by 7, Philadelphia took the field again with the ball on their own 19. Deavers lined up on the ball, in the gap between Freedom right tackle Jim Schank and Blackstone. Deavers alignment was exactly what Lafond had hoped for when he had called the play. With a combined weight of 600 pounds, his two best run-blockers could double team, Deavers. Success running the ball at Dallas' best player would slow Deavers down and help Philly establish momentum of their own. Unfortunately for Lafond and his offense, things didn't go as planned. Schank's lack of quickness and Blackstone's lackadaisical effort were no match for the Dallas linebacker. Deavers slipped between the two would be blockers and dropped Matthieu for a four yard loss.

Deavers and his teammates dominated the rest of the first half and took a 21-0 lead into the break. The score would have been more lopsided, if not for two Dallas fumbles deep in Freedom territory.

Joe spent half time with the offense, listening to Lafond and his assistant's scheme up ways to move the ball. But the coaches' words were lost on him. While Lafond dissected defensive fronts on a white board, Joe thought of nothing but his fatigue. His ribs were sore, his arms and legs heavy; and for the first time in his life, he didn't want to play football. The thoughts swam in his head until he was drowning in shame.

On their way out for the half, Pickell met Joe in the tunnel and said, "If you're ever gonna get your head out of your ass now would be a good time."

"Don't start coach," Joe replied with a trace of weariness.

"Seriously Blackstone, Deavers is kicking your ass all over the field. At least when you're on defense he isn't there to dominate you, you should think about making a play. Forget about a sack; a tackle or even a QB pressure would be fantastic at this point."

Joe stopped, wheeled around, and held a finger in front of Pickell. "Get the fuck outta my face."

Pickell swiped Joe's hand aside. "Fucking waste," he said. "You stick to offense and stay the hell away from me." He pushed by and marched out of the tunnel

The Freedom defense took the field to start the second half without Blackstone. They gave up a long drive but held Dallas to a field goal. Down 24-0 Philly was back on offense at their own 21.

Pickell's words had stung, but the look Dwayne gave Joe in the huddle was a far greater blow. The shame and self-guilt it generated ignited a spark within Joe. He cast aside his self-pity, resolved to get back in the fight.

Philly came out with three receivers to the left and Joe as the lone target on the right. Deavers was lined up over Joe, in a good position to jam him, if he released on a pass. And that's exactly what the big man tried to do when Joe came off the ball, but Joe eluded Deavers and ran free into the secondary.

Pergine caught the snap and looked to his left, but no one was open. He twisted to his right to dodge a defender and saw Blackstone a step behind Deavers. Pergine fired the ball down the seam, and Blackstone caught it in stride.

Using reserves he had seldom needed, Joe outran the entire Dallas defense for a touchdown. The Freedom sideline came to life while Joe loitered in the end zone to catch his breath.

Mealey turned to Lafond and said, "Nice call, hopefully, it lights a fire under our ass."

"I'd be happy if it ignites one under Blackstone," Lafond replied.

Pickell's defense kept Dallas off the board for the rest of the 3rd quarter. Rejuvenated by Joe's catch, the offense started living up to its reputation. Rookie receiver Ryan Barrett took a short pass forty-six yards for another score. Trailing by ten, with a 3rd and 7 on the Dallas 14-yard, Philadelphia was back in the game when the quarter ended.

In the first half, Deavers had dominated the matchup between the, two top rookies, but Joe had held his own to start the second half. All of a sudden, the one-sided battle was living up to the hype. With Philadelphia on the verge of another score, the game had become a direct reflection of the private battle between the two stars.

Philly broke the huddle to start the 4th quarter, and Joe lined up on the left. Deavers was on the opposite side, aligned over Barrett in the slot. Joe read the coverage and assumed Dallas was playing man to man. He knew the linebacker covering him was not fast enough and the strong safety was shaded to the outside and in no position to help double him. A clean release off the line would leave him open in the middle of the field for an easy touchdown. Had Joe been paying attention in meetings that week, he would have recognized Dallas was in a zone coverage disguised as man to man.

Pergine had been paying attention, and he'd watched plenty of film. He knew exactly how the defense would react when the ball was snapped. "Blue laser — Blue laser — Hut,HUT," he barked. Pergine caught the snap and immediately locked on to his tight end. As he'd anticipated, the big man came off the ball untouched. Pergine reared back and lofted a beautiful spiral when Blackstone broke to the middle of the field.

The pass was a bit overthrown, but Joe's powerful strides ate up the turf. Right before it sailed over his head, Joe vaulted off the ground with his arms stretched skyward.

Unable to contain himself, Pergine broke into a broad smile as Blackstone clutched the ball high in the air. It was a tremendous catch, in fact, it was exactly what Pergine had imagined before he overthrew the ball.

As Joe dropped from the sky, so did his focal point. He saw a golden flash from Deavers' teeth a split second before the collision. Pain exploded from his jaw and chest, and a second impact propelled him into darkness.

Flags flew, and the ball bounced in the air. Dallas' free safety dove and gathered it in before it hit the ground, Barrett tagged him down, but not even the hostile fans seemed to care. The crowd stood, and murmur rolled through the stadium as medical personnel rushed the field. Joe lay motionless as a group of EMT's, doctors and trainers gathered around.

CHAPTER 45

Everywhere Joe looked he found himself surrounded.
Each face was gruesome and familiar, they belonged to dead
men. They stood over him; calling to him; reaching for him.
Joe went for his gun, but it wasn't there. He tried to stand, but
his body failed him. A headless figure, Junior Calabrese,
lunged at him with a knife. Joe's feeble efforts to protect
himself were of no use. The knife sunk deep into his chest and
his vision turned crimson. He stopped struggling, fell still and
waited for death to come.
***

Horrified, Carrie stood in the middle of her living room,
staring at the TV. Troy was there also, behind her on the edge
of his seat. She watched the replay in slow motion and clasped
a hand over her mouth, muffling a sob. When a commercial
interrupted her nightmare, Carrie looked at her brother with
wet eyes and said, "Troy this is my fault."

Trying his best to project a reassuring tone, Troy said,
"Carrie … calm down, it's going to be okay."

Carrie shook her head. "No, no, no you said it yourself,
he hasn't looked the same. I shouldn't have acted the way I
did; this is my fault."

Troy stood and hugged his sister. "This is Joe, he'll be
alright."

Coverage of the game resumed, and Carrie and Troy turned to the broadcast. A camera was focused on the crowd around Joe. Carrie thought she saw Joe move. Relief flooded through her momentarily until she saw what was going on. Another camera filled the screen with Joe's face, it was knotted in anguish, and his eyes were wide with fear. He was struggling, trying to get away from the men gathered around him. Joe was saying something, but the only sound she could hear was the concerned voices of the men announcing the game. A spasm rocked Joe's body, and he roared with pain. Carrie jumped back and shrieked. "My God."

The disturbing image changed and showed players from both teams kneeling on the perimeter. Carrie was focused on one particular player when a faceless voice said, "Our thoughts and prayers are with Joe Blackstone. Injuries are part of the game, but in all my years I've never seen a more vicious hit."

Carrie hurried to the kitchen and grabbed her keys from the counter.

"Where are you going?" asked Troy.

She stopped by the door to put a jacket on and looked at her brother. "Dallas." Carrie tore out of the house before Troy could respond.

Alone in his sister's living room, Troy listened to her car pull away and said, "About time."

CHAPTER 46

Confused, Joe woke in a dark room. He tilted his head to survey the surroundings, throbbing pain in his skull rewarded the effort. Realizing he was in a hospital, Joe eased back into the pillow. Sorting through a cluster of hazy memories, he recalled Pickell yelling at him at half time. The recollection filled him with shame. Joe was thankful Carrie had not been there to witness his poor performance. He had dreamt about her; she'd held his hand in hers as they talked. He couldn't remember what they talked about, only the happiness it brought him. The partial memory and her absence, hurt more than his head.

Joe heard footsteps in the hall. Risking the pain, he turned toward to the door. A silhouette appeared in the opening, but the bright lights outside his room forced Joe to shield his eyes.

"Oh good you're awake, how do you feel?"

Joe's heart skipped a beat. "Carrie? What … how … I don't understand, when did you get here? Where is here?"

"You're still in Dallas. I got here last night," Carrie said. She set a cup of coffee on a small table, sat on the edge of his bed, and rested her hand on his arm. "We talked most of the night, but I'm not surprised you don't remember, you were pretty messed up."

Joe squeezed his eyes shut, opened them, and focused on Carrie again. "I thought I was dreaming, am I dreaming now?"

Carrie leaned in close and whispered, "No baby, you're not dreaming."

He pulled her close, the simple task sent a fresh jolt of pain through his body. It was a happy trade-off for Carrie's full lips and the tenderness with which she kissed him. When she eased back, her emerald eyes warmed his heart.

"Do you remember what happened?" she asked.

"No, but if I'd known it would get you to come see me, I'd have done it sooner."

Despite a measure of guilt, Joe's smile made her laugh. "You're not right," said Carrie, chuckling.

"Clearly not," Joe replied, still smiling despite his physical discomfort.

"You got hurt in the game."

"I did?"

"Yeah, in case you haven't noticed this isn't the Ritz Carlton."

"Very funny … what happened?"

Carrie's expression turned serious. "It was Deavers," she said. "You went up for a pass, it was high, and he hit you right in the head when you were stretched out for the ball. It was a cheap shot, Joe, everybody says so. The league fined him and gave him a two-game suspension; it's bullshit they should've kicked him out forever."

Unable to remember what happened and unsure how to respond, Joe changed the subject. "What time did you get here?"

"I got in around midnight, we talked for a long time before you fell asleep. Do you remember anything?"

Joe's forehead creased, and he said, "I don't know, maybe. I thought I'd dreamt you were here, but I don't remember what we talked about. How'd you get here so fast?"

The answer to his question arrived, Sky Marie Taylor strode into the room and said, "Good you're up. It's nice of you to join us sleeping beauty. I hope you're a bit more coherent this morning?"

Joe looked back and forth between the two women and wondered if his eyes were playing tricks on him. Finally, he asked, "How on earth did you two hook up and why on earth is it so dark in here?"

Ms. Taylor answered, "The doctor wants your room to remain dark until he's had a chance to examine you. And why are you surprised the two of us would find a way to contact one another?"

"Nothing, either of you, do would ever surprise me." Joe's expression conceded the point as much as his words.

"I contacted some people I knew at the studio and asked if they could get me Ms. Taylor's number, which they did. When I called her to check on you, she insisted on chartering a jet and flew me here.

Joe looked toward Ms. Taylor and said, "Thank you."

"Nonsense Joseph, we take care of our family, this was the least I could do."

Joe's eyes conveyed his appreciation.

"Did you tell him?" Ms. Taylor asked.

"No, not yet."

The sudden change of tone in both womens' voices twisted Joe's face with worry. "Tell me what?"

Carrie's voice conveyed her unease. "Junior Calabrese said something when Troy and I were in the Cabin. At the time, I was half unconscious and didn't understand what it meant. He was talking about how someone had called him about you and said something like, '*the Jew was paying us*". I had no idea what it meant, I must've blocked it out."

Joe's jaw tightened, and his pulse began to race.

"I was watching the game when you got hurt," Carrie said. "All these doctors and trainers crowded around you, but the players kept their distance. They stayed back, far enough, so they weren't in the way. At one point, the camera panned past the guy's kneeling on the perimeter, and I saw Jeff Pergine. His hand was on his mouth like he was upset, but his eyes … they were … it was as if he were smiling. I think his hand was on his mouth to cover a smile. I know it sounds crazy, but what if Calabrese was referring to Harvey Litt when he said, *Jew*?"

Joe's expression conveyed his thoughts on the matter. "It's not crazy." He sat up and threw his feet over the side of the bed.

Carrie took hold of him, and panic rattled her voice. "Whatta you doin'?"

Joe tried to stand but lost his balance and fell back on the mattress.

Ms. Taylor stepped in front of him and saw the storm in his eyes. "Joseph, I need you to listen." She waited for him to meet her gaze and said, "I don't know if Jeff had anything to do with what happened to Carrie and Troy, but I don't like what I've heard. I will get to the bottom of this, me Joseph, not you. You need to rest and move on with your life. If you want things to change, you need to change. Have faith in me and let me fight this battle."

Carrie could tell Joe was struggling with Ms. Taylor's request. She put her hand on his and said, "Joe please, I love you, but you scare me, you're scaring me now." His eyes softened. "The man I've known since I was a kid is kind and caring, I love him. The man I saw at the camp is a different person, I understand why he did what he did, Troy and I owe our lives to him, but he scares me. Let him go, stay with me, be with me. You've done enough, you don't need to be him anymore."

CHAPTER 47

Pergine could not stop watching clips of the hit, and Blackstone's ensuing meltdown. Each time he saw the play, it brought the same smile to his face as it had during the game. Dallas had dominated the rest of the way, beating his team 38-14. But Blackstone was done for the year, if not ever; Pergine didn't care about anything else. The spotlight was back on him, as it should be.

Wednesday, Pergine was listening to music at his locker before the morning meeting when his phone rang. He ignored it, but continued attempts by the same caller, prompted him to answer, "What is it, Harvey?"

"Jeff, thank God I got you, we've got a problem," Harvey said in a breathy explosion of words.

Pergine rolled his eyes. "What is it now?"

"The thing with your teammate, I think he knows."

"Hold on." Pergine walked out of the locker room, down the hall, through the lobby, and out into the early sun. He continued until he was far enough from the building so he couldn't be overheard. In a voice bristling with contempt, Pergine said, "Blackstone don't know shit, after what Deavers did to him, I doubt he knows his name."

"Jeff I'm telling you something's up, my guy at your bank say's the feds were in there looking for large withdrawals and transfers."

"He said they were looking at my account specifically?" Jeff asked with a hint of anxiety.

"Well no ... but it's too much of a coincidence."

"Harvey, what the hell is wrong with you? Do you have any idea how many accounts they could've been looking at? Christ, they're probably after some fucking drug dealer. Besides, I gave you cash for Calabrese, so unless you screwed up, they can't touch us. Now do me a favor and drop this shit," Pergine ended the call.

When he got back to his locker, Pollard was waiting for him. "Hey, John, what's up?"

"Not much," Pollard answered. "Ms. Taylor would like to see you if you have a minute." It wasn't so much a question as it was an order.

"Yeah sure John," Pergine said. He jerked a thumb toward his teammates, who were filing out, on their way to the team meeting. "But coach Mealey won't be happy if I'm late."

Pollard brushed the concern aside. "No worries," he said. "Ms. Taylor will smooth everything over with coach."

Pergine shrugged and followed Pollard. *She's gonna ask me to attend another fucking charity event*, he thought and started thinking of a graceful way to decline. When they arrived at the owner's office, Pollard held the door, and Pergine strolled in. More annoyed than surprised to find Mealey seated inside, Pergine flashed his trademark smile and asked, "What's going on?"

Unbeknownst to Pergine, the other people in the room were no longer fooled by his façade. His contemptuous personality had been revealed.

The owner, GM, and coach were all repulsed, but Mealey had the shortest temper and was struggling to keep himself in check.

Seated behind her desk, Ms. Taylor met Pergine's phony smile with one of her own. She motioned to a chair and said, " Thanks for coming up Jeff, have a seat. We don't want to take too much of your time, but we thought it best to discuss this matter privately."

Pergine sat beside Mealey and glanced over his shoulder at a spot where Pollard remained standing. "So what's so important the three of you need to speak with me privately?" he asked with a trace of nervousness.

The room was silent until Ms. Taylor stood and strode to the row of windows behind her desk. She spoke with her back to the room. "My husband was a great man, and he worked his ass off his entire life. While Jonathan was alive, he never enjoyed the kind of on-field success we've had since he passed, but make no mistake, he played a huge part in it. I learned a great deal from him, from both his successes and failures. I've used those lessons as a blueprint on how to run this franchise. He had one rule above all, it was the cornerstone of everything he did in life, and it continues to be the cornerstone of this franchise." Ms. Taylor whirled around and fastened her attention on Pergine. "Do you know what that rule is Jeff?"

"I'm sorry ma'am, I don't."

"I don't expect you would," Ms. Taylor said, her disappointment evident.

"Excuse me?" Pergine asked.

She held his stare and walked back to her desk. "My husband believed, you should surround yourself with good people and give them the tools needed to be successful."

"Hard to argue with that logic," Pergine said and shot Mealey a questioning look, but the coach's scowl offered no answers.

"Yes, it's an excellent way to approach things, and we try and do it here. But it wasn't his number one rule … no." Her smile swelled with disdain, but the gesture was lost on Pergine. "He believed the real path to success was avoiding the pitfalls along the way. Jonathan knew real magic could only happen if you avoided fool's gold. He believed it was every bit as important to keep bad people out, as it was to bring the best in. My husband didn't think one rotten apple would spoil the bunch, he believed it would sink the ship. A bad person with talent can often be a temptation too great to resist. My husband's first rule was to always resist that temptation. And we did until one player came along with too many measurables to resist. John and I made a mistake," — she frowned — "we ignored our most important rule, and brought a rotten apple into our organization."

Blinded by arrogance, Pergine couldn't see the obvious. "Ms. Taylor there's no way you could have known, Blackstone fooled us all."

Unable to contain himself, Mealey exploded from his chair and hollered, "You fucking disgust me."

Pergine jumped to his feet. "What the hell's your problem?" he asked towering over the coach. "You upset because your little experiment failed?"

"Gentleman please," hollered Ms. Taylor, slamming her hand on the desk. The two men stopped. She met Pergine's hateful glare and spoke to him as if he were a child. "Jeff … you're the player I'm referring to. I failed this organization, and I failed my husband's memory by making you a part of this team, I'm ashamed."

"I don't deserve to be spoken to like this, not by some uppity broad," Pergine said, swatting a hand in Mealey's direction, "or a rookie coach who still thinks he's in college."

"You're right Jeff, I agree, we shouldn't be speaking to you like this," Ms. Taylor said and buzzed her secretary. "Jenny, be a dear and send my guest in please."

Pergine deflated when Harvey Litt was escorted into the room by two men. He noted their cheap suits and thought, *feds*.

A bead of sweat trickled on Litt's forehead, and he avoided eye contact as he shuffled in.

"Jeff, you know Harvey, I believe he works for you?"

What the hell is this? Pergine ignored Ms. Taylor and scrambled for an answer.

Ms. Taylor raised her voice. "Jeff" This time, Pergine acknowledged her and she said. "Harvey works for you, correct?"

"No," said Pergine.

Ms. Taylor raised a brow. "No? … I'm confused, I've seen him with you at many public appearances. Are you saying you've never paid Mr. Litt for his services?"

Pergine waved his hands in a jittery manner and said, "No … I mean … wait, hold on a minute. I know Harvey, we're friends. Sometimes I do hire him for public relations stuff, but no, he does not work for me. Harvey works for himself, he has lots of clients."

Ms. Taylor pursed her lips in feigned thought and said. "I see, so Harvey does," — she held her fingers up and made quotation marks — "'*public relations stuff*'."

Regaining some confidence, Pergine said, "Yes, that's right. Now I don't know what the hell game you all are playing, but I'm done listening to this shit." He turned for the door with an air of defiance.

Pollard blocked Pergine's path, pointed to an empty chair and said, "Ms. Taylor isn't done, so you need to sit your ass back down." His stern expression bent Pergine to his will.

Pergine returned to his seat, and everyone else remained standing. Ms. Taylor placed her hands on her desk, leaned forward and said, "I heard some concerning things about you, so John and I did some digging. We learned all about your friend here and his *public relations* work. Once we got ahold of Harvey, it didn't take much convincing to get him to cooperate. We already had a pretty good idea what you two had done, and Harvey was eager to confirm it."

Pergine pointed at Harvey and said, "I don't know what the hell he told you, but he's been acting strange lately. If he's made some kind of a mistake or gotten himself into trouble that's on him, not me."

"Agent Capperella, if you would be so kind." Ms. Taylor held her hand out, and the senior agent gave her a small recording device. She hit play and laid it on her desk.

Pergine's stomach sank as his own words exposed him. When the recording ended, he tore his eyes from the little black box and looked at Ms. Taylor. "He should've never been here, I'm the star, this is my team."

"No." Ms. Taylor set her jaw and said, "This is my team." She turned to the two FBI agents. "Would you please remove this monster from my building."

Pergine and Litt were escorted out. When they got to the lobby, Joe and Carrie were waiting for them. Pergine locked eyes with Joe and, for the first time, saw what lay behind Joe's glacial stare. The color drained from his face, and a chill ran down his spine.

Luckily for Litt, his watery eyes shielded him from the same experience and the nightmares sure to follow.

Ms. Taylor joined Joe and Carrie as the two criminals were taken away. His surprise evident, Joe asked, "How on earth did you pull this off so quickly?"

A cunning smile tugged at Ms. Taylor's lips. "You're not the only one with tricks up their sleeve. I had Harvey's computer hacked and threatened to share what I found on it with Anthony Calabrese. In exchange for my discretion and a reduced sentence, which I helped broker, he became very cooperative.

Joe's expression displayed his approval. "Nicely done Ms. Taylor."

"Thank You," Carrie added.

"No, I owe you both thanks and an apology. I'm so sorry for everything those two put you, though. And I thank you for having the strength to survive it, and for helping to stop them. If there's ever anything I can do to repay you, please don't hesitate to ask."

Joe looked at Carrie and back to Ms. Taylor. "There is one thing."

CHAPTER 48

Without Blackstone, Philadelphia stumbled in the aftermath of Pergine's arrest and lost their remaining games. Finishing 11-5 they still made the playoffs, but there was little optimism in the City of Brotherly Love. One local paper dubbed their postseason appearance *a cruel twist of fate.*

What no one outside the Freedom front office knew, was Joe started working out again the day after Pergine was taken into custody. Unwilling to give up his chance at a normal life, his dream, or the season, Joe had asked for Ms. Taylor's assistance, in finding an isolated place to train. He and Carrie needed time to heal, physically and emotionally. Both knew time alone would be the best way to start.

Ms. Taylor knew the perfect spot, her ranch in Texas. Her jet delivered the couple to her properties private airstrip, and they stayed there for the rest of the regular season.

The property had a large gym and thousands of acres for Joe to train on. The first few workouts had been some of the most painful of Joe's life. His body was weak, and his head throbbed, but he had pushed forward. By the second week, his headaches had faded, and Joe began to feel like himself again. Whether he was training, reading, eating or just relaxing, Carrie was there, every day. Her presence put him at ease and allowed his hostility to fade away. The gentle giant with the quick grin had returned, and it was he, who put Carrie at ease. The fear she'd experienced when she was taken, and her fear of Joe, became a distant memory. Each, the best medicine for the others ailments, Joe and Carrie, healed together.

Before long, Joe was stronger, healthier and happier than he had ever been. When he had called Ms. Taylor to inform her he was ready to go, she sent the team doctor to check on him. The man had marveled at Joe's conditioning and the speed of his recovery. He passed his physical with flying colors and was cleared to play.

For the entirety of their stay, none of the people who worked the ranch had struck a conversation with Joe or Carrie. While polite, and eager to assist any request, the staff had allowed their famous guest a wide berth.

They were preparing to board Ms. Taylor's jet for the flight back to Philadelphia when one of the ranch hands stopped Joe. The tall, lean, middle-aged man, had brown eyes with hard lines from years of working outside. He didn't appear the type to ask for an autograph, but Joe was more than happy to oblige. Instead, he handed Joe a newspaper and said, "Here on this ranch we're all proud Texans, but I want you to know, everyone here will be pulling for you. I'm sure you'll make us proud." He shook Joe's hand, tipped his hat to Carrie and walked off.

An attendant took their bags, and Joe looked at the paper the man had handed him. The front page of the Dallas Star had a picture of Deavers hitting Joe in mid-air with the headline, *Deavers Devastates*. A caption below it read, *Dallas' hard hitting Lucius Deavers has established himself as the best player in pro football.*

Carrie couldn't see what Joe was looking at, but she saw the corners of his mouth twitch into a tight smile. "What is it?" she asked.

"Something I've been waiting for my entire life ... a rival."

CHAPTER 49

Initially, Ms. Taylor, Pollard, and Mealey had informed the team Joe was done for the season. Unlike their boss, the coach and GM believed he was. But they had all agreed it was better to limit expectations than risk a letdown if he couldn't return.

Joe greeted his teammates in the locker room when they arrived for Wednesday's practice. Surprised and happy to see him, they were all anxious to learn how he was doing. When he told them how he felt and he was cleared to play, any doubts they had about their playoff chances disappeared. A quiet confidence charged the entire organization in a way not seen since Philadelphia's last championship.

Invigorated by his return, Joe's teammates were ready to pick up any slack should he be rusty or less than one-hundred percent. But what they saw in practice bolstered their expectations, Joe Blackstone was back, and he looked better than ever.

Pergine's arrest was still dominating national news. Not even the upcoming playoffs had been able to supplant it from the front page of the sports section. As soon as word got out he was going to play, a fresh wave of reporters descended on Ms. Taylor's team. Each one was in search of a new angle to the Pergine story. Having anticipated such, she closed practice to the media and insisted Joe and Carrie move into her guest house until things cooled off.

***

Freedom fans did not know what to expect from Blackstone, but his mere presence gave them hope. Dejected only days before, they poured into South Philadelphia before sunup on game-day. It didn't matter the football gods were garnishing the city with a good old fashion nor'easter, or that their team was a six-point home underdog. The entire region was buzzing, and the home crowd couldn't wait to be part of the excitement.

Unaffected by the gusting winds and a thick blanket of snow, which smothered Arizona's performance, Philadelphia did not disappoint. Dominating from the opening kickoff, they won 42-10. Joe caught nine passes for one-hundred-forty-six yards and 2 TD's, adding four sacks and a forced fumble on defense. Matthieu ran for two scores, and Hopewell capped off a career day with scoring passes to Wilmot and Barrett.

The following week, Philadelphia traveled to the Great Northwest. It was their second trek to Seattle in three weeks, and an opportunity to avenge the 31-13 loss they suffered on the previous trip.

Saturday night, Joe joined the defense, for their final meeting of the week. He normally met with Lafond and the offense the night before a game, but Pickell had requested his presence.

Philly's DC started the meeting with a highlight reel of Seattle's left tackle, Bradley Hendricks. Hendricks was one of the best to ever play the position and a sure-fire first ballot Hall of Famer. He'd only given up one sack the entire season, and it was to Lucius Deavers. On screen, a pancake block against an all-pro linebacker evoked a few quips from Pickell's unit. Next, a graceful pass-block against another highly regarded player garnered their appreciation. Each clip displayed a combination of Hendricks talents and validate his standing among his peers. Joe had watched plenty of film on Seattle, and their stud tackle, but nothing as impressive as these cut outs.

When the video ended Pickell surveyed the room. His gaze settled on Joe and he said, "That ugly bastard is one of the best four or five players in the league. You're better. Kick his ass, and we'll win this fucking game."

The hair stood straight on the back of Joe's neck, and he gave Pickell a slow nod. A fire was rising within him, but it was different, the anger which had fueled him for so long was gone. It reminded him of a different time, an innocent time when his soul was pure, and his heart was full.

Anxious to call Carrie, Joe hurried back to the room when the meeting was over. Dwayne wasn't there yet but would be soon, so he stepped out on the balcony for some privacy. Joe pulled his phone out of his pocket, dialed Carrie and let the cold air wash over him.

She answered on the second ring. "Hey there, I was hoping you'd call."

"You here hoping? Of course, I'd call," Joe said.

"Good, because I miss you."

Joe closed his eyes and held the phone to his ear without saying a word.

"Joe ... are you there? Are you okay?"

"I'm better than okay." Joe took a deep breath of crisp air and said, "I'm happy, you make me happy. You make me feel like … like it's okay; like I might deserve to be happy."

"Oh baby, of course, you deserve to be happy. I love you so much."

They talked for a long while before wishing one another goodnight. Afterward, Joe stayed outside, observing the lights that brightened a starless night.

When Dwayne got back to the room, he spotted Joe outside on the phone and thought, *nope, not even a jacket.* He tried to watch TV on his iPad but kept glancing in Joe's direction. By the time Dwayne finished his second episode on Banshee, he was freezing. He hopped off his bed, plodded across the rug and pulled the door open. "Jesus Blackstone, you trying to freeze to death out there?"

"No," Joe said, his inflection free and easy. "Enjoying the view." He backed away from the railing, crossed the balcony and slipped inside.

Dwayne closed the door and asked, "Yo man, you okay?"

"I'm better than okay, much better."

Joe fell asleep, thinking how much better than okay he was going to be, come game time.
***

Seattle won the toss and elected to receive, after a good return their offense started on their own 36-yard line. A broad frame eclipsed half the stadium as Hendricks approached the line of scrimmage. Standing in the man's shadow, Joe looked up and said, "You're a big motherfucker ain't ya."

Hendricks mouth twisted into a snarl but he said nothing.

Everyone in the WFL knew Seattle liked to run the ball behind their big tackle on the first play. Joe was counting on it. Anticipating the snap, he got a great jump off the ball. He came up under the taller man and shot both his hands into the center of the Hendricks' chest. Joe's hips exploded forward, and all of the future Hall of Famer's 365 pounds left the turf. Joe hurled the giant into the backfield.

Hendricks walloped his own running back, and both players crashed to the turf. The Philly defense mauled Joe. Excitement resonated on the Freedom sideline and a stunned Seattle crowd fell silent. After struggling to his feet, Hendricks walked back to the huddle trying to make sense of what had happened.

On 2nd down, Hendricks stepped to the line less sure of himself than he had been on the previous play. Joe read his puzzled expression and said, "Sorry big man, I'm a huge fan of yours, but today isn't going to be your day."

By game's end, Joe had set a new WFL record, recording 8 sacks. As if that wasn't enough, he tacked on fourteen receptions, for two-hundred-three yards and two touchdowns. When Mealey was asked about Blackstone and his team's performance after their 45-3 win he said, "I've never been around a group of players who came closer to playing a perfect game than these men did today. It all starts with Joe Blackstone. He's our leader, and today he contributed the greatest individual performance I've ever seen. I hope everyone who watched him today appreciated what they saw."

A herd of reporters congregated around Hendricks, at his locker. He sat near motionless with his head down, staring at the floor. And he hadn't said much until Philadelphia reporter Bud Perkins shouted, "Bradley were you one-hundred percent today? Where you playing injured?"

Agitated, Hendricks lifted his head and asked, " Who said that?"

"I did, Bradley." Perkins raised his hand from the back. Anxious to clear the line of fire his fellow reporters fanned out and allowed Perkins to step forward.

Fatigue broke the surface when Hendricks frowned at Perkins and said, "Coming into today, I was as healthy as any player out there." His low voice offered further evidence of exhaustion. "I got my ass kicked, it's that simple. I've been playing this game since I was a kid, and to put it bluntly, I've always believed, I was the baddest mother fucker on the field. Everyone in the league felt the same way at some point, or they would've never made it here. In my case, it never stopped being true, at least not until today." Hendricks' shoulders sagged. "Half the game I had a tight end helping me with pass protection, a fucking tight end. I haven't needed help with a protection scheme since I was a rookie. Not that it did any good, we still couldn't stop the guy. As for the run, you all saw what happened on the first play. I'm pissed we lost, and I wish I could have done more, but I'm not embarrassed. I played the best I could. Usually, that's good enough to kick ass out there, but today Blackstone was at a different level."

***

Lucius Deavers watched the Hendricks interview from his living room. Still, unbeaten, Deavers' team had thrashed their opponent the day before. Now they would host Philadelphia, with a trip to the WFL Championship on the line.

The broadcast jumped from Seattle to New York, and studio experts dissected Blackstone's amazing game, but Deavers paid them no mind. His focus was on a small picture of Philadelphia's Star, in the upper right-hand corner of his 80" TV. He hit pause and his eyes burned into the frozen image. "You should have stayed out Blackstone, 'cause this time, you ain't ever gonna get back up." For twenty minutes Deavers was glued to the screen. The entire time, his own words echoed in his head, amplifying his rage.

CHAPTER 50

The days leading to Philly's showdown in Dallas, saw another surge, in what was already an unprecedented media storm. Each day, the gated lot at the Freedom facility swelled above capacity, and news trucks lined the streets. Pollard brought in extra security to handle the flood.

The night before they flew to Dallas, Joe stayed late after practice to study more film. But he was troubled with his team's game plan and couldn't concentrate. Realizing he needed to speak with Lafond, Joe went looking for him and found him in Mealey's office. He tapped on the open door and asked, "You guys have a minute?"

Both coaches turned. "Hey Joe, come in, have a seat," Mealey said and waved him inside. "I thought all the guys were gone for the night."

"I'm the last one." Joe walked around the table sat across from the two men.

Lafond paused the film he and Mealey had been watching and said, "Coach and I were taking another look at Dallas' defense."

"That's what I wanted to talk to you about."

"What's on your mind?" Mealey asked.

Joe took a moment to choose his words. "I don't want to be disrespectful, but…"

"Speak freely," Mealy said.

Joe looked at Lafond. "I don't like the offensive game plan."

"Oh?" Lafond cocked a brow and asked, "What specifically don't you like?"

"We've been aggressive all season, but this week, it seems our only goal is not to get beat. We're putting too much emphasis on Deavers." Joe's tone was neither combative nor defensive, more matter of fact.

"Deavers is a special player," Mealey answered for his Coordinator. "We can't ignore it."

"He's good, I'm not gonna deny it, but we can't run an offense while trying to play defense," said Joe. His eyes hardened, and he leaned forward. "Don't run away from him, let's run over him. This isn't gonna be like last time, I'm gonna kick his ass."

Lafond glanced at Mealey. But the head coach was locked on Joe and pulled no punches. "You played him tough in the second half last time before you got dinged. But he took it to you pretty good in the first. And we need you on defense this week. Last time you only played offense in the second half." Mealey's intensity rose, reflecting what he saw in front of him. "You think you got the juice to play both ways and take Deavers one on one?"

Deadpan, Joe's answered, "No ... I don't *think* it, I KNOW IT."

Mealey matched Joe's expression and said, "We appreciate the input. Why don't you head on home now and get some rest."

"Thanks." Joe stood and said, "I'll see you guys tomorrow."

After Joe had gone, Lafond turned to Mealey and asked, "What do you think?"

"Did you see the look in the man's eyes?" A crooked grin hinted at Mealey's jubilation. "We better take another look at the game plan."

CHAPTER 51

Two hours before pre-game warm-ups Joe walked the field. Angus Young's guitar and Cliff William's bass had never sounded better. Joe was reborn. His team was ready, and he couldn't wait for kickoff. As it had in every game since his return, a blaze of love and hope warmed in his soul. But it wasn't the only reason Joe so amped up, today he was going to do something he never had. He was about to play a worthy opponent, an opponent who would test him, who would push him and who had once beaten him.

An unfamiliar stream of emotions poured from the challenge. They carried Joe through pre-game and placed him in the middle of Philadelphia's locker room moments before kickoff. "Listen up," he shouted. The room went silent, players and coaches alike gathered around. "We've had a crazy season, the kind that would've torn most teams apart, but not us. We've won big, and we've lost big, on and off the field, yet look where we are now." He gave his words time to simmer; the grit within his teammate's time to reveal itself. "We can avenge two of those losses today, and the prize is a trip to the championship." Joe glanced at the floor when he lifted his head his eyes glistened. "My presence caused a lot of problems … but you all stood by me. Ms. Taylor, John Pollard and every guy in this room picked me up. You carried me when it would've been easier to turn your back … Thank you." Joe's jaw twitched, and his voice rose. "I promise … if you slip. If you can't push yourself any further. If you collapse in exhaustion … I'll be there to pick you up. I owe you guys, and I'll carry you if need be, because, no matter what we're gonna win this fucking game!"

***

The Hills, Pete Cooper, Adam and AJ Owad were with Ms. Taylor and a select group in the visiting owner's box. When Ms. Taylor learned Joe and Carrie had requested tickets for their friends, she insisted on flying them to Dallas and hosting them in her box.

Moments before the teams took the field, there was a commotion at the back of Mrs. Taylor's suite. A familiar voice joked from the door. "I sure as hell hope your boys are ready Sky Marie. I'm a Texan and all, but if I hear the Vice President yap about Dallas anymore, I may drop him from next year's ticket."

Everyone gawked while Ms. Taylor stood to greet her new guest. "Mr. President I'm so happy you made it."

"Are you kidding me? I wouldn't miss this one for the world." With a playful smile, he winked at the group from Maine. "And I mean that, literally."

Everyone laughed, and introductions were made, not that any were needed, they all knew whom he was. And thanks to the Secret Service and his chief of staff the President knew all about Joe's friends.

President Flynn rested a hand on AJ's shoulder and said, "I heard you had one heck of a season young man."

"We, yeah, it was …" AJ stumbled for a response and finally said, "Yeah, we did pretty good."

"Pretty good! You call an undefeated State Championship season pretty good?"

AJ's face burned red, and he smiled. "I guess it was pretty awesome, sir." Everyone chuckled.

"I hear you're interested in attending the Naval Academy after high school, is that right?" The President asked.

"Yes, sir, I do."

The President handed AJ a card. "Keep your grades up, and when the time comes give me a call, I'd be more than happy to write your letter of recommendation." AJ's jaw dropped. "I called your dad a while back for a favor, so if there's ever anything I can do for your family to repay it, consider it done."

AJ's nose crinkled, giving him a toothy smile. "My dad … did you a favor?" AJ asked bewildered.

"He sure did." The President looked at Adam. "His did us all a favor."

***

While President Flynn was entertaining Ms. Taylor's guest, Joe and his teammates took the field. The home fans showered Philadelphia with a chorus of boos until Dallas emerged, triggering applause.

Deavers was shouting unheard obscenities at Joe from across the field when their teams lined up for the opening kickoff. Dallas' return man fielded the ball four yards deep in his own end zone and took it out. He sliced down the visiting sideline and hurdled a would-be tackler at the nineteen. A touchdown-saving dive by the Freedom kicker knocked him out of bounds near midfield. An official marked the ball at the Philadelphia 49-yard line. The crowd thundered approval, and the stadium trembled.

Joe lined up on the outside shoulder of Dallas' left tackle Jeff Winslow. Expecting to be double teamed, he was surprised to see the offense in a spread set with no tight end. But when he glanced in the backfield, he understood his opponents' plan.

Abandoning the run game, Dallas had replaced their talented halfback with Max Conner, a blocking specialist. Conner's singular, but key, responsibility was to protect their all-pro quarterback, Hayes Nolte.

Joe blasted forward on the snap and beat Winslow to the edge. Met by Conner, he hurtled the 6'2", 265 pound ball of muscle, but not in time. Nolte delivered a quick pass, which turned into a fourteen yard gain. Five straight completions capped off an opening drive score for Dallas.

The instant Joe got to the sideline, Pickell gave him a *'What the fuck are you guys doing out there?'* look.

Joe started Philly's first offensive series on the right side of the formation. He was disappointed when Deavers lined up on the opposite side of the field. The first play was a toss to Matthieu in Joe's direction. He got excellent leverage on the outside linebacker and pinned him inside, sealing the middle backer as well. Joe was still driving both men across the grain of the defense when the whistle blew. Deavers had run Matthieu down from the backside and dropped him for a two yard loss.

Next, Lafond called a pass, but Deavers made the play again. He hit Hopewell and jarred the ball loose. Dallas recovered at the Freedom 9-yard line, giving their offense 1st and Goal.

Frustrated and back on defense, Joe made no effort to elude Winslow; he charged through him. As Joe bulled his way over the tackle, Conner dove at his knee. The fullback had telegraphed his move, giving Joe time to react. But when he tried to hurdle Conner, Joe found his left foot anchored to the ground. Winslow was clinging to his ankle. Joe yanked against Winslow's grip as Conner's shoulder crashed into the side of his knee.

Joe was looking up, at the cavernous dome when he heard the crowd. With his knee burning, Joe rolled onto his side and climbed to his feet. He limped to the sideline trailing by two scores.

Lafond pointed at Joe's knee and asked, "You okay?"

Joe ignored the question. "Coach, if Deavers is gonna try and blow everything up from the backside, use me as the H-back. I can run motion at him and lead the play or wham block on the backside."

Lafond was shaking his head yes before Joe finished speaking. "Yeah, I like it." He glanced at Joe's knee one last time, before turning to Hopewell and telling him which formations they would use.

Trailing 14-0, Joe lined up on the left side of the formation, a yard off the line of scrimmage. Again, Deavers was on the opposite side. On the snap, Matthieu dashed to his left. Deavers beat Philly's right tackle, Jim Schank, off the edge and charged hard from the backside. He was closing fast when Hopewell tossed the ball in Matthieu's direction

Ignoring his knee, Joe pivoted to his right and barreled back into Matthieu's wake. Deavers never saw it coming. The impact stabbed Joe's right shoulder and sent a stinger down his arm. But the sound Dallas' star made when he hit the ground, more than compensated for his pain. When he popped up, Joe was pleased to see Matthieu had gained 12 on the play.

Deavers rushed at Joe from behind, hollering, "I'm gonna kill you man, you're mine."

Joe wheeled around and shoved the bigger man, knocking him off balance. Officials and players from both teams stepped between them, and Deavers let loose with another barrage of threats.

On the sideline, Lafond looked at Mealey and said, "Coach I'm not sure how much of that Joe can take. They chopped his knee pretty good on that last score."

"Mark, call the play and let that big fucker lead the way. You saw what he did to Deavers, his knee can't be hurt too bad."

Hoping Mealey was right, Lafond called a similar play out of the same formation

This time, Joe went in motion before the snap and met Deavers at the point of attack. When they collided, Joe mauled the massive linebacker and drove him backward.

Dallas' cornerback lost sight of Matthieu behind the two behemoths. By the time he recovered, it was too late. Philly's star back got outside, made a great cut, which left the safety grasping at air and jetted the rest of the way for a touchdown.

Joe was jogging off the field when Deavers cut in front of him and screamed, "I'm gonna kick your fucking ass, Blackstone." Again, players from both sides rushed between the two.

Joe held his ground. "How's that working out for you?"

Blinded by rage and oblivious to his teammates' pleas, Deavers continued his rant. "Ain't gonna be like last time muthafucka, you ain't ever going to wake up this time."

We'll see about that, Joe thought and turned to his sideline without another a word.

Pickell grabbed Joe as he was coming off the field. "We've got to get to Nolte, or we're never gonna stop these assholes."

"I'm on it," Joe said. "But first I need to teach Winslow and Conner a little lesson."

"Okay, hurry it the hell up would you."

After the kick, Joe strode back on the field and waited for Winslow to break the huddle. When he did, Joe pointed at him and said, "You shouldn't have pulled the cheap shot bullshit." Joe grimaced and shook his head. "Big mistake."

Winslow spit on the turf at Joe's feet but said nothing.

Nolte barked out the cadence and sent both players hurtling into one another. Joe hammered Winslow, and the big tackle staggered back, but Joe didn't try to get past him. Instead, his left hand gripped the joint at Winslow's right elbow. Joe locked his fingers around the back of the arm and drove his thumb deep into the tissue at the front of the joint. Winslow howled, the searing pain would have dropped him to his knees had Joe not been holding him up.

With the play still unfolding, Joe pulled Winslow into him until their facemask were touching. "I can do this all day, and I know shit that'll hurt much worse and do a lot more damage." The whistle blew, and Joe released his grip. Winslow dropped to a knee and grabbed his arm. "How about you and Conner lay off the cheap shots and play some football," Joe warned.

Winslow looked up. When he saw the cold look on Joe's face, he knew the man wasn't bluffing. Still holding his arm, he struggled to his feet and said, "Whatever you say, Blackstone, I'm cool but Conner ain't gonna stop, he's Deavers boy."

"I'll take care of Conner."

Dallas had completed a pass for eleven yards on the previous play. Winslow and his teammates broke the huddle with another 1st and 10, but his bravado was gone, and he approached the line with apprehension.

Nolte looked over the Philly defense and barked out adjustments.

Joe hollered across the line. "Sorry man forgot to tell you, this may hurt a bit."

Winslow's eyes darted back and forth, searching for help, which wasn't there. His body stiffened, and his mouth ran dry. The ball was snapped, and Blackstone was into him before he could take a step. A blow to his chest rocked him back on his heels.

Joe latched onto Winslow's pads and accelerate. With a final burst, he hurled the 340 pound lineman at Conner.

Winslow's feet came off the ground. Anticipating a hard landing, he gritted his teeth and closed his eyes.

Conner was ready to chop Joe's knee again, but he froze when Winslow's broad back filled his vision. Caught off guard, he didn't escape the flailing mass and his season came to an abrupt end.

Winslow opened his eyes. He was looking straight up at the bottom of the jumbotron. The awkward lump beneath his back and muffled screams assured him, he wasn't on the turf. He twisted to his left and rolled off. An awful cry blasted him in the ear. He shook the ringing from his head and pushed himself up. When he looked down and saw Conner's leg, Winslow heaved his breakfast all over the turf.

Conner withered in agony. His foot was bent sharply in the wrong direction, and a bone was sticking out of his right leg. Medics rushed to his side. Players from both teams recoiled from the gruesome scene.

On the sideline, Pickell slapped Mealey on the arm and pointed at Blackstone. "That's a bad mother fucker right there."

Speechless, Mealey nodded his agreement.

Dallas had gained eight yards on the play, but the drive and they were forced to punt. Utilizing an extensive range of formations and motions to counteract Deavers alignment, Philadelphia drove the length of the field. On 2nd and 7 from the Dallas 12, Hopewell stepped up in the pocket and lobbed a perfect pass to Wilmot in the back of the end zone. The same moment Wilmot caught the pass, Schank tripped over someone's foot and toppled into Hopewell's knee.

The play ignited everyone on the Freedom sideline except Mealey. "Goddammit."

Hopewell's backup, Rich Wesselt, heard Mealey's comment and asked, "What? What is it, coach?"

"He's done." Mealey motioned to Hopewell, who was on his back clutching his knee. "You better start warming up."

Over the final nine minutes of the half, Wesselt threw a pick-six and fumbled, which set up another Dallas score. With 20 seconds left, Philadelphia took a knee on their own 36-yard line, bring the half to a close with Dallas ahead 28-14.

CHAPTER 52

The last time Philly was in the locker room the atmosphere had been electric, the air thick with excitement and the outcome promising. Now, they returned deflated and resigned to their fate. A few hollow cries to rally were shouted as players filed in, but the expression on every face was dismal. Except one.

Joe moved to the exact spot he had stood when he addressed the team before the game. His teammates split into offensive and defensive units. A chorus of adjustments began on each side of the room; Joe lingered in the middle. Mealey spotted him and waved him toward the offensive group, but he didn't move.

What the hell Blackstone. Get your ass over here, Mealey thought and was about to scream it, but the intensity etched on Joe's face stopped him. "Everybody listen up." He made a gesture toward Joe and said, "Blackstone, you got something to say?"

Every pair of eyes in the room settled on Joe. He looked back and forth between the two groups. "I see a bunch of guys who've given up, and I can't for the life of me figure out why? We know what we need to do to beat these assholes, but we haven't been doing it. We've got two quarters of football left to go out there and get it right. If you guys are spent, if you've got nothing left … fine, I'll pick up the slack." Joe scanned the room. His fiery eyes challenged each man. "I know everyone in here has a hell of a lot of fight left, but you need to find it. Until then, I told you guys I'd pick you up and carry you if had to. Well goddammit, that's exactly what I'm gonna do." Joe locked eyes with Mealey. "Put me in at quarterback, and we'll win this thing."

Reinvigorated, his players looked at Mealey, but he wasn't convinced. "Blackstone listen--"

"I know the offense, and I've been preparing for this all year," Joe said, refusing to give in. "I'm a Quarterback and always have been. Besides, if I'm back there we don't have to worry about Deavers."

"Oh yeah, how's that?" asked Mealey.

"Because I'm better."

Anticipation from the entire team bore down on Mealey. After an agonizing silence, he set his jaw and said, "Fuck it, let's see whatcha got kid."

A silent exchange between player and coach conveyed Joe's gratitude. He looked away from Mealey and liked what he saw. "Coach is willing to roll with me, how 'bout you guys?"

"Hell yeah," Wilmot hollered.

The team erupted and rallied around their leader.

On their way out for the second half, Pickell lumbered up beside Joe. "Nice speech," he said.

"What's the matter grandpa." Joe looked Pickell. "You don't think I can play quarterback?"

"Shit, I'll be surprised if you can't."

"So, what's the problem?"

"How the hell's our defense gonna stop these guys without you?"

Joe pulled up. "You must be getting hard of hearing old man. I asked coach to put me in at QB. I didn't say anything about sitting out on D."

***

Watching from above, AJ spotted Joe taking snaps. He tapped on Cooper's arm, and his words came in a flurry. "Coach, they're gonna put Joe in at quarterback."

Cooper had noticed the same thing. He swelled with pride and said, "Looks that way, don't it."

President Flynn overheard their exchange. He excused himself from a conversation. Approaching Cooper and AJ, he pointed down at the field. "Are they putting Joe in at quarterback?" he asked.

"No other reason for him to be taking snaps, Mr. President," answered Cooper.

It didn't take long, before every person in the booth, stadium and watching from around the country came to the same conclusion.

Ms. Taylor looked at Carrie, who was grinning ear-to-ear, and asked, "My God Carrie what are you so happy about? You know how highly I think of Joe, but I don't know about this."

"I haven't seen Joe play quarterback since I was a kid," Carrie said. "But I can remember it like it was yesterday, you know why?"

"Alright, I'll play along," Ms. Taylor said. "Why?"

"Because I'd never seen *anybody* do *anything* so perfectly. We're going to win this game," Carrie promised.

A couple of Ms. Taylor's guest responded to Carrie's statement with snickers. She ignored them, but Ms. Taylor cast a stern look in their direction.

The younger of the two put his hands in the air. "Sorry Ms. Taylor, we didn't mean any disrespect. But this looks a little desperate," he said.

"Son." Cooper's voice boomed with such authority he garnered the attention of everyone in the booth. Even the President hung on the edge of his seat waiting for the coach to continue. "I've been around this sport my whole life, and I've seen them all. Joe would be great at any position, but his true calling is quarterback, he's the best I ever saw."

The young man Cooper addressed withered and melted into the back of the room.

Ms. Taylor looked at Cooper and said, "Coach, I hear what you're saying, and God knows I hope you're right. But when Joe played for you, he was a right-handed quarterback. With his injury, he'll have to play left handed, what makes you so sure he can?"

"Because he's Joe Blackstone, ma'am."

***

Philadelphia started the second half by fumbling the kickoff. Helpless on the sideline, Joe watched as Dallas recovered the loose ball at the Freedom 6-yard line. A deafening roar rained on the field. The ground was still shaking when Joe and the defense trotted out on the field.

With Conner out of the game, Dallas returned to their normal offense. Eddie Drake was back in at tailback, Joe smothered him for a three yard loss on first down. On the next play, Joe forced Nolte to throw the ball away. Dallas lined up in the shotgun on 3rd and 13. Nolte caught the snap and lofted a pass into the back corner of the end zone. The receiver leaped over Philly corner, Moo Moo Thompson, and snagged the jump ball. Nolte raised his arms in the air signalling a touchdown, but the play wasn't over.

As Moo Moo was falling to the turf, he clung to the receiver, punched the ball and jarred it free. The pass fell incomplete, but a yellow flag cut Philly's celebration short.

"Son of a bitch," hollered Pickell.

The call was pass interference. Dallas received a fresh set of downs, and the ball was spotted on the 1-yard line.

Pickell had to be restrained from storming onto the field. Moo Moo and the rest of the team were still protesting the call while Dallas huddled for the next play.

Standing in the end zone, Joe hollered, "Let it go, it was a bad call but let it go, let's stop these assholes."

"Yeah let's stop these motherfuckers," said Atkins, and the middle linebacker called the play. "Pirate goal line, pirate goal line."

As they broke the huddle, Joe grabbed Atkins and said, "Switch with me."

"What?" Atkins asked, panicked.

"Just switch," Joe said again. "Set the edge, and I'll take care of the rest."

Mealey tore his headset off. "What the hell's Blackstone doing?" He looked at his DC. "Kevin, what the hell's he doing?"

Pickell threw his hands in the air. "No idea."

In pirate goal line, two interior linemen angled into the inside gaps. This clogged the middle and defended against the quarterback sneak. Dallas had anticipated this, so they called a dive to the tailback. Typically, the play would send the ball carrier through one of the inside gaps. But, in short yardage situations, with the defense focused on filling those gaps, the tailback would leap over the line instead. It was a simple play, and one Drake excelled at.

Nolte took the snap, pivoted away from the line and handed the ball to his charging tailback. Drake exploded off his feet and vaulted toward the end zone.

The same way Dallas had expected Philly's play call, Joe had expected theirs. When Drake left the ground, Joe was already in the air. The sound of his forearm striking Dallas' tailback reverberated throughout the stadium.

The savage blow instantly reversed Drake's momentum. He ricocheted back and crashed to the turf at the 4-yard line.

In as impressive of a display ever seen in professional sports, Blackstone cleared the entire line of scrimmage and landed on his feet in the Dallas backfield. The crowd was silent.

Forty yards away, Wilmot flinched. "Holly shit!" He said.

The next two plays were equally disastrous for the home team. Dallas settled for a field goal, pushing the lead to 31-14.

Joe gathered with Lafond and Mealey on the sideline. The OC scrolled down his play chart and said, "Let's start with a simple G power so we can see what they're going to throw at you."

"Coach, we don't have time to see what they wanna do," Joe said. "Let's run what we want."

Lafond looked at Mealey, whose expression indicated he agreed with his new QB. Turning back to Joe, Lafond asked, "You have something in mind?"

"You bet your ass I do."

Joe's jog out to the offense was a journey through time. Dark memories, always close to the surface, flashed before his eyes and faded away. Visions of his youth and the promise it once held filled the void. When he reached the huddle, and every eye looked to him for leadership, the best of his past became the present.

Deavers was in a tirade. His rant was more of a disturbance than eighty-thousand hostile fans. Foam Anderson, Philly's big left tackle said, "Don't worry about him Legend we got you're back."

"I know you do," Joe said. "But let him come free on this play."

"WHAT?" Foam asked.

"It's cool, don't worry. I'm gonna set the tone. Receivers, be ready to break off your route if I leave the pocket. Except you Wilmot, no matter what you stay vertical."

Philadelphia broke the huddle. Joe stood in the shotgun with Matthieu slightly behind and to his left. Joe looked at Deavers and winked.

"You're finished Blackstone," — Deavers was jumping up and down like a wildman — "I'm going to lay you out, you better say good night because you're going to sleep you, bitch."

"Blue 23 — Blue 23 — HUT." Joe caught the snap, dropped his left foot and held the ball out for his back.

Deavers charged, and his eyes bore into Joe as Matthieu flashed between them. Focused on the unblocked defender, Joe took a slide step and meshed the ball into Matthieu's midsection. The gold in Deavers' teeth gleamed as he hurled himself forward. Joe pulled the ball free the instant before contact; palmed Deavers' helmet with his right hand and drove him to the turf as he sprinted from the pocket.

The run fake had frozen several Dallas defenders. Barrett and Bates were open underneath, but Joe spotted Wilmot running stride for stride with the cornerback. Time slowed. Joe remembered an old football saying, 'if he's even … he's leaving,' and a grin spread across his face.

Lafond saw Joe look at Wilmot. "No, no," he hollered. "HE'S TOO DEEP …" Joe stopped and launched a missile. "Holly shit!" Lafond gasped. Seventy-eight yards later, Wilmot gathered it in without breaking stride.

Everyone in Ms. Taylor's booth was on their feet. "Holy cow, did you see that throw? Incredible," said the President.

The group from Fairfield were all thinking the same thing, but it was Troy who responded. "Mr. President you're in for a treat because he's just getting started."

Unable to believe their own eyes, the crowd looked up and searched the massive video screens for a replay. But the home team opted not to relive their opponent's highlight. The stadium grew restless. Fans shook their head in disbelief but couldn't shake their sense of foreboding.

Despite Joe's disruptive presence, Nolte mounted another drive into Philadelphia territory. Utilizing the short passing game, he drained valuable time off the clock before stalling at the Freedom 44-yard line. A terrific punt on 4th down pinned Philly at their own 3-yard line with 3:02 left in the 3rd quarter.

Deavers was in a frenzy when he took the field. Spittle on the side of his mouth gave him the resemblance of a rabid dog.

Back in the shotgun, Joe barked out the cadence. "Red 17 — Red 17 — HUT."

Matthieu feigned a block on Deavers and Joe retreated from the rush. Deep in the pocket, Joe lofted the ball back to his left. Matthieu caught it near the sideline and followed a wall of blockers for a thirty-four yard gain.

Well after the throw, Deavers planted the crown of his helmet on Joe's chin. He landed on top when they hit the ground and goaded. "How you like me now pretty boy?"

A kaleidoscope of colors danced in Joe's vision.

"Get the fuck off of him asshole," yelled Schank, as he latched on to Deavers and tore him off. The Dallas linebacker ripped himself free, scrambled to his feet and started spewing obscenities.

Still woozy, Joe hauled himself up and stepped in front of his right tackle. "It's okay big fella." He jerked his thumb over his shoulder. "Dumbo here was congratulating me on his fifteen yard penalty," Joe said as he pulled Schank back toward their huddle.

When he finally saw the flag, Deavers unleashed another tirade. "Fuck you, Blackstone, you're a dead man, you're dead." His teammates grabbed him, and the officials threatened to give Deavers a penalty if he didn't back off.

On the next play, Deavers was to Joe's right, on Schank's outside shoulder. When Joe called for the ball, Deavers bull rushed right through Schank. He was in the backfield almost as fast as the snap, forcing Joe to the left.

Amidst the chaos, time stood still, the crowd noise evaporated and Joe's mind filtered out anything unessential to his task. He anticipated the course of two defenders in front of him and countered with his own precise movement. All the while, tracking Deavers approach by the sound of his stampeding cleats.

Unconsciously, Lafond twisted his body to help Joe escape. He cringed when Joe pulled up to throw the ball.

Deavers thrust himself at Joe's back. Like a sixth sense, Joe sensed it coming and ducked. Deavers somersaulted over the top of his head but never touched him.

Lafond hopped in the air. "Holly shit," he said to anyone in earshot. "Did you see that?"

Forty yards down the field, Dwayne had looked back in time to see Joe duck and Deavers go flying. When Joe cut back, reversing his course, Dwayne broke off his route and headed across the field, mirroring Joe's movement.

Scrambling to his right, Joe dodged three defenders and de-cleated Dallas' 350 pound nose guard with a vicious stiff arm. As he was nearing the sideline, he found an open receiver down field and unleashed a frozen rope.

The ball screamed toward Dwayne. It arrived in a flash and stung his hands when he made the catch. He brought it into his body and turned up field. The strong safety was closing fast. Instead of running out of bounds, Dwayne tried to cut back inside. But his right cleat bit the turf and his ankle rolled. The sharp pain and sudden loss of balance spun him to his right and caused his grip to loosen on the ball.

Timing it perfectly, the safety punched the exposed ball and knocked it free. A scramble ensued, and Dallas recovered the ball at their own 8-yard line. His ankle severely sprained, Dwayne had to be helped from the field as the 3rd quarter came to a close with Dallas leading 34-21.

During the TV timeout, Joe standing was with the coaches. He was watching the trainers attend to Dwayne when Pickell said, "You need to make a play right now, don't let these assholes eat the clock up on us."

With his eye still on Dwayne, Joe said, "No problem, go with two extra DB's in the dime package. I'll take care of the rest."

"Yeah let's do it," Mealey agreed. He followed Joe's stare. "Wilmot's done for the day, without his speed on the field Dallas is gonna sit on our routes. The passing windows are gonna be damn tight out there."

"We'll be okay," assured Joe.

True to his word, Joe and the defense were up to the task. But a facemask on third and long gave Dallas a first down. Three more rushing attempts by the home team netted only four yards but drained valuable time off the clock. With 10:37 left in the game Dallas punted the ball.

As Mealey had feared, his receivers were struggling without Wilmot's speed in the game. Two aggressive plays by Dallas' secondary resulted in incompletions for Philly and left them with a 3rd and 10 at their own 24-yard line.

For the first time all game, Deavers was quiet. Deciding to rectify that, Joe called his play and the snap count; the entire offense started laughing. They were still snickering when they broke the huddle. "Yo … big ugly," Joe called out to Deavers. "What's the matter cat got your tongue?"

Deavers snarled at Joe. "Fuck you, Blackstone. I'm dropping you on this play asshole."

Joe stood in the shotgun with Matthieu to his right. Adjusting the cadence, he yelled, "Deavers is a dipshit … Deavers is a dip-shit … dip-shit … DIP-SHIT."

Deavers barreled forward, trouncing anyone in his path. When he was three yards away, Joe flipped a shovel pass to Matthieu, lowered his shoulder and slammed into Deavers with everything he had. The sound of shattering bone rang out like a gunshot, an agonizing howl followed.

Matthieu's run after the catch was highlight reel material. Which was good, because it's the only way his team would ever see it. Their attention was glued to the ear piercing screams.

The whistle blew, and Freedom trainers broke from the sideline, but they stopped short when Joe hopped to his feet. It was Deavers who was still on the turf, thrashing with a ghastly bend above the elbow on his right arm. His legs writhed, and he pounded the surface with his other arm, desperately trying to escape his anguish. His teammates knelt around him, troubled by what they saw, and anxious about its effect on their chance to win.

Staring at Deavers, Joe backed to the sideline. The burn in his right shoulder had never felt better.

"Blackstone, you okay?" asked Mealey.

Joe continued glaring at the wreckage until a hand on his arm broke his trance, and he snapped his head around.

Mealey let go. The fury in Joe's eyes sent a chill down his spine but quickly vanished. "You okay?" he asked again.

"I'm good," answered Joe. "I, ah … I got sick of him."

Pickell guffawed, both Mealey and Joe turned in his direction. "That's a fucking understatement," he said, still laughing.

On the next play, Joe dropped back to pass. Under heavy pressure, he tucked the ball and took off.

Dallas' middle linebacker was shadowing Joe's movement and was in good position to defend the play. He dashed forward and braced himself for the tackle, but an anvil hit the front of his helmet and took him off his feet.

After hammering the linebacker with a stiff arm, Joe shot between the Dallas safeties and raced untouched to the end zone. A hush blanketed the home fans, and Philadelphia soared.

Spirits were high in Ms. Taylor's booth. Carrie taunted the two men who had doubted Joe with a, *I told you so,* smirk. President Flynn and AJ witnessed the exchange and shared a laugh.

Dallas wasn't finished. When they got back on the field, their offense started moving the ball, sinking Philly's hopes with each first down. Clutch throws by Nolte, and a pass interference penalty, pushed them over midfield with 3:16 left to play.

On 3rd and 3, Nolte pitched the ball to his right away from Joe. As soon as the running back bubbled away from the line of scrimmage, Joe knew they were in trouble. Affirming his concern, Dallas' tailback, pulled up and fired a spiral down the middle of the field. The tight end caught the ball at the 19-yard line. A diving tackle by Gino Sayer's prevented the score, but Dallas had 1st and goal on the 1-yard line with less than three minutes to play.

"Timeout," hollered Mealey over an invigorated crowd. "TIMEOUT!" He gathered his team. Expecting to see disappointment and doubt he was encouraged by their resolve. "This game ain't over gentlemen, we still have a job to do. We've made up a lot of ground this half but we ain't done yet." Heads nodded in agreement and jaws were set tight with determination. "Now go keep those pricks off the board and let's win this thing."

Playing conservative and satisfied to milk the clock, Dallas ran three straight quarterback sneaks. They lost a yard each time but forced Philadelphia to use their final two timeouts. Following the two-minute warning, the two teams lined up for the biggest play of the game. A field goal would give Dallas a nine-point lead and clinch the win.

Joe was ten yards off the ball when the Dallas kicker set his feet. Anticipating the snap, he streaked toward the line and catapulted off the ground as the ball was snapped.

Two distinct sounds were heard, a loud pop when the kicker's foot connected with the ball and a hard slap when Joe's outstretched hands batted it to the ground. The ensuing bedlam resulted in a 1st and 10 for Philadelphia at their own 12 with 1.44 to play. Tension hung in the air as both teams huddled up.

All eyes stared at Joe. A tremendous peace settled upon him. "We've got eighty-eight yards to go. Is there a single one of you who has any doubt?" No one said a word, they didn't have to, their determination spoke loud and clear. Joe nodded. "Okay then, let's cowboy up and win this thing."

To ensure Joe stayed in the pocket, Dallas assigned two linebackers with the job of spying him. Their only responsibility was to hover at the line of scrimmage and mirror his movement. Six defensive backs dropped into coverage, leaving three men to rush.

Four short passes moved the ball to the Dallas forty-six. But three straight incompletions left Philly with a 4th and 10 and only 0:38 to play. They caught a break when Joe noticed Showtime Lloyd was tighter to the line than he had been all day. He called an audible. "Kill—Kill, Red one gladiator—Red one gladiator—HUT."

As he'd expected, Showtime blitzed off the edge. Giving ground, Joe sprinted to his right. The two linebackers tasked with shadowing him joined the chase.

Above the field, Carrie clasped her hands together, and her knuckles turned white. Three defenders were closing in on Joe's as he neared the sideline. "Throw it," she jumped out of her seat and shouted, "THROW IT!"

At the last possible moment, Joe heaved the ball. The three defenders hit him, and all four players tumbled out of bounds. But no one saw the collision because everyone was watching the flight of the ball. The entire building held its breath until it touched down in Barrett's outstretched hands.

The rookie breezed across the goal line, and pandemonium broke loose in Ms. Taylor's suite.

"Goddammit," Cooper hollered slapping his hat across his thigh. "Damn zebras are gonna try and steal this thing."

A giant yellow flag was blown up on the jumbotron. "Holding #64 offense, repeat 4th down," The referee announced.

Joe huddled the offense facing 4th and 20 with 0:21 to go. Unglued, Schank was babbling something unintelligible. "Hey," Joe hollered, "knock it off." Schank and everyone else who was hanging their head snapped to attention "It's a penalty, big deal. We can quit and feel sorry for ourselves or stop fucking around. What's it gonna be?"

"Let's do it," Matthieu said.

Head's nodded all around.

Philadelphia lined up in an empty backfield with Bates and Matthieu to the left and three receivers to the right.

"—Hut,HUT." Joe caught the snap and took a five-step drop.

The two linebackers sat at the line of scrimmage. Allowing a big cushion, four Dallas defenders retreated with the three receivers running deep.

Joe pumped the ball downfield and sprinted to his left. When the two spy linebackers turned to pursue him, they were hit by Matthieu and Bates. Both defenders landed hard on their back.

Joe's strides ate up long chunks of yardage as he glided past the Dallas sideline. The defensive backs angled toward him, rapidly narrowing the distance. Leaving Joe with no option but to step out once he reached the first down marker.

Joe was about to step out. Ms. Taylor glanced at the scoreboard to check the game clock. "What the hell is he doing?" She heard the president shout.

Joe had stayed in bounds and was circling backward, toward the middle of the field. He spotted Lafond jumping up and down on the sideline, no doubt screaming at him to get out of bounds. *No way,* thought Joe.

"Watch this Mr. President," said Cooper; everyone from Fairfield echoed his confidence.

Gathered speed like a freight train, Joe left diving defenders in his wake. Showtime was the last to fall as Joe blasted down the Freedom sideline.

Thundering across the turf Joe separated himself from more than the Dallas defense, he left behind a decade of anger and violence. The moment before his teammates swarmed him in the end zone, Joe imagined his parents sitting among the stunned Dallas crowd, happy and cheering for their son.

EPILOGUE

Two weeks later, Joe led Philadelphia to the WFL Championship, earning MVP honors. After attending the victory parade in Philadelphia Joe and Carrie returned to Maine.

A week had passed, and they were sitting in front of a fire at Carrie's house when she said, "As much as I've enjoyed the peace and quiet of these past few days, I need to get back to work. My agent called, and they wanna start filming in Philly again."

"You mind if I tag along?" asked Joe.

Carrie smiled and said, "I was kinda hopin' you would."

Joe's eyes filled with mischief.

Recognizing the look, Carrie asked, "Whatta you thinkin'?"

"Well since you're gonna be kinda busy I might play some hoops while I'm there."

"'Play some hoops'," — Carrie's head flinched back— "like in a men's league?"

"Think bigger."

Acknowledgements

This first draft of this story was written around 1984 — I was in 8th grade— it was three pages long, and my teacher hated it. I couldn't possibly thank everyone who contributed to what I hope is a much-improved version, but I'd like to acknowledge a few. Martin Sturla, Kevin Pickell, Marc Fecteau, Bill Lucchesi, Bruce Roderick, Dwayne Wilmot, Betty Pickell, Chuck and Lieu Barrett, thank you for struggling through my early drafts and providing much-needed feedback. My thanks go out to the real Earl "Pete" Cooper and Mike Mealey for teaching me I didn't have to be perfect, but my effort did. Mom, Dad & Dad, thank you for allowing me to dream, showing me how to work hard and giving me grit.

Selfishly, I put a lot of time into this project, and it came at the expense of my family. I'm forever grateful for your patience and understanding, hope I made you proud. Skye & Joe, yes we can go to Rita's now; Colleen you can have the kitchen table back, I'll be outside cleaning the pool—and working on book two.

Last but not least, thank you for reading Legend, I hope you enjoyed it. There has never been a larger, more accessible, selection of books than there is today. I'm humbled you choose mine.

If an author tells you they're not interested in their readers' feedback, I assure you, they're lying. I'm no different. Glowing reviews are the lifeblood of any successful book, and I'd certainly like yours if you feel it's warranted. Either way, I'd love to hear from you timyoungfiction@gmail.com.

For news on appearances and upcoming books follow me at; Facebook: @timothyryoungfiction

Twitter: @TimYoungFiction
Instagram: @timothy_young_fiction

46166766R00192

Made in the USA
Middletown, DE
24 July 2017